CATALYST   the pearson custom library for chemistry

General College Chemistry
CHE111/CHE112
Arapahoe Community College

Pearson Learning Solutions

New York   Boston   San Francisco
London   Toronto   Sydney   Tokyo   Singapore   Madrid
Mexico City   Munich   Paris   Cape Town   Hong Kong   Montreal

Senior Vice President, Editorial and Marketing: Patrick F. Boles
Executive Marketing Manager: Nathan L. Wilbur
Senior Acquisition Editor: Debbie Coniglio
Operations Manager: Eric M. Kenney
Development Editor: Christina Martin
Editorial Assistant: Jeanne Martin
Production Manager: Jennifer Berry
Art Director: Renée Sartell
Cover Designer: Kristen Kiley

Cover Art: Courtesy of Photodisc, Age Fotostock America, Inc. and Photo Researchers.

Pyrex, pHydrion, Chem3D Plus, Apple, Macintosh, Chemdraw, Hypercard, graphTool, Corning, Teflon, Mel-Temp, Rotaflow, Tygon, Spec20, and LambdaII UV/Vis are registered trademarks.

Chem3D Plus is a registered trademark of the Cambridge Soft Corp.

The information, illustration, and/or software contained in this book, and regarding the above mentioned programs, are provided "as is," without warranty of any kind, express or implied, including without limitation any warranty concerning the accuracy, ade or completeness of such information. Neither the publisher, the authors, nor the copyright holders shall be responsible for any c attributable to errors, omissions, or other inaccuracies contained in this book. Nor shall they be liable for direct, indirect, special, inci- dental, or consequential damages arising out of the use of such information or material.

The authors and publisher believe that the lab experiments described in this publication, when conducted in conformity with the safety precautions described herein and according to the school's laboratory safety procedures, are reasonably safe for the students for whom this manual is directed. Nonetheless, many of the described experiments are accompanied by some degree of risk, including human error, the failure or misuse of laboratory or electrical equipment, mismeasurement, spills of chemicals, and exposure to sharp objects, heat, body fluids, blood or other biologics. The authors and publisher disclaim any liability arising from such risks in connections with any of the experiments contained in this manual. If students have questions or problems with materials, procedures, or instructions on any experiment, they should always ask their instructor for help before proceeding.

This special edition published in cooperation with Pearson Learning Solutions.

Printed in the United States of America.

Please visit our web site at *www.pearsoncustom.com/custom-library/catalyst*.

Attention bookstores: For permission to return any unsold stock, contact us at *pe-uscustomreturns@pearson.com*.

Pearson Learning Solutions, 501 Boylston Street, Suite 900, Boston, MA 02116
A Pearson Education Company
www.pearsoned.com

ISBN 10: 0-536-36833-3
ISBN 13: 978-0-536-36833-1

Laboratory Safety:
General Guidelines

1. Notify your instructor immediately if you are pregnant, color blind, allergic to any insects or chemicals, taking immunosuppressive drugs, or have any other medical condition (such as diabetes, immunologic defect) that may require special precautionary measures in the laboratory.

2. Upon entering the laboratory, place all books, coats, purses, backpacks, etc. in designated areas, not on the bench tops.

3. Locate and, when appropriate, learn to use exits, fire extinguisher, fire blanket, chemical shower, eyewash, first aid kit, broken glass container, and cleanup materials for spills.

4. In case of fire, evacuate the room and assemble outside the building.

5. Do not eat, drink, smoke, or apply cosmetics in the laboratory.

6. Confine long hair, loose clothing, and dangling jewelry.

7. Wear shoes at all times in the laboratory.

8. Cover any cuts or scrapes with a sterile, waterproof bandage before attending lab.

9. Wear eye protection when working with chemicals.

10. Never pipet by mouth. Use mechanical pipeting devices.

11. Wash skin immediately and thoroughly if contaminated by chemicals or microorganisms.

12. Do not perform unauthorized experiments.

13. Do not use equipment without instruction.

14. Report all spills and accidents to your instructor immediately.

15. Never leave heat sources unattended.

16. When using hot plates, note that there is no visible sign that they are hot (such as a red glow). Always assume that hot plates are hot.

17. Use an appropriate apparatus when handling hot glassware.

18. Keep chemicals away from direct heat or sunlight.

19. Keep containers of alcohol, acetone, and other flammable liquids away from flames.

20. Do not allow any liquid to come into contact with electrical cords. Handle electrical connectors with dry hands. Do not attempt to disconnect electrical equipment that crackles, snaps, or smokes.

21. Upon completion of laboratory exercises, place all materials in the disposal areas designated by your instructor.

22. Do not pick up broken glassware with your hands. Use a broom and dustpan and discard the glass in designated glass waste containers; never discard with paper waste.

23. Wear disposable gloves when working with blood, other body fluids, or mucous membranes. Change gloves after possible contamination and wash hands immediately after gloves are removed.

24. The disposal symbol indicates that items that may have come in contact with body fluids should be placed in your lab's designated container. It also refers to liquid wastes that should not be poured down the drain into the sewage system.

25. Leave the laboratory clean and organized for the next student.

26. Wash your hands with liquid or powdered soap prior to leaving the laboratory.

27. The biohazard symbol indicates procedures that may pose health concerns.

The caution symbol points out instruments, substances, and procedures that require special attention to safety. These symbols appear throughout this manual.

Measurement Conversions

Metric to American Standard	American Standard to Metric

Length

1 mm = 0.039 inches	1 inch = 2.54 cm
1 cm = 0.394 inches	1 foot = 0.305 m
1 m = 3.28 feet	1 yard = 0.914 m
1 m = 1.09 yards	1 mile = 1.61 km

Volume

1 mL = 0.0338 fluid ounces	1 fluid ounce = 29.6 mL
1 L = 4.23 cups	1 cup = 237 mL
1 L = 2.11 pints	1 pint = 0.474 L
1 L = 1.06 quarts	1 quart = 0.947 L
1 L = 0.264 gallons	1 gallon = 3.79 L

Mass

1 mg = 0.0000353 ounces	1 ounce = 28.3 g
1 g = 0.0353 ounces	1 pound = 0.454 kg
1 kg = 2.21 pounds	

Temperature

To convert temperature:

$$°C = \frac{5}{9}(F - 32) \qquad °F = \frac{9}{5} + 32$$

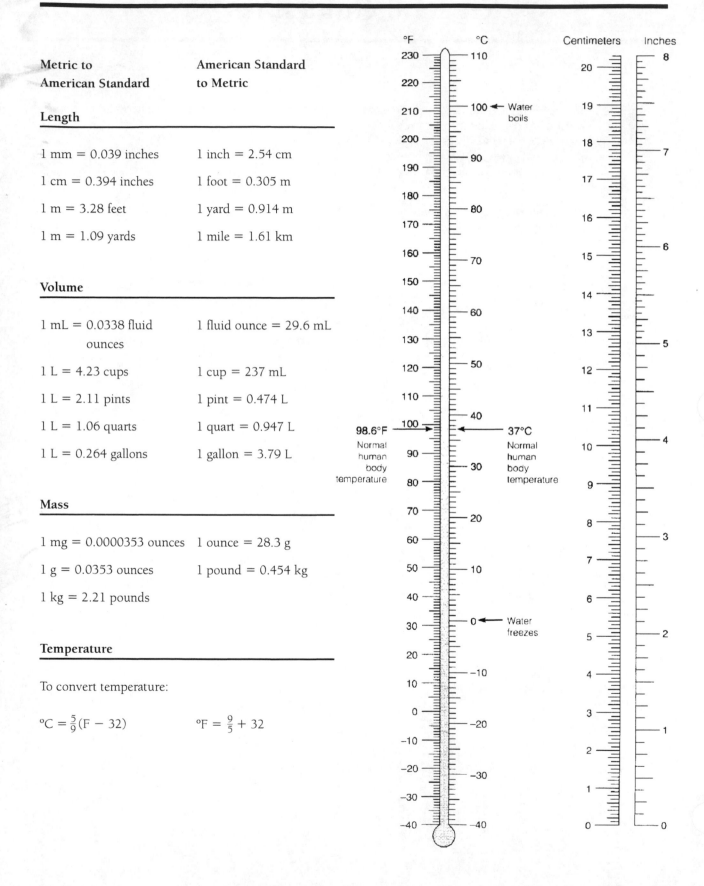

Contents

Laboratory Safety and Work Instructions

Attention Student! Read the following carefully because your instructor may give you a quiz on this material.

The laboratory can be—but is not necessarily—a dangerous place. When intelligent precautions and a proper understanding of techniques are employed, the laboratory is no more dangerous than any other classroom. Most of the precautions are just common-sense practices. These include the following:

1. Wear *approved* eye protection (including splash guards) at all times while in the laboratory. (*No one will be admitted without it.*) Your safety eye protection may be slightly different from that shown, but it must include shatterproof lenses and side shields to provide protection from splashes.

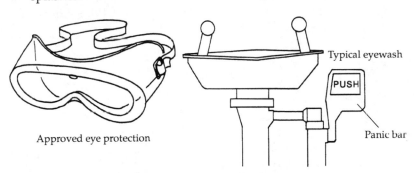

Approved eye protection

Typical eyewash

PUSH

Panic bar

The laboratory has an eyewash fountain available for your use. In the event that a chemical splashes near your eyes, you should use the fountain *before the material runs behind your eyeglasses and into your eyes.* The eyewash has a "panic bar," which enables its easy activation in an emergency.

2. Wear shoes at all times. (*No one will be admitted without them.*)

3. Eating, drinking, and smoking are strictly prohibited in the laboratory at all times.

4. Know where to find and how to use all safety and first-aid equipment (see the first page of this book).

5. Consider all chemicals to be hazardous unless you are instructed otherwise. ***Dispose of chemicals as directed by your instructor.*** Follow the explicit instructions given in the experiments.

6. If chemicals come into contact with your skin or eyes, wash immediately with copious amounts of water and then consult your laboratory instructor.

7. Never taste anything. Never directly smell the source of any vapor or gas. Instead, by means of your cupped hand, bring a small sample to your nose. Chemicals are not to be used to obtain a "high" or clear your sinuses.

Waft toward
your nose

8. Perform in the fume exhaust hood any reactions involving skin-irritating or dangerous chemicals, or unpleasant odors. This is a typical fume exhaust hood. Exhaust hoods have fans to exhaust fumes out of the

hood and away from the user. The hood should be used when you are studying noxious, hazardous, and flammable materials. It also has a shatterproof glass window, which may be used as a shield to protect you from minor explosions. Reagents that evolve toxic fumes are stored in the hood. Return these reagents to the hood after their use.

9. Never point a test tube that you are heating at yourself or your neighbor—it may erupt like a geyser.

10. Do not perform *any* unauthorized experiments.

11. Clean up all broken glassware *immediately.*

12. Always pour acids into water, not water into acid, because the heat of solution will cause the water to boil and the acid to spatter. "Do as you oughter, pour acid into water."

13. Avoid rubbing your eyes unless you *know* that your hands are clean.

14. When inserting glass tubing or thermometers into stoppers, *lubricate the tubing and the hole in the stopper with glycerol or water.* Wrap the rod in a towel and grasp it as close to the end being inserted as possible. Slide the glass into the rubber stopper with a twisting motion. Do not push. Finally, remove the excess lubricant by wiping with a towel. Keep your hands as close together as possible in order to reduce leverage.

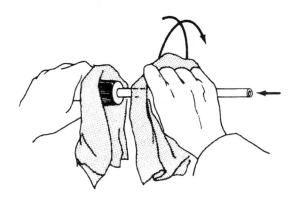

15. For safety purposes, always place the ring stand as far back on the laborator bench as comfortable, with the long edges of the base perpendicular to the front of the bench.

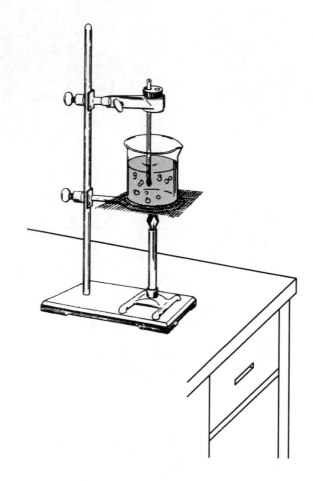

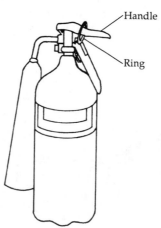

Handle

Ring

16. NOTIFY THE INSTRUCTOR IMMEDIATELY IN CASE OF AN ACCIDENT.

17. Many common reagents—for example, alcohols, acetone, and especially ether—are highly flammable. *Do not use them anywhere near open flames.*

18. Observe all special precautions mentioned in experiments.

19. Learn the location and operation of fire-protection devices.

In the unlikely event that a large chemical fire occurs, carbon dioxide fire extinguishers are available in the lab (usually mounted near one of the exits in the room). A typical carbon dioxide fire extinguisher is shown below.

In order to activate the extinguisher, you must pull the metal safety ring from the handle and then depress the handle. Direct the output from the extinguisher at the base of the flames. The carbon dioxide smothers the flames and cools the flammable material quickly. If you use the fire extinguisher, be sure to turn the extinguisher in at the stockroom so that it can be refilled immediately. If the carbon dioxide extinguisher does not extinguish the fire, evacuate the laboratory immediately and call the fire department.

One of the most frightening and potentially most serious accidents is the ignition of one's clothing. Certain types of clothing are hazardous in the laboratory and must *not* be worn. Since *sleeves* are most likely to come closest to flames, ANY CLOTHING THAT HAS BULKY OR LOOSE SLEEVES SHOULD NOT BE WORN IN THE LABORATORY. Ideally, students should wear laboratory coats with tightly fitting sleeves. Long hair also presents a hazard and must be tied back.

If a student's clothing or hair catches fire, his or her neighbors should take prompt action to prevent severe burns. Most laboratories have a water shower for such emergencies. A typical laboratory emergency water shower has the following appearance:

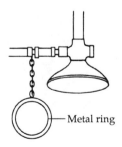
Metal ring

In case someone's clothing or hair is on fire, immediately lead the person to the shower and pull the metal ring. Safety showers generally dump 40 to 50 gallons of water, which should extinguish the flames. These showers generally cannot be shut off once the metal ring has been pulled. Therefore, the shower cannot be demonstrated. (Showers are checked for proper operation on a regular basis, however.)

19. Whenever possible, use hot plates in place of Bunsen burners.

BASIC INSTRUCTIONS FOR LABORATORY WORK

1. Read the assignment *before* coming to the laboratory.
2. Work independently unless instructed to do otherwise.
3. Record your results directly onto your report sheet or notebook. DO NOT RECOPY FROM ANOTHER PIECE OF PAPER.
4. Work conscientiously to avoid accidents.
5. Dispose of excess reagents as instructed by your instructor. NEVER RETURN REAGENTS TO THE REAGENT BOTTLE.
6. Do not place reagent-bottle stoppers on the desk; hold them in your hand. Your laboratory instructor will show you how to do this. Replace the stopper on the same bottle, never on a different one.
7. Leave reagent bottles on the shelf where you found them.
8. Use only the amount of reagent called for; avoid excesses.
9. Whenever instructed to use water in these experiments, use distilled water unless instructed to do otherwise.
10. Keep your area clean.
11. Do not borrow apparatus from other desks. If you need extra equipment, obtain it from the stockroom.
12. When weighing, do not place chemicals directly on the balance.
13. Do not weigh hot or warm objects. Objects should be at room temperature.
14. Do not put hot objects on the desktop. Place them on a wire gauze or heat-resistant pad.

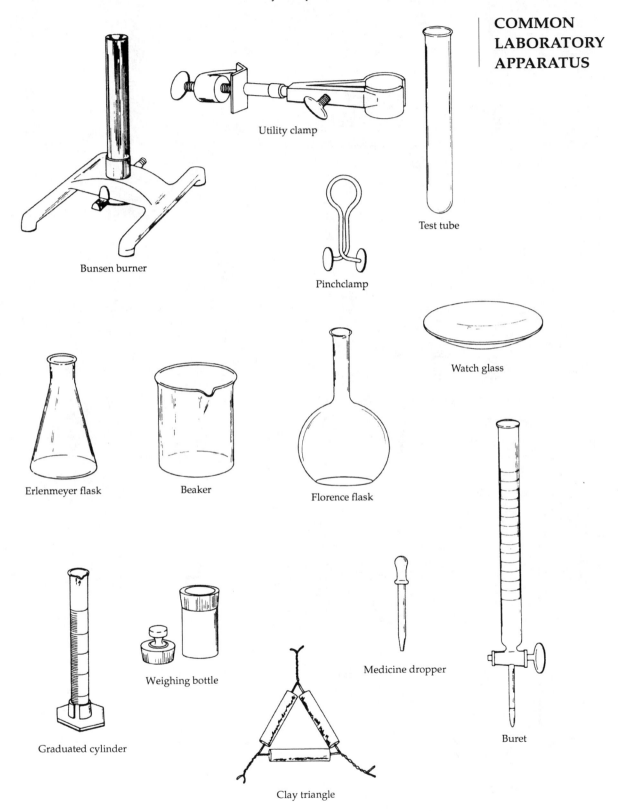

COMMON LABORATORY APPARATUS

Utility clamp

Test tube

Bunsen burner

Pinchclamp

Watch glass

Erlenmeyer flask

Beaker

Florence flask

Graduated cylinder

Weighing bottle

Medicine dropper

Buret

Clay triangle

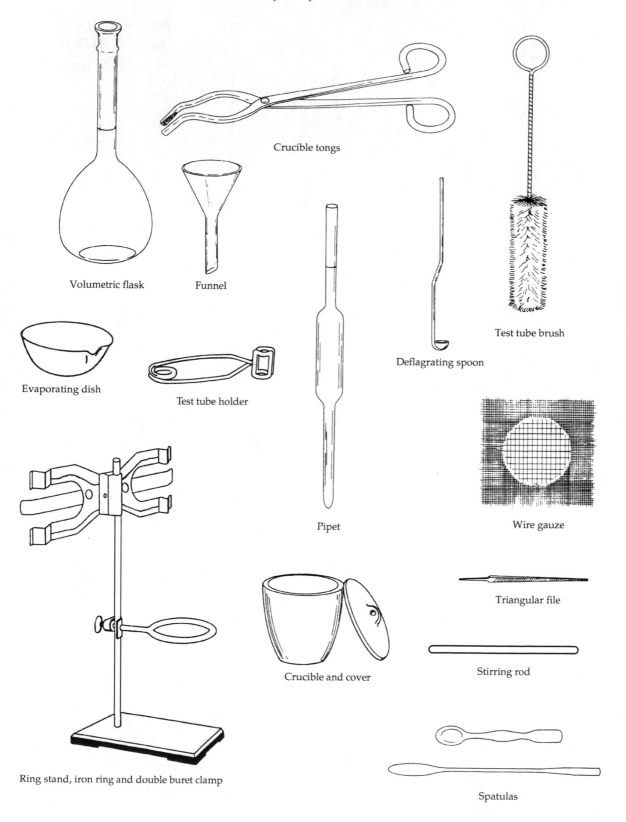

Volumetric flask

Funnel

Crucible tongs

Test tube brush

Evaporating dish

Test tube holder

Deflagrating spoon

Pipet

Wire gauze

Triangular file

Crucible and cover

Stirring rod

Ring stand, iron ring and double buret clamp

Spatulas

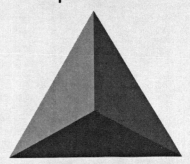

Basic Laboratory Techniques

OBJECTIVE

To learn the use of common, simple laboratory equipment.

APPARATUS AND CHEMICALS

Apparatus

balance	Bunsen burner and hose
150- and 250-mL beakers	meter stick
50- and 125-mL Erlenmeyer flasks	10-mL pipet
50- or 100-mL graduated cylinder	rubber bulb for pipet
barometer	ring stand and iron ring
clamp	thermometer
large test tube	

Chemicals

ice	antifreeze (ethylene glycol)

DISCUSSION

Chemistry is an experimental science. It depends upon careful observation and the use of good laboratory techniques. In this experiment, you will become familiar with some basic operations that will help you throughout this course. Your success as well as your safety in future experiments will depend upon your mastering these fundamental operations.

Because every measurement made in the laboratory is really an approximation, it is important that the numbers you record reflect the accuracy and precision of the device you use to make the measurement. Our system of weights and measures, the metric system, was originally based mainly upon fundamental properties of one of the world's most abundant substances: water. The system is summarized in Table 1. Conversions within the metric system are quite simple once you have committed to memory the meaning of the prefixes given in Table 2 and you use dimensional analysis.

In 1960 international agreement was reached, specifying a particular choice of metric units in which the basic units for length, mass, and time are the meter, the kilogram, and the second. This system of units, known as the International System of Units, is commonly referred to as the SI system and is preferred in scientific work. A comparison of some common SI, metric, and English units is presented in Table 3.

In Table 1, the prefix *means* the power of 10. For example, 5.4 *centi*meters means 5.4×10^{-2} meter; *centi-* has the same meaning as $\times 10^{-2}$.

From *Laboratory Experiments*, Tenth Edition, John H. Nelson and Kenneth C. Kemp. Copyright © 2006 by Pearson Education, Inc. Published by Prentice Hall, Inc. All rights reserved.

TABLE 1 Units of Measurement in the Metric System

Measurement	Unit and definition
Mass or weight	Gram (g) = mass of 1 cubic centimeter (cm^3) of water at 4°C and 760 mm Hg Mass = quantity of material Weight = mass × gravitational force
Length	Meter (m) = 100 cm = 1000 millimeters (mm) = 39.37 in.
Volume	Liter (L) = volume of 1 kilogram (kg) of water at 4°C
Temperature	°C, measures heat intensity: $°C = \frac{5}{9}(°F - 32)$ or $°F = \frac{9}{5}°C + 32$
Heat	1 calorie (cal), amount of heat required to raise 1 g of water 1°C: 1 cal = 4.184 joules (J)
Density	d, usually g/mL, for liquids, g/L for gases, and g/cm^3 for solids $d = \dfrac{mass}{unit\ volume}$
Specific gravity	sp gr, dimensionless: $sp\ gr = \dfrac{density\ of\ a\ substance}{density\ of\ a\ reference\ substance}$

TABLE 2 The Meaning of Prefixes in the Metric System

Prefix	Meaning (power of 10)	Abbreviation
femto-	10^{-15}	f
pico-	10^{-12}	p
nano-	10^{-9}	n
micro-	10^{-6}	μ
milli-	10^{-3}	m
centi-	10^{-2}	c
deci-	10^{-1}	d
kilo-	10^{3}	k
mega-	10^{6}	M
giga-	10^{9}	G

TABLE 3 Comparison of SI, Metric, and English Units

Physical quantity	SI unit	Some common metric units	Conversion factors between metric and English units
Length	Meter (m)	Meter (m) Centimeter (cm)	$1\ m = 10^2\ cm$ $1\ m = 39.37\ in.$ $1\ in. = 2.54\ cm$
Volume	Cubic meter (m^3)	Liter (L) Milliliter (mL)*	$1\ L = 10^3\ cm^3$ $1\ L = 10^{-3}\ m^3$ $1\ L = 1.06\ qt$
Mass	Kilogram (kg)	Gram (g) Milligram (mg)	$1\ kg = 10^3\ g$ $1\ kg = 2.205\ lb$ $1\ lb = 453.6\ g$
Energy	Joule (J)	Calorie (cal)	1 cal = 4.184 J
Temperature	Kelvin (K)	Degree celsius (°C)	$0K = -273.15°C$ $°C = \frac{5}{9}(°F - 32)$ $°F = \frac{9}{5}°C + 32$

*A mL is the same volume as a cubic centimeter: $1\ mL = 1\ cm^3$.

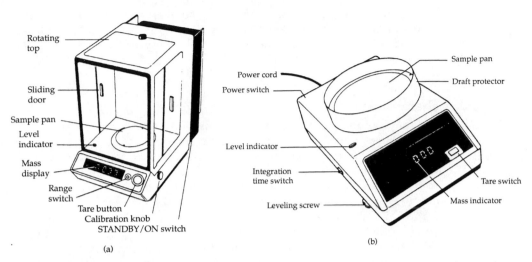

▲ FIGURE 1 Digital electronic balances. The balance gives the mass directly when an object to be weighed is placed on the pan. (a) Analytical balance. (b) Top loader.

EXAMPLE 1

Convert 6.7 nanograms to milligrams.

SOLUTION:

$$(6.7 \text{ ng})\left(\frac{10^{-9} \text{ g}}{1 \text{ ng}}\right)\left(\frac{1 \text{ mg}}{10^{-3} \text{ g}}\right) = 6.7 \times 10^{-6} \text{ mg}$$

Notice that the conversion factors have no effect on the magnitude (only the power of 10) of the mass measurement.

The quantities presented in Table 1 are measured with the aid of various pieces of apparatus. A brief description of some measuring devices follows.

Laboratory Balance

A laboratory balance is used to obtain the mass of various objects. There are several varieties of balances, with various limits on their accuracy. Two common kinds of balances are depicted in Figure 1. These single-pan balances are found in most modern laboratories. Generally they are simple to use, but they are very *delicate* and *expensive*. The amount of material to be weighed and the accuracy required determine which balance you should use.

Meter Rule

The standard unit of length is the meter (m), which is 39.37 in. in length. A metric rule, or meterstick, is divided into centimeters (1 cm = 0.01 m; 1 m = 100 cm) and millimeters (1 mm = 0.001 m; 1 m = 1000 mm). It follows that 1 in. is 2.54 cm. (Convince yourself of this, since it is a good exercise in dimensional analysis.)

Graduated Cylinders

Graduated cylinders are tall, cylindrical vessels with graduations scribed along the side of the cylinder. Since volumes are measured in these cylinders by measuring the height of a column of liquid, it is critical that the cylinder have a uniform diameter along its entire height. Obviously, a tall cylinder with a small diameter will be more accurate than a short one with a large diameter. A liter (L) is divided into milliliters (mL), such that 1 mL = 0.001 L, and 1 L = 1000 mL.

Thermometers

Most thermometers are based upon the principle that liquids expand when heated. Most common thermometers use mercury or colored alcohol as the liquid. These thermometers are constructed so that a uniform-diameter capillary tube surmounts a liquid reservoir. To calibrate a thermometer, one defines two reference points, normally the freezing point of water (0°C, 32°F) and the boiling point of water (100°C, 212°F) at 1 atm of pressure (1 atm = 760 mm Hg).* Once these points are marked on the capillary, its length is then subdivided into uniform divisions called *degrees*. There are 100° between these two points on the Celsius (°C, or centigrade) scale and 180° between those two points on the Fahrenheit (°F) scale.

Pipets

Pipets are glass vessels that are constructed and calibrated so as to deliver a precisely known volume of liquid at a given temperature. The markings on the pipet illustrated in Figure 2 signify that this pipet was calibrated to deliver (TD) 10.00 mL of liquid at 25°C. *Always* use a rubber bulb to fill a pipet. NEVER USE YOUR MOUTH! A TD pipet should not be blown empty.

It is important that you be aware that every measuring device, regardless of what it may be, has limitations in its accuracy. Moreover, to take full advantage of a given measuring instrument, you should be familiar with or evaluate its accuracy. Careful examination of the subdivisions on the device will indicate the maximum accuracy you can expect of that particular tool. In this experiment you will determine the accuracy of your 10-mL pipet. The approximate accuracy of some of the equipment you will use in this course is given in Table 4.

Not only should you obtain a measurement to the highest degree of accuracy that the device or instrument permits, but you should also record the reading or measurement in a manner that reflects the accuracy of the instrument. For example, a mass obtained from an analytical balance should be observed and recorded to the nearest 0.0001 g, or 0.1 mg. If the same object were weighed on a top-loading balance, its mass is recorded to the nearest 0.001 g. This is illustrated in Table 5.

PROCEDURE | ## A. The Meterstick

Examine the meterstick and observe that one side is ruled in inches, whereas the other is ruled in centimeters. Measure and record the length and width of your lab book in both units. Mathematically convert the two measurements to show that they are equivalent.

B. The Graduated Cylinder

Examine the 100-mL graduated cylinder and notice that it is scribed in milliliters. Fill the cylinder approximately half full with water. Notice that the *meniscus* (curved surface of the water) is concave (Figure 3).

---

*1 mm Hg is also called 1 torr.

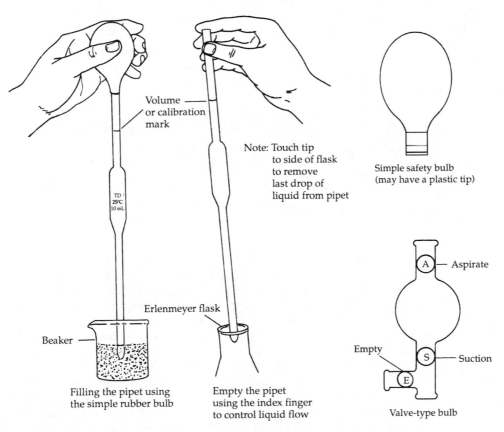

▲ FIGURE 2 A typical volumetric pipet, rubber bulbs, and the pipet-filling technique.

TABLE 4 Equipment Accuracy

Equipment	Accuracy
Analytical balance	±0.0001 g (±0.1 mg)
Top-loading balance	±0.001 g (±1 mg)
Meterstick	±0.1 cm (±1 mm)
Graduated cylinder	±0.1 mL
Pipet	±0.02 mL
Buret	±0.02 mL
Thermometer	±0.2°C

TABLE 5 Significant Figures Used In Recording Mass

Analytical balance	Top loader
85.9 g (incorrect)	85.9 g (incorrect)
85.93 g (incorrect)	85.93 g (incorrect)
85.932 g (incorrect)	85.932 g (correct)
85.9322 g (correct)	

The *lowest* point on the curve is always read as the volume, never the upper level. Avoid errors due to parallax; different and erroneous readings are obtained if the eye is not perpendicular to the scale. Read the volume of water to the nearest 0.1 mL. Record this volume. Measure the maximum amount of water that your largest test tube will hold. Record this volume.

C. The Thermometer and Its Calibration

This part of the experiment is performed to check the accuracy of your thermometer. These measurements will show how measured temperatures (read from thermometer) compare with true temperatures (the boiling and freezing points of water). The freezing point of water is 0°C; the boiling point

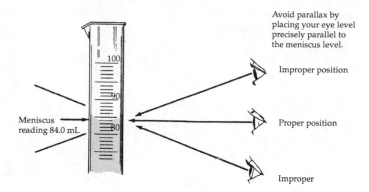

Avoid parallax by placing your eye level precisely parallel to the meniscus level.

Improper position

Proper position

Improper

Meniscus reading 84.0 mL

▲ **FIGURE 3** Proper eye position for taking volume readings.

depends upon atmospheric pressure and is calculated as shown in Example 2. Place approximately 50 mL of ice in a 250-mL beaker and cover the ice with distilled water. Allow about 15 min for the mixture to come to equilibrium and then measure and record the temperature of the mixture. *Theoretically, this temperature is 0°C.* Now, set up a 250-mL beaker on a wire gauze and iron ring as shown in Figure 4. Fill the beaker about half full with distilled water. Adjust your burner to give maximum heating and begin heating the water. *(Time can be saved if the water is heated while other parts of the experiment are being conducted.)* Periodically determine the temperature of the water with the thermometer, but be careful not to touch the walls of the beaker with the thermometer bulb. Record the boiling point (b.p.) of the water. Using the data given in Example 2, determine the *true boiling point at the observed*

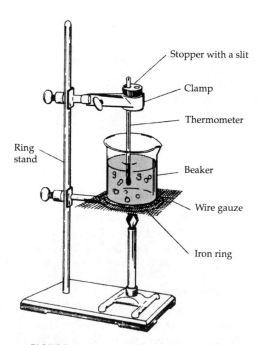

Stopper with a slit

Clamp

Thermometer

Ring stand

Beaker

Wire gauze

Iron ring

▲ **FIGURE 4** Apparatus setup for thermometer calibration.

atmospheric pressure. Obtain the atmospheric pressure from your laboratory instructor. Determine the temperature correction to be applied to your thermometer readings.

EXAMPLE 2

Determine the boiling point of water at 659.3 mm Hg.

SOLUTION: Temperature corrections to the boiling point of water are calculated using the following formula:

b.p. correction = (760 mm Hg − atmospheric pressure) × (0.037°C/mm)

The correction at 659.3 mm Hg is therefore

b.p. correction = (760 mm Hg − 659.3 mm Hg) × (0.037°C/mm) = 3.7°C

The true boiling point is thus

$$100.0°C − 3.7°C = 96.3°C$$

Using the graph paper provided, construct a thermometer-calibration curve like the one shown in Figure 5 by plotting observed temperatures versus true temperatures for the boiling and freezing points of water.

D. Using the Balance to Calibrate Your 10-mL Pipet

Weighing an object on a single-pan balance is a simple matter. Because of the sensitivity and the expense of the balance (some cost more than $2500), you must be careful in its use. Directions for operation of single-pan balances vary with make and model. Your laboratory instructor will explain how to use the balance. Regardless of the balance you use, proper care of the balance requires that you observe the following:

1. Do not drop an object on the pan.
2. Center the object on the pan.
3. Do not place chemicals directly on the pan; use a beaker, watch glass, weighing bottle, or weighing paper.

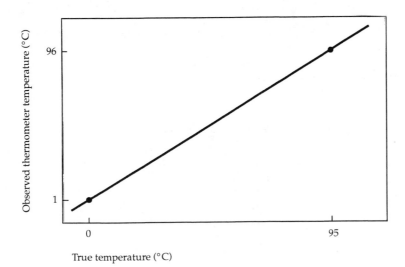

▲ **FIGURE 5** Typical thermometer-calibration curve.

4. Do not weigh hot or warm objects; objects must be at room temperature.
5. Return all weights to the zero position after weighing.
6. Clean up any chemical spills in the balance area.
7. Inform your instructor if the balance is not operating correctly; do not attempt to repair it yourself.

The following method is used to calibrate a pipet or other volumetric glassware. Obtain about 40 mL of distilled water in a 150-mL beaker. Allow the water to sit on the desk while you weigh and record the mass of an empty, dry 50-mL Erlenmeyer flask (tare) to the nearest 0.1 mg. Measure and record the temperature of the water. Using your pipet and rubber bulb, pipet exactly 10 mL of water into this flask and weigh the flask with the water in it (gross) to the nearest 0.1 mg. Obtain the mass of the water by subtraction (gross − tare = net). Using the equation below and the data given in Table 6, obtain the volume of water delivered and therefore the volume of your pipet.

$$\text{Density} = \frac{\text{mass}}{\text{volume}} \qquad d = \frac{m}{V}$$

Normally, density is given in units of grams per milliliter (g/mL) for liquids, grams per cubic centimeter (g/cm^3) for solids, and grams per liter (g/L) for gases. Repeat this procedure in triplicate—that is, deliver and weigh exactly 10 mL of water three separate times.

EXAMPLE 3

Using the procedure given above, a mass of 10.0025 g was obtained for the water delivered by one 10-mL pipet at 22°C. What is the volume delivered by the pipet?

SOLUTION: From the density equation given above, we know that

$$V = \frac{m}{d}$$

For mass we substitute our value of 10.0025 g. For the density, consult Table 6. At 22°C, the density is 0.997770 g/mL. The calculation is

$$V = \frac{10.0025 \text{ g}}{0.997770 \text{ g/mL}} = 10.0249 \text{ mL}$$

which must be rounded off to 10.02, because the pipet's volume can be determined only to within a precision of ±0.02 mL.

TABLE 6 Density of Pure Water at Various Temperatures

T (°C)	d (g/mL)	T (°C)	d (g/mL)
15	0.999099	22	0.997770
16	0.998943	23	0.997538
17	0.998774	24	0.997296
18	0.998595	25	0.997044
19	0.998405	26	0.996783
20	0.998203	27	0.996512
21	0.997992	28	0.996232

The *precision* of a measurement is a statement about the internal agreement among repeated results; it is a measure of the reproducibility of a given set of results. The arithmetic mean (average) of the results is usually taken as the "best" value. The simplest measure of precision is the *average deviation from the mean.* The average deviation is calculated by first determining the mean of the measurements, then calculating the deviation of each individual measurement from the mean and, finally, averaging the deviations (treating each as a positive quantity). Study Example 4 and then, using your own experimental results, calculate the mean volume delivered by your 10-mL pipet. Also calculate for your three trials the individual deviations from the mean and then state your pipet's volume with its average deviation.

EXAMPLE 4

The following volumes were obtained for the calibration of a 10-mL pipet: 10.10, 9.98, and 10.00 mL. Calculate the mean value and the average deviation from the mean.

SOLUTION:

$$\text{Mean} = \frac{10.10 + 9.98 + 10.00}{3} = 10.03$$

Deviations from the mean: $|\text{value} - \text{mean}|$

$$|10.10 - 10.03| = 0.07$$
$$|9.98 - 10.03| = 0.05$$
$$|10.00 - 10.03| = 0.03$$

Average deviation from the mean

$$= \frac{0.07 + 0.05 + 0.03}{3} = 0.05$$

The reported value is therefore 10.03 ± 0.05 mL.

E. Measuring the Density of Antifreeze

Weigh a dry 50-ml flask to the nearest 0.1 mg, and record its mass. Using your pipet, measure a 10-mL sample of antifreeze solution into the 50-mL flask, weigh the flask and its contents, and record this mass. Repeat these measurements two more times to give you an indication of the precision of your measurements. Use the measured mass and volume to calculate the density of the antifreeze for each measurement. Using the three values for the density, calculate the mean density and the average deviation from the mean for your determinations.

You should be able to answer the following questions before beginning this experiment:

PRE LAB QUESTIONS

1. What are the basic units of length, mass, volume, and temperature in the SI system?

2. What is the number of significant figures in each of the following measured quantaties? (a) 2578 g; (b) 0.010 mL; (c) 1.010 mL; (d) 3.72×10^{-3} cm.

3. What is the length of a crystal of copper sulfate in centimeters that is 0.125 inches long?

4. DNA is approximately 2.5 nm in length. If an average man is 6 ft tall, how many DNA molecules could be stacked end to end in an average man?

5. A liquid has a volume of 3.70 liters. What is its volume in mL? In cm^3?

6. If an object weighs 0.092 g, what is its mass in mg?

7. Why should you never weigh a hot object?

8. Why is it necessary to calibrate a thermometer and volumetric glassware?

9. What is precision?

10. Define the term *density*. Can it be determined from a single measurement?

11. What is the density of an object with a mass of 1.663 g and a volume of 0.2009 mL?

12. Weighing an object three times gave the following results: 9.2 g, 9.1 g, and 9.3 g. Find the mean mass and the average deviation from the mean.

13. Normal body temperature is 37.0°C. What is the corresponding Fahrenheit temperature?

14. What is the mass in kilograms of 750 mL of a substance that has a density of 0.930 g/mL?

15. An object weighs exactly 5 g on an analytical balance that has an accuracy of 0.1 mg. To how many significant figures should this mass be recorded?

REPORT SHEET | EXPERIMENT

Basic Laboratory Techniques

A. The Meterstick

Length of this lab book   _____ in. _____ cm _____ mm _____ m

Width of this lab book   _____ in. _____ cm _____ mm _____ m

Using an equation (including units), show that the above measurements are equivalent.

Area of this lab book (show calculations)   _____ cm^2

B. The Graduated Cylinder

Volume of water in graduated cylinder   _____ mL

Volume of water contained in largest test tube   _____ mL

C. The Thermometer and Its Calibration

Observed temperature of water-and-ice mixture   _____ °C

Temperature of boiling water   _____ °C

Observed atmospheric pressure   _____ mm Hg

True (corrected) temperature of boiling water   _____ °C

Thermometer correction   _____ °C

D. Using the Balance to Calibrate Your 10-mL Pipet

Temperature of water used in pipet   _____ °C

Corrected temperature   _____ °C

	Trial 1	Trial 2	Trial 3
Mass of Erlenmeyer plus ~10 mL H$_2$O (gross mass)	_____	_____	_____ g
Mass of Erlenmeyer (tare mass)	_____	_____	_____ g
Mass of ~10 mL of H$_2$O (net mass)	_____	_____	_____ g

Volume delivered by 10-mL _____   _____   _____ mL
pipet (show calculations)

Mean volume delivered by 10-mL pipet (show calculations)   _____ mL

	Trial 1	Trial 2	Trial 3
Individual deviations from the mean	_____	_____	_____

Average deviation from the mean (show calculations)   _____ mL

Volume delivered by your 10-mL pipet _____ mL ± _____ mL

E. Measuring the Density of Antifreeze

Temperature of antifreeze   _____ °C

	Trial 1	Trial 2	Trial 3
Mass of flask + antifreeze	_____	_____	_____ g
Mass of empty flask	_____	_____	_____ g
Mass of antifreeze	_____	_____	_____ g
Density of antifreeze (show calculation below)	_____	_____	_____ g

Mean (average) density

Average deviation from the mean
(show calculation below)

QUESTIONS

1. What is the number of significant figures in each of the following measured quantities? (a) 2513 kg; (b) 0.0034 g; (c) 5.060 mL; (d) 0.01060 cm; (e) 1.245×10^{-6} L.

2. Carry out the following operations, and express the answer with the appropriate number of significant figures and units. (a) (5.231 mm)(7.1 mm); (b) 72.3 g/1.2 mL; (c) 12.21 g + 0.0132 g; (d) 31.03 g + 12 mg.

3. Drug medications are often prescribed on the basis of body weight. The adult dosage of Elixophyllin, a drug used to treat asthma, is 6 mg/kg of body mass. Calculate the dose in milligrams for a 150-lb person.

4. A man who is 5 ft 10 in. tall weighs 170 lb. What is his height in centimeters and his mass in kilograms?

5. Determine the boiling point of water at 698.5 mm Hg.

6. A pipet delivers 9.98 g of water at 20°C. What volume does the pipet deliver?

7. A pipet delivers 9.04, 9.02, 9.08, and 9.06 mL in consecutive trials. Find the mean volume and the average deviation from the mean.

8. A 141-mg sample was placed on a watch glass that weighed 9.203 g. What is the weight of the watch glass and sample in grams?

9. (a) Using the defined freezing and boiling points of water, make a plot of degrees Fahrenheit versus degrees Celsius on the graph paper provided.

   (b) Determine the Celsius equivalent of 40°F using your graph. The relationship between these two temperature scales is linear (i.e., it is of the form $y = mx + b$). Determine the equation that relates degrees Fahrenheit to degrees Celsius.

   (c) Compute the Celsius equivalent of 40°F using this relationship.

Thermometer Calibration Curve

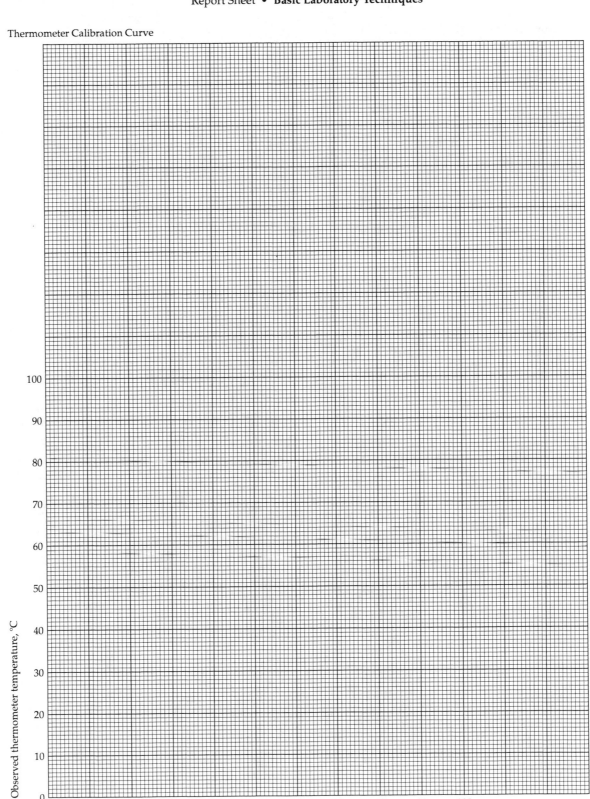

Observed thermometer temperature, °C

True temperature, °C

Fahrenheit—Celsius Graph

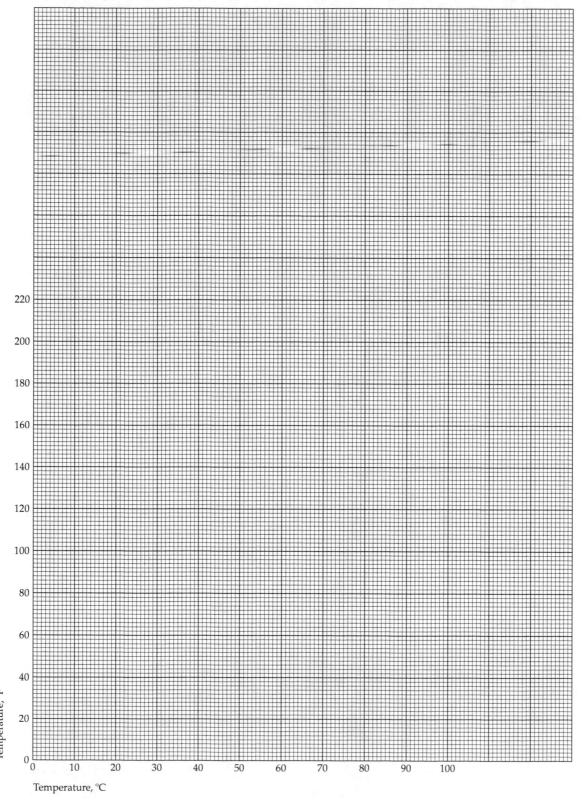

Temperature, °F

Temperature, °C

Answers to Selected
Pre Lab Questions

1. The basic units of measurement in the SI system are mass, kilogram; temperature, K; volume, m^3; length, meter; energy, joule.

3. $(0.125 \text{ in})(2.54 \text{ cm/in}) = 0.318 \text{ cm}$

5. $(3.70 \text{ L})(1000 \text{ mL/L}) = 3700 \text{ mL} = 3700 \text{ cm}^3$

7. Convection currents will tend to buoy the object and thus lead to an inaccurately low mass. Moreover, hot objects can damage the balance.

8. Thermometers and volumetric glassware are designed to be accurate, but their manufacture is subject to human error, and they should be calibrated.

9. Precision is a measure of the internal consistency of a replicate set of data.

10. Density is mass per unit volume. The determination of density requires a measurement of both mass and volume and so could not be done with a single unitary measurement.

12. $$\text{mean} = \frac{9.3 + 9.1 + 9.2}{3} = 9.2$$

$$\text{average deviation from mean} = \frac{0.1 + 0.1 + 0.0}{3} = 0.07$$

14. $d = \dfrac{m}{v}; \quad m = dv = (0.930 \text{ g/mL})(750 \text{ mL}) = 698 \text{ g}$

$698 \text{ g} = 0.698 \text{ kg}.$

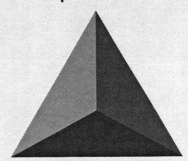

Experiment

Identification of Substances by Physical Properties

To become acquainted with procedures used in evaluating physical properties and the use of these properties to identify substances.

OBJECTIVE

APPARATUS AND CHEMICALS

Apparatus

balance	Bunsen burner and hose
50-mL beakers (2)	stirring rod
250-mL beaker	dropper
50-mL Erlenmeyer flask	boiling chips
10-mL graduated cylinder	thermometer
large test tubes (2)	spatula
small test tubes (6)	small watch glass
test-tube rack	capillary tubes (5)
10-mL pipet	tubing with right-angle bend
ring stand and ring	utility clamp
wire gauze	two-hole stopper
no. 3 two-hole stopper	small rubber bands (or small
with one of the holes slit	sections of $^1/_4$-in. rubber tubing)
to the side or a buret clamp	rubber bulb for pipet

Chemicals

ethyl alcohol	cyclohexane
toluene	naphthalene
soap solution	two unknowns (one liquid; one solid)

DISCUSSION

Properties are those characteristics of a substance that enable us to identify it and to distinguish it from other substances. Direct identification of some substances can readily be made by simply examining them. For example, we see color, size, shape, and texture, and we can smell odors and discern a variety of tastes. Thus, copper can be distinguished from other metals on the basis of its color.

Physical properties are those properties that can be observed without altering the composition of the substance. Whereas it is difficult to assign definitive values to such properties as taste, color, and odor, other physical properties, such as melting point, boiling point, solubility, density, viscosity, and refractive index, can be expressed quantitatively. For example, the melting point of copper is 1087°C and its density is 8.96 g/cm³. As you probably realize, a specific combination of properties is unique to a given substance, thus making it possible to identify most substances just by careful determination of several properties. This is so important that large books have been compiled listing characteristic properties of many known substances. Many

From *Laboratory Experiments*, Tenth Edition, John H. Nelson and Kenneth C. Kemp. Copyright © 2006 by Pearson Education, Inc. Published by Prentice Hall, Inc. All rights reserved.

scientists, most notably several German scientists during the latter part of the nineteenth century and earlier part of the twentieth, spent their entire lives gathering data of this sort. Two of the most complete references of this type that are readily available today are The Chemical Rubber Company's *Handbook of Chemistry and Physics* and N. A. Lange's *Handbook of Chemistry*.

In this experiment, you will use the following properties to identify a substance whose identity is unknown to you: solubility, density, melting point, and boiling point. The *solubility* of a substance in a solvent at a specified temperature is the maximum weight of that substance that dissolves in a given volume (usually 100 mL or 1000 mL) of a solvent. It is tabulated in handbooks in terms of grams per 100 mL of solvent; the solvent is usually water.

Density is an important physical property and is defined as the mass per unit volume:

$$d = \frac{m}{V}$$

Melting or freezing points correspond to the temperature at which the liquid and solid states of a substance are in equilibrium. These terms refer to the *same* temperature but differ slightly in their meaning. The *freezing point* is the equilibrium temperature when approached from the liquid phase—that is, when solid begins to appear in the liquid. The *melting point* is the equilibrium temperature when approached from the solid phase—that is, when liquid begins to appear in the solid.

A liquid is said to boil when bubbles of vapor form within it, rise rapidly to the surface, and burst. Any liquid in contact with the atmosphere will boil when its vapor pressure is equal to atmospheric pressure—that is, the liquid and gaseous states of a substance are in equilibrium. Boiling points of liquids depend upon atmospheric pressure. A liquid will boil at a higher temperature at a higher pressure or at a lower temperature at a lower pressure. The temperature at which a liquid boils at 760 mm Hg is called the *normal* boiling point. To account for these pressure effects on boiling points, people have studied and tabulated data for boiling point versus pressure for a large number of compounds. From these data, nomographs have been constructed. A *nomograph* is a set of scales for connected variables (see Figure 5 for an example); these scales are so placed that a straight line connecting the known values on some scales will provide the unknown value at the straight line's intersection with other scales. A nomograph allows you to find the correction necessary to convert the normal boiling point of a substance to its boiling point at any pressure of interest.

PROCEDURE | A. Solubility

Qualitatively determine the solubility of naphthalene (mothballs) in three solvents: water, cyclohexane, and ethyl alcohol. (**CAUTION:** *Cyclohexane is highly flammable and must be kept away from open flames.*) Determine the solubility by adding two or three small crystals of naphthalene to 2 to 3 mL (it is not necessary to measure either the solute weight or solvent volume) of each of these three solvents in separate, clean, *dry* test tubes. Make an attempt to keep the amount of naphthalene and solvent the same in each case. Place a cork in each test tube and shake briefly. Cloudiness indicates insolubility. Record your conclusions on the report sheet using the abbreviations s (soluble), sp (sparingly soluble), and i (insoluble). Into each of three more clean, *dry* test tubes place 2 or 3 mL of these same solvents and add 4 or 5 drops of toluene in place of naphthalene. Record your observations. The formation of two layers indicates immiscibility (lack of solubility). Now repeat these experiments using each of the three solvents (water, cyclohexane, and ethyl alcohol) with your solid and liquid unknowns and record your observations.

SAVE your solid and liquid unknowns for Parts B, C, and D, but dispose of the other chemicals in the marked refuse container. Do not dispose of them in the sink.

B. Density

Determine the densities of your two unknowns in the following manner.

The Density of a Solid Weigh about 1.5 g of your solid unknown to the nearest 0.001 g and record the mass. Using a pipet or a wash bottle, half fill a *clean, dry* 10-mL graduated cylinder with a solvent in which your unknown is *insoluble*. Be *careful* not to get the liquid on the inside walls, because you do not want your solid to adhere to the cylinder walls when you add it in a subsequent step. Read and record this volume to the nearest 0.1 mL. Add the weighed solid to the liquid in the cylinder, being careful not to lose any of the material in the transfer process and ensuring that all of the solid is beneath the surface of the liquid. Carefully tapping the sides of the cylinder with your fingers will help settle the material to the bottom. Do not be concerned about a few crystals that do not settle, but if a large quantity of the solid resists settling, add one or two drops of a soap solution and continue tapping the cylinder with your fingers. Now read the new volume to the nearest 0.1 mL. The difference in these two volumes is the volume of your solid (Figure 1). Calculate the density of your solid unknown.

You may recall that by measuring the density of metals in this way, Archimedes proved to the king that the charlatan alchemists had in fact not transmuted lead into gold. He did this after observing that he weighed less in the bathtub than he did normally by an amount equal to the weight of the fluid displaced. According to legend, upon making his discovery, Archimedes emerged from his bath and ran naked through the streets shouting *Eureka!* (I have found it).

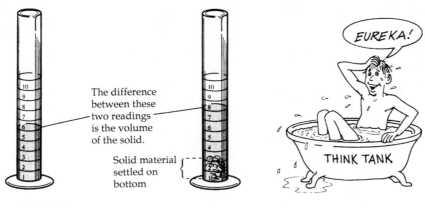

The difference between these two readings is the volume of the solid.

Solid material settled on bottom

▲ FIGURE 1

The Density of a Liquid   Weigh a clean, *dry* 50-mL Erlenmeyer flask to the nearest 0.0001 g. Obtain at least 15 mL of the unknown liquid in a clean, *dry* test tube. Using a 10-mL pipet, pipet exactly 10 mL of the unknown liquid into the 50-mL Erlenmeyer flask and quickly weigh the flask containing the 10 mL of unknown to the nearest 0.0001 g. Using the calibration value for your pipet, if you calibrated it, and the weight of this volume of unknown, calculate its density. Record your results and show how (with units) you performed your calculations. SAVE the liquid for your boiling-point determination.

C. Melting Point of Solid Unknown

Obtain a capillary tube and a small rubber band. Seal one end of the capillary tube by carefully heating the end in the edge of the flame of a Bunsen burner until the end *completely* closes. Rotating the tube during heating will help you to avoid burning yourself (Figure 2).

Pulverize a small portion of your solid-unknown sample with the end of a test tube on a clean watch glass. Partially fill the capillary with your unknown by gently tapping the pulverized sample with the open end of the capillary to force some of the sample inside. Drop the capillary into a glass tube about 38 to 50 cm in length, with the sealed end down to pack the sample into the bottom of the capillary tube. Repeat this procedure until the sample column is roughly 5 mm in height. Now set up a melting-point apparatus as illustrated in Figure 3.

Place the rubber band about 5 cm above the bulb on the thermometer and out of the liquid. Carefully insert the capillary tube under the rubber band with the closed end at the bottom. Place the thermometer with attached capillary into the beaker of water so that the sample is covered by water, the thermometer does not touch the bottom of the beaker, and the open end of the capillary tube is above the surface of the water. Heat the water slowly while gently agitating the water with a stirring rod. Observe the sample in the capillary tube while you are doing this. At the moment that the solid

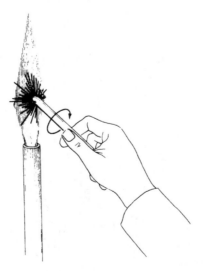

▲ FIGURE 2 Sealing one end of a capillary tube.

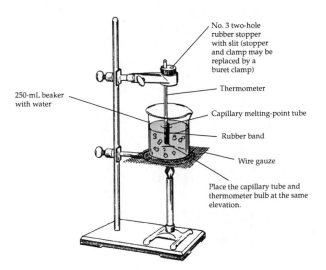

▲ FIGURE 3 Apparatus for melting-point determination.

melts, record the temperature. Also record the melting-point range, which is the temperature range between the temperature at which the sample begins to melt and the temperature at which all of the sample has melted. Using your thermometer-calibration curve, correct these temperatures to the true temperatures and record the melting point and melting-point range. These temperatures may differ by only 1°C or less.

D. Boiling Point of Liquid Unknown

To determine the boiling point of your liquid unknown, put about 3 mL of the material you used to determine the density into a clean, dry test tube. Fit the test tube with a two-hole rubber stopper that has one slit; insert your thermometer into the hole with the slit and one of your right-angle-bend glass tubes into the other hole, as shown in Figure 4. Add one or two small

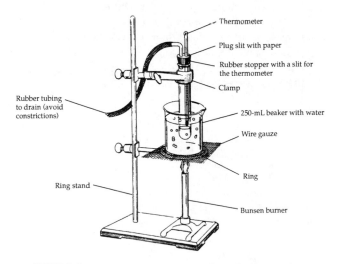

▲ FIGURE 4 Apparatus for boiling-point determination.

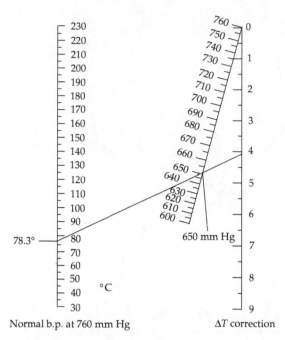

Normal b.p. at 760 mm Hg   ΔT correction

▲ **FIGURE 5** Use of nomograph for boiling-point correction for ethyl alcohol to 650 mm Hg.

boiling chips to the test tube to ensure even boiling of your sample. Position the thermometer so that it is about 1 cm above the surface of the unknown liquid. Clamp the test tube in the ring stand and connect to the right-angle-bend tubing a length of rubber tubing that reaches to the sink. Assemble your apparatus as shown in Figure 4. (**CAUTION:** *Be certain that there are no constrictions in the rubber tubing. Your sample is flammable. Keep it away from open flames.*)

Heat the water gradually and watch for changes in temperature. The temperature will become constant at the boiling point of the liquid. Record the observed boiling point. Correct the observed boiling point to the true boiling point at room atmospheric pressure using your thermometer-calibration curve. The normal boiling point (b.p. at 1 atm = 760 mm Hg) can now be calculated (see Example 1, below) using the nomograph provided in Figure 5. Your boiling-point correction should not be more than +5°C.

EXAMPLE 1

What will be the boiling point of ethyl alcohol at 650 mm Hg when its normal boiling point at 760 mm Hg is known to be 78.3°C?

SOLUTION: The answer is easily found by consulting the nomograph in Figure 5. A straight line drawn from 78.3°C on the left scale of normal boiling points through 650 mm Hg on the pressure scale intersects the temperature correction scale at 4°C. Therefore,

$$\text{normal b.p.} - \text{correction} = \text{observed b.p.}$$
$$78.3°C - 4.0°C = 74.3°C$$

TABLE 1 Physical Properties of Pure Substances

Substance	Density (g/mL)	Melting point (°C)	Boiling point (°C)	Solubility[a] in Water	Solubility[a] in Cyclohexane	Solubility[a] in Ethyl alcohol
Acetanilide	1.22	114	304	sp	sp	s
Acetone	0.79	−95	56	s	s	s
Benzophenone	1.15	48	306	i	s	s
Bromoform	2.89	8	150	i	s	s
2,3-Butanedione	0.98	−2.4	88	s	s	s
t-Butyl alcohol	0.79	25	83	s	s	s
Cadmium nitrate · 4H$_2$O	2.46	59	132	s	i	s
Chloroform [b]	1.49	−63.5	61	i	s	s
Cyclohexane	0.78	6.5	81.4	i	s	s
p-Dibromobenzene	1.83	86.9	219	i	s	s
p-Dichlorobenzene	1.46	53	174	i	s	s
m-Dinitrobenzene	1.58	90	291	i	s	s
Diphenyl	0.99	70	255	i	s	s
Diphenylamine	1.16	53	302	i	s	s
Diphenylmethane	1.00	27	265	i	s	s
Ether, ethyl propyl	1.37	−79	64	s	s	s
Hexane	0.66	−94	69	i	s	s
Isopropyl alcohol	0.79	−98	83	s	s	s
Lauric acid	0.88	43	225	i	s	s
Magnesium nitrate · 6H$_2$O	1.63	89	330[c]	s	i	s
Methyl alcohol	0.79	−98	65	s	i	s
Methylene chloride[b]	1.34	−97	40.1	i	s	s
Naphthalene	1.15	80	218	i	s	sp
α-Naphthol	1.10	94	288	i	i	s
Phenyl benzoate	1.23	71	314	i	s	s
Propionaldehyde	0.81	−81	48.8	s	i	s
Sodium acetate · 3H$_2$O	1.45	58	123	s	i	sp
Stearic acid	0.85	70	291	i	s	sp
Thymol	0.97	52	232	sp	s	s
Toluene	0.87	−95	111	i	s	s
p-Toluidine	0.97	45	200	sp	s	s
Zinc chloride	2.91	283	732	s	i	s

[a] s = soluble; sp = sparingly soluble; i = insoluble.

[b] Toxic. Most organic compounds used in the lab are toxic.

[c] Boils with decomposition.

Similar calculations could be done for the compounds in Table 1 at any pressure listed on the nomograph in Figure 5. In this experiment you will observe a boiling point at a pressure other than at 760 mm Hg, and you wish to know its normal boiling point. In order to estimate its normal boiling point, assume that, for example, your observed boiling point is 57.0°C and the observed pressure is 650 mm Hg. Use your observed boiling point of 57.0°C as if it were the normal boiling point and find the correction for a pressure of 650 mm Hg. Using the nomograph, you can see that the correction is 3.8°C. You would then add this correction to your observed boiling point to obtain an approximate normal boiling point:

$$57°C + 3.8°C = 60.8°C, \text{ or } 61°C$$

By consulting Table 1, you can find the compound that best fits your data; in this example, the data are for chloroform.

E. Unknown Identification

Your unknowns are substances contained in Table 1. Compare the properties that you have determined for your unknowns with those in the table. Identify your unknowns and record your results.

Dispose of your unknowns in the appropriate marked refuse containers.

PRE LAB QUESTIONS

Before beginning this experiment in the laboratory, you should be able to answer the following questions:

1. List five physical properties.

2. An 1.192-mL sample of an unknown has a mass of 9.02 g. What is the density of the unknown?

3. Are the substances diphenyl and acetone solids or liquids at room temperature?

4. Could you determine the density of cadmium nitrate using water? Why or why not?

5. What would be the boiling point of hexane at 670 mm Hg?

6. Why do we calibrate thermometers and pipets?

7. Is chloroform miscible with water? With cyclohexane?

8. When water and toluene are mixed, two layers form. Is the bottom layer water or toluene? (See Table 1.)

9. What solvent would you use to determine the density of zinc chloride?

10. The density of a solid with a melting point of 42° to 44°C was determined to be 0.87 ± 0.02 g/mL. What is the solid?

11. The density of a liquid whose boiling point is 55° to 57°C was determined to be 0.77 ± 0.05 g/mL. What is the liquid?

12. Which has the greater volume, 10 g of acetone or 10 g of toluene? What is the volume of each?

Name _____ Desk _____

Date _____ Laboratory Instructor _____

Liquid unknown no. _____

Solid unknown no. _____

REPORT SHEET | EXPERIMENT

Identification of Substances by Physical Properties

A. Solubility

	Water	Cyclohexane	Ethyl alcohol
Naphthalene	_____	_____	_____
Toluene	_____	_____	_____
Liquid unknown	_____	_____	_____
Solid unknown	_____	_____	_____

B. Density

Solid

Final volume of liquid in cylinder	_____ mL	
Initial volume of liquid in cylinder	_____ mL	Diphenylamine data
Volume of solid	_____ mL	
Mass of solid	_____ g	Density of solid _____ g/mL (show calculations)

Liquid

Volume of liquid	_____ mL	
Volume of liquid corrected for the pipet correction	_____ mL	
Mass of 50-mL Erlenmeyer plus 10 mL of unknown	_____ g	Isopropyl alcohol data
Mass of 50-mL Erlenmeyer	_____ g	
Mass of liquid	_____ g	Density _____ g/mL (show calculations)

C. Melting Point of Solid Unknown

Observed melting point   _____ °C

Corrected (apply thermometer
correction to obtain)   _____ °C

Observed melting-point range   _____ °C

Corrected (apply thermometer
correction to obtain)   _____ °C

D. Boiling Point of Liquid Unknown

Barometric pressure   _____ mm Hg

Observed   _____ °C

Corrected (apply thermometer
correction to obtain)   _____ °C

Estimated true (normal) b.p. (apply
pressure correction to obtain)   _____ °C

E. Unknown Identification

Solid unknown   _____

Liquid unknown   _____

QUESTIONS

1. Is p-toluidine a solid or a liquid at room temperature?

2. What solvent would you use to measure the density of lauric acid?

3. Convert your densities to kg/L and compare these values with those in g/mL.

4. If air bubbles were trapped in your solid beneath the liquid level in your density determination, what error would result in the volume measurement, and what would be the effect of this error on the calculated density?

5. A liquid unknown was found to be insoluble in water and soluble in cyclohexane and alcohol; the unknown was found to have a boiling point of 145°C at 658 mm Hg. What is the substance? What could you do to confirm your answer?

6. A liquid that has a density of 0.80 ± 0.01 g/mL is soluble in cyclohexane. What liquids may this be?

7. What is the boiling point of toluene at 600 mm Hg?

Consult a handbook or the internet for the following questions and specify the source used.

_____

8. Osmium is the densest element known. What are its density and melting point?

9. What are the colors of $CoCl_2$ and $CoCl_2 \cdot 6H_2O$?

10. What are the formula, molar mass, and color of potassium permanganate?

NOTES AND CALCULATIONS

Answers to Selected Pre Lab Questions

1. Melting points, boiling points, solubility properties, color, and densities are five physical properties.

3. Diphenyl, m.p. 70°C, is a solid and acetone, m.p. −95°C, is a liquid at room temperature because room temperature is normally about 20°C.

4. The density of cadmuim nitrate could not be determined in water because it is soluble in water. It could be determined in cyclohexane because it is not soluble in cyclohexane.

6. Thermometers, pipets, and other pieces of laboratory equipment are mass produced and subject to human error. Consequently, they should always be calibrated.

7. Chloroform is not miscible with water but is miscible with cyclohexane.

11. The liquid is acetone. (See Table 1.)

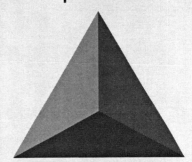

Separation of the Components of a Mixture

OBJECTIVE

To become familiar with the methods of separating substances from one another using decantation, extraction, and sublimation techniques.

APPARATUS AND CHEMICALS

Apparatus

balance	50- or 100-mL graduated cylinder
Bunsen burner and hose	clay triangles (2) or wire gauze (2)
tongs	ring stands (2)
evaporating dishes (2)	iron rings (2)
watch glass	glass stirring rods

Chemicals

unknown mixture of sodium chloride, ammonium chloride, and silicon dioxide

DISCUSSION

Most of the matter we encounter in everyday life consists of mixtures of different substances. Mixtures are combinations of two or more substances in which each substance retains its own chemical identity and therefore its own properties. Whereas pure substances have fixed compositions, the composition of mixtures can vary. For example, a glass of sweetened tea may contain either a little or a lot of sweetener. The substances making up a mixture are called *components*. Mixtures such as cement, wood, rocks, and soil do not have the same composition, properties, and appearance throughout the mixture. Such mixtures are called *heterogeneous*. Mixtures that are uniform in composition, properties, and appearance throughout are called *homogeneous*. Such mixtures include sugar water and air. Homogeneous mixtures are also called solutions. Mixtures are characterized by two fundamental properties:

- Each of the substances in the mixture retains its chemical identity.
- Mixtures are separable into these components by physical means.

If one of the substances in a mixture is preponderant—that is, if its amount far exceeds the amounts of the other substances in the mixture—then we usually call this mixture an impure substance and speak of the other substances in the mixture as impurities.

The preparation of compounds usually involves their separation or isolation from reactants or other impurities. Thus the separation of mixtures into their components and the purification of impure substances are frequently encountered problems. You are probably aware of everyday problems of this sort. For example, our drinking water usually begins as a mixture of silt, sand, dissolved salts, and water. Since water is by far the largest component in this mixture, we usually call this impure water. How do we purify it? The separation of the components of mixtures is based upon the fact that each component has different physical properties. The components of mixtures are always pure substances, either compounds or elements, and each pure substance possesses a unique set of properties. The properties of every sample of a pure substance are identical under the same conditions of temperature and pressure. This means that once we have determined that a sample of sodium chloride, (table salt) NaCl, is water soluble and a sample of silicon dioxide (sand), SiO_2, is not, we realize that all samples of sodium chloride are water soluble and all samples of silicon dioxide are not.

Likewise, every crystal of a pure substance melts at a specific temperature, and at a given pressure, every pure substance boils at a specific temperature.

Although there are numerous physical properties that can be used to identify a particular substance, we will be concerned in this experiment merely with the separation of the components and not with their identification. The methods we will use for the separation depend on differences in physical properties, and they include the following:

1. *Decantation.* This is the process of separating a liquid from a solid (sediment) by gently pouring the liquid from the solid so as not to disturb the solid (Figure 1).
2. *Filtration.* This is the process of separating a solid from a liquid by means of a porous substance—a filter—which allows the liquid to pass through but not the solid (see Figure 1). Common filter materials are paper, layers of charcoal, and sand. Silt and sand can be removed from our drinking water by this process.
3. *Extraction.* This is the separation of a substance from a mixture by preferentially dissolving that substance in a suitable solvent. By this process a soluble compound is usually separated from an insoluble compound.
4. *Sublimation.* This is the process in which a solid passes directly to the gaseous state and back to the solid state without the appearance of the liquid state. Not all substances possess the ability to be sublimed. Iodine, naphthalene, and ammonium chloride (NH_4Cl) are common substances that easily sublime.

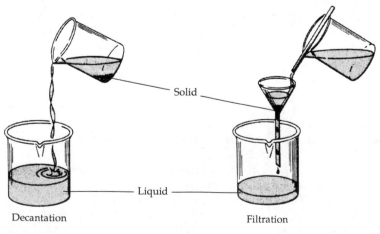

Solid

Liquid

Decantation

Filtration

▲ FIGURE 1

The mixture that you will separate contains three components: $NaCl$, NH_4Cl, and SiO_2. Their separation will be accomplished by heating the mixture to sublime the NH_4Cl, extracting the $NaCl$ with water, and finally drying the remaining SiO_2, as illustrated in the scheme shown in Figure 2. Carefully weigh a clean, dry evaporating dish to the nearest 0.01 g. Then obtain from your instructor a 2- to 3-g sample of the unknown mixture in the evaporating dish. Write the unknown number on your report sheet. If you obtain your unknown from a bottle, shake the bottle to make the sample mixture as uniform as possible. Weigh the evaporating dish containing the sample and calculate the sample mass to the nearest 0.001 g.

Place the evaporating dish containing the mixture on a clay triangle (or wire gauze), ring, and ring-stand assembly IN THE HOOD as shown in Figure 3. Heat the evaporating dish with a burner until white fumes are no longer formed (a total of about 15 min). Heat carefully to avoid spattering, especially when liquid is present. Occasionally shake the evaporating dish gently, using crucible tongs during the sublimation process.

Allow the evaporating dish to cool until it reaches room temperature and then weigh the evaporating dish with the contained solid. NEVER WEIGH HOT OR WARM OBJECTS! The loss in mass represents the amount of NH_4Cl in your mixture. Calculate this.

Add 25 mL of water to the solid in this evaporating dish and stir gently for 5 min. Next, weigh another clean, dry evaporating dish and watch glass. Decant the liquid carefully into the second evaporating dish, *which you have weighed*, being careful not to transfer any of the solid into the second evaporating dish. Add 10 mL more of water to the solid in the first evaporating dish, stir, and decant this liquid into the second evaporating dish as before. Repeat with still another 10 mL of water. This process extracts the soluble

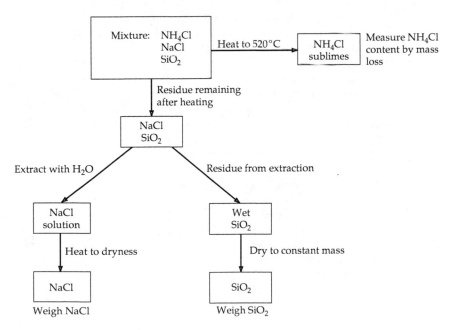

▲ **FIGURE 2** Flow diagram for the separation of the components of a mixture.

NOTE: To sublime NH$_4$Cl, do not use the watch glass; to dry NaCl and SiO$_2$, use the watch glass on top of the evaporating dish. Heat slowly—do not flame the edges of the watch glass that extend beyond the edge of the evaporating dish.

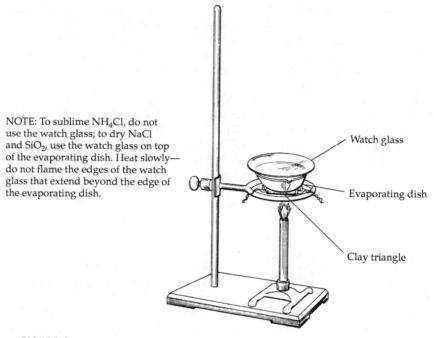

Watch glass

Evaporating dish

Clay triangle

▲ FIGURE 3

NaCl from the sand. You now have two evaporating dishes—one containing wet sand, and the second a solution of sodium chloride.

Place the evaporating dish containing the sodium chloride solution carefully on the clay triangle on the ring stand. Begin gently heating the solution to evaporate the water. Take care to avoid boiling or spattering, especially when liquid is present. Near the end, cover the evaporating dish with the watch glass that was weighed with this evaporating dish, and reduce the heat to prevent spattering. While the water is evaporating, you may proceed to dry the SiO$_2$ in the other evaporating dish as explained in the next paragraph, if you have another Bunsen burner available. When you have dried the sodium chloride completely, no more water will condense on the watch glass, and it, too, will be dry. Let the evaporating dish and watch glass cool to room temperature on a wire gauze and weigh them. The difference between this mass and the mass of the empty evaporating dish and watch glass is the mass of the NaCl. Calculate this mass.

Place the evaporating dish containing the wet sand on the clay triangle on the ring stand and cover the evaporating dish with a clean, dry watch glass. Heat slowly at first until the lumps break up and the sand appears dry. Then heat the evaporating dish to dull redness and maintain this heat for 10 min. Take care not to overheat, or the evaporating dish will crack. When the sand is dry, remove the heat and let the dish cool to room temperature. Weigh the dish after it has cooled to room temperature. The difference between this mass and the mass of the empty dish is the mass of the sand. Calculate this mass. Dispose of the sand in the marked container.

Calculate the percentage of each substance in the mixture using an approach similar to that shown in Example 1.

The accuracy of this experiment is such that the combined total of your three components should be in the neighborhood of 99%. If it is less than this, you have been sloppy. If it is more than 100%, you have not sufficiently dried the sand and salt.

EXAMPLE 1

What is the percentage of SiO_2 in a 2.56-g sample mixture if 1.25 g of SiO_2 has been recovered?

SOLUTION: The percentage of each substance in such a mixture can be calculated as follows:

$$\% \text{ Component} = \frac{\text{mass component in grams} \times 100}{\text{mass sample in grams}}$$

Therefore, the percentage of SiO_2 in this particular sample mixture is

$$\% \text{ } SiO_2 = \frac{1.25 \text{ g} \times 100}{2.56 \text{ g}} = 48.8\%$$

Before beginning this experiment in the laboratory, you should be able to answer the following questions:

PRE LAB QUESTIONS

1. Classify each of the following as a pure substance or a mixture; if a mixture, state whether it is heterogeneous or homogeneous: (a) concrete (b) tomato juice (c) marble (d) seawater (e) iron.

2. Suggest a way to determine whether a colorless liquid is pure water or a salt solution without tasting it.

3. What distinguishes a mixture from an impure substance?

4. Define the process of sublimation.

5. How do decantation and filtration differ? Which should be faster?

6. Why should one never weigh a hot object?

7. How does this experiment illustrate the principle of conservation of matter?

8. A mixture was found to contain 1.05 g of SiO_2, 0.69 g of cellulose, and 2.17 g of calcium carbonate. What is the percentage of SiO_2 in this mixture?

9. How could you separate a mixture of zinc chloride and cyclohexane?

10. How could you separate zinc chloride from SiO_2?

11. A student found that her mixture was 13% NH_4Cl, 18% $NaCl$, and 75% SiO_2. Assuming her calculations are correct, what did she most likely do incorrectly in her experiment?

12. Why is the NaCl extracted with water three times as opposed to only once?

NOTES AND CALCULATIONS

REPORT SHEET | EXPERIMENT

Separation of the Components of a Mixture

A. Mass of Evaporating Dish and Original Sample _____ g

    Mass of evaporating dish _____ g

    Mass of original sample _____ g

    Mass of evaporating dish after subliming NH_4Cl _____ g

    Mass of NH_4Cl _____ g

    Percent of NH_4Cl (show calculations) _____ %

B. Mass of Evaporating Dish, Watch Glass, and NaCl _____ g

    Mass of evaporating dish and watch glass _____ g

    Mass of NaCl _____ g

    Percent of NaCl (show calculations) _____ %

C. Mass of Evaporating Dish and SiO_2 _____ g

    Mass of evaporating dish _____ g

    Mass of SiO_2 _____ g

    Percent of SiO_2 (show calculations) _____ %

D. Mass of Original Sample   _____ g

   Mass of determined $(NH_4Cl + NaCl + SiO_2)$ _____ g

   Differences in these weights   _____ g

   $$\text{Percent recovery of matter} = \frac{\text{g matter recovered}}{\text{g original sample}} \times 100 =$$ _____ %

   Account for your errors

QUESTIONS

1. Could the separation in this experiment have been done in a different order? For example, if the mixture were first extracted with water and then the extract and the insoluble residue both heated to dryness, could you determine the amounts of NaCl, NH_4Cl, and SiO_2 originally present? Why or why not?

Consult a handbook to answer these questions.

2. How could you separate barium sulfate, $BaSO_4$, from NH_4Cl?

3. How could you separate barium chloride, $BaCl_2$, from calcium sulfate $CaSO_4$?

4. How could you separate tellurium dioxide, TeO_2, from SiO_2?

5. How could you separate benzophenone from α-naphthol? (See Table 1)

Answers to Selected Pre Lab Questions

3. A mixture differs from an impure substance only in the relative amounts of materials. If the substance contains primarily one component, it is called an impure substance. If, on the other hand, it contains several components in similar amounts, it is called a mixture. In reality, all impure substances are mixtures.

4. Sublimation is the process by which a substance changes physical states from the solid to the gaseous and back to the solid state without passing through the liquid state.

5. Filtration differs from decantation in that the liquid phase passes through a semipermeable substance such as a filter, whereas in decantation the liquid phase is separated from the solid phase by carefully pouring off the liquid. Decantation does not involve the use of another substance to achieve the separation, and is faster than filtration.

6. A hot object creates a buoyancy effect by radiating energy in the form of heat and will appear to have a reduced mass. In addition the hot object may cause damage to the delicate balance and so should be allowed to cool to room temperature before it is weighed.

7. All of the original sample should be recovered; thus the sum of the weights of the components, NH_4Cl, SiO_2, and $NaCl$, should precisely equal the total weight of the sample as no matter is being converted into energy in this experiment.

9. Zinc chloride is insoluble in cyclohexane and can be removed by filtering it from the cyclohexane.

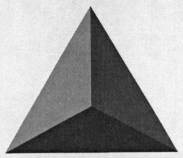

Chemical Formulas

To become familiar with chemical formulas and how they are obtained.

Apparatus

balance	250-mL beaker
Bunsen burner	evaporating dish
50-mL graduated cylinder	ring stand and ring
wire gauze	stirring rod
crucible and cover	clay triangle
carborundum boiling chips or	
glass beads	

Chemicals

granular zinc	copper wire
powdered sulfur	6 M HCl

Chemists use an abbreviated notation to indicate the exact chemical composition of compounds (chemical formulas). We then use these chemical formulas to indicate how new compounds are formed by chemical combinations of other compounds (chemical reactions). However, before we can learn how chemical formulas are written, we must first acquaint ourselves with the symbols used to denote the elements from which these compounds are formed.

Symbols and Formulas

We use one or two letters (with the first letter capitalized) to denote a chemical element. These symbols are derived, as a rule, from the first two letters or first syllable of the element's name.

Many elements are found in nature in molecular form; that is, two or more of the same type of atom are tightly bound together. The resultant "package" of atoms, or *molecule*, as it is termed, behaves in many ways as a single distinct object or unit. For example, the oxygen normally found in air consists of molecules that contain two oxygen atoms. We represent this molecular form of oxygen by the chemical formula O_2. The subscript in the formula tells us that two oxygen atoms are present in each oxygen molecule.

Compounds that are composed of molecules are called *molecular compounds*, and they may contain more than one type of atom. For example, a molecule of water consists of two hydrogen atoms and one oxygen atom and is represented by the chemical formula H_2O. The absence of a subscript on the O implies there is one oxygen atom per water molecule. Another compound composed of these same elements, but in different proportions, is hydrogen peroxide, H_2O_2. The physical and chemical properties of these two compounds are very different. We shouldn't be surprised, for they are two different substances.

Chemical formulas that indicate the *actual* numbers and types of atoms in a molecule are called *molecular formulas*, whereas chemical formulas that indicate only the *relative* numbers of atoms of a type in a molecule are called *empirical formulas*. The subscripts in an empirical formula are always the smallest whole-number ratios. For example, the molecular formula for hydrogen peroxide is H_2O_2, whereas its empirical formula is HO. The molecular formula for glucose is $C_6H_{12}O_6$; its empirical formula is CH_2O. For many substances the molecular formula and empirical formula are identical, as is the case for water, H_2O, and sulfuric acid, H_2SO_4.

Atomic Weights

It is important to know something about masses of atoms and molecules. With a mass spectrometer we can measure the masses of individual atoms with a high degree of accuracy. We know, for example, that the hydrogen-1 atom has a mass of 1.6735×10^{-24} g and the oxygen-16 atom has a mass of 1.674×10^{-24} g. Because it is cumbersome to express such small masses in grams, we use a unit called the *atomic mass unit*, or amu. An amu equals 1.66054×10^{-24} g. Most elements occur as mixtures of isotopes. The average atomic mass of each element expressed in amu is also known as its *atomic weight*. The atomic weights of the elements listed both in the table of elements and in the periodic table inside the front and back covers of this book, respectively, are in amu.

Formula and Molecular Weights

The *formula weight* of a substance is merely the sum of the atomic weights of all atoms in its chemical formula. For example, nitric acid, HNO_3, has a formula weight of 63.0 amu.

$$FW = (AW \text{ of } H) + (AW \text{ of } N) + 3(AW \text{ of } O)$$
$$= 1.0 \text{ amu} + 14.0 \text{ amu} + 3(16.0 \text{ amu})$$
$$= 63.0 \text{ amu}$$

If the chemical formula of a substance is its molecular formula, then the formula weight is also called the *molecular weight*. For example, the molecular formula for formaldehyde is CH_2O. The molecular weight of formaldehyde is therefore

$$MW = 12 \text{ amu} + 2(1.0 \text{ amu}) + 16.0 \text{ amu}$$
$$= 30.0 \text{ amu}$$

For ionic substances such as NaCl that exist as three-dimensional arrays of ions, it is not appropriate to speak of molecules. Similarly, the terms molecular weight and molecular formula are inappropriate for these ionic substances. It is correct to speak of their formula weight, however. Thus, the formula weight of NaCl is

$$FW = 23.0 \text{ amu} + 35.5 \text{ amu}$$
$$= 58.5 \text{ amu}$$

Percentage Composition from Formulas

New compounds are made in laboratories every day, and the formulas of these compounds must be determined. The compounds are often analyzed for their *percentage composition*, i.e., the percentage by mass of each element present in the compound. The percentage composition is useful information in establishing the formula for the substance. If the formula of a compound is known, calculating its percentage composition is a straight-forward matter. In general, the percentage of an element in a compound is given by

$$\frac{(\text{Number of atoms of element})(\text{AW})}{\text{FW of compound}} \times 100$$

If we want to know the percentage composition of formaldehyde, CH_2O, whose formula weight is 30.0 amu, we proceed as follows:

$$\%C = \frac{12.0\ \text{amu}}{30.0\ \text{amu}} \times 100 = 40.0\%$$

$$\%H = \frac{2(1.0\ \text{amu})}{30.0\ \text{amu}} \times 100 = 6.7\%$$

$$\%O = \frac{16.0\ \text{amu}}{30.0\ \text{amu}} \times 100 = 53.3\%$$

The Mole

Even the smallest samples we use in the laboratory contain an enormous number of atoms. A drop of water contains about 2×10^{21} water molecules! The unit that the chemist uses for dealing with such a large number of atoms, ions, or molecules is the *mole*, abbreviated mol. Just as the unit dozen refers to 12 objects, the mole refers to a collection of 6.02×10^{23} objects. This number is called Avogadro's number. Thus, a mole of water molecules contains 6.02×10^{23} H_2O molecules, and a mol of sodium contains 6.02×10^{23} Na atoms. The mass (in grams) of 1 mol of a substance is called its *molar mass*. The molar mass (in grams) of any substance is numerically equal to its formula weight.

Thus:

One CH_2O molecule has a mass of 30.0 amu; 1 mol CH_2O has a mass of 30.0 g
and contains 6.02×10^{23} CH_2O molecules

One Na atom has a mass of 23.0 amu; 1 mol Na has a mass of 23.0 g
and contains 6.02×10^{23} Na atoms

It is a simple matter to calculate the number of moles of any substance whose mass and formula we know. For example, suppose we have one quart of rubbing alcohol (generally isopropyl alcohol) and know its density to be 0.785 g/mL and we want to know how many moles this is. First we need to convert the volume to our system of units. Since 1 qt is 0.946 L and 1 L contains 1000 mL, our quart of isopropyl alcohol is

$$(1\ \text{qt})\left(\frac{0.946\ \text{L}}{\text{qt}}\right)\left(\frac{1000\ \text{mL}}{\text{L}}\right) = 946\ \text{mL}$$

We can now calculate the mass:

$$946 \text{ mL} \times 0.785 \text{ g/mL} = 743 \text{ g}$$

We next need the chemical formula for isopropyl alcohol. This is C_3H_7OH. The molecular weight is, therefore,

Weight carbon	$3 \times 12.0 = 36.0$ amu
Weight hydrogen	$8 \times 1.0 = 8.0$ amu
Weight oxygen	$1 \times 16.0 = 16.0$ amu
Molecular weight	$C_3H_7OH = 60.0$ amu

Hence,

$$\text{moles of } C_3H_7OH = (743 \text{ g } C_3H_7OH)\left(\frac{1 \text{ mol } C_3H_7OH}{60.0 \text{ g } C_3H_7OH}\right) = 12.4 \text{ mol}$$

Thus our quart of rubbing alcohol contains 12.4 mol of isopropyl alcohol. It should now be apparent to you how much information is contained in a chemical formula.

Empirical Formulas from Analyses

The empirical formula for a substance tells us the relative number of atoms of each element in the substance. Thus, the formula H_2O indicates that water contains two hydrogen atoms for each oxygen atom. This ratio applies on the molar level as well; thus, 1 mol of H_2O contains two mol of H atoms and 1 mol of O atoms. Conversely, the ratio of the number of moles of each element in a compound gives the subscripts in a compound's empirical formula. Thus, the mole concept provides a way of calculating the empirical formula of a chemical substance. This is shown in the following example.

EXAMPLE 1

While you are working in a hospital laboratory, a patient complaining of severe stomach cramps and labored respiration dies within minutes of being admitted. Relatives of the patient later tell you that he may have ingested some rat poison. You therefore have his stomach pumped to verify this and also to determine the cause of death. One of the more logical things to do would be to attempt to isolate the agent that caused death and perform chemical analyses on it. Let's suppose that this was done, and the analyses showed that the isolated chemical compound contained, by weight, 60.0% potassium, 18.5% carbon, and 21.5% nitrogen. What is the chemical formula for this compound?

SOLUTION: One simple and direct way of making the necessary calculations is as follows. Assume you had 100 g of the compound. This 100 g would contain

$$(100 \text{ g})(0.600) = 60.0 \text{ g potassium}$$
$$(100 \text{ g})(0.185) = 18.5 \text{ g carbon}$$
$$(100 \text{ g})(0.215) = 21.5 \text{ g nitrogen}$$

Divide each of these masses by the appropriate atomic weight to obtain the number of moles of each element in the 100 g:

$$60.0 \text{ g K}\left(\frac{1 \text{ mol K}}{39.0 \text{ g K}}\right) = 1.54 \text{ mol K}$$

$$18.5 \text{ g C}\left(\frac{1 \text{ mol C}}{12.0 \text{ g C}}\right) = 1.54 \text{ mol C}$$

$$21.5 \text{ g N}\left(\frac{1 \text{ mol N}}{14.0 \text{ g N}}\right) = 1.54 \text{ mol N}$$

Then divide each number by 1.54 to determine the simplest whole-number ratio of moles of each element. (In general, after determining the number of moles of each element, we determine the simplest whole-number ratio by dividing each number of moles by the smallest number of moles. In this example all the numbers are the same.)

$$K = \frac{1.54}{1.54} = 1.00$$

$$C = \frac{1.54}{1.54} = 1.00$$

$$N = \frac{1.54}{1.54} = 1.00$$

The ratio obtained in this case is 1.00, and we conclude that the formula is KCN. This is the simplest, or empirical, formula because it uses as subscripts the smallest set of integers to express the correct ratios of atoms present. Because KCN is a common rat poison, we may justifiably conclude that the relatives' suggestion of rat-poison ingestion as the probable cause of death is correct.

Molecular Formulas from Empirical Formulas

The formula obtained from percentage composition is *always* the empirical formula. We can obtain the molecular formula from the empirical formula if we know the molecular weight of the compound. *The subscripts in the molecular formula of a substance are always a whole-number multiple of the corresponding subscripts in its empirical formula.* The multiple is found by comparing the formula weight of the empirical formula with the molecular weight. For example, suppose we determined the empirical formula of a compound to be CH_2O. Its formula weight is

$$FW = 12.0 \text{ amu} + 2(1.0 \text{ amu}) + 16.0 \text{ amu} = 30.0 \text{ amu}$$

Suppose the experimentally determined molecular weight is 180. Then, the molecule has six times the mass ($180/30.0 = 6.00$) and must, therefore, have six times as many atoms as the empirical formula. The subscripts in the empirical formula must be multiplied by 6 to obtain the molecular formula: $C_6H_{12}O_6$.

In this experiment, you will determine the empirical formulas of two chemical compounds. One is copper sulfide, which you will prepare according to the following chemical reaction:

$$x\text{Cu}(s) + y\text{S}(s) \longrightarrow \text{Cu}_x\text{S}_y(s)$$

The other is zinc chloride, which you will prepare according to the chemical reaction

$$x\text{Zn}(s) + y\text{HCl}(aq) \longrightarrow \text{Zn}_x\text{Cl}_y(s) + \frac{y}{2}\text{H}_2(g)$$

The objective is to determine the combining ratios of the elements (that is, to determine x and y) and to balance the chemical equations given above.

PROCEDURE | ## A. Zinc Chloride

Clean and dry your evaporating dish and place it on the wire gauze resting on the iron ring. Heat the dish with your Bunsen burner, gently at first, and then more strongly, until all of the condensed moisture has been driven off. This should require heating for about 5 min. Allow the dish to cool to room temperature on a wire gauze (do not place the hot dish on the countertop) and weigh it. Record the mass of the empty evaporating dish to the nearest 0.01 g.

Obtain a sample of granular zinc from your laboratory instructor and add about 0.5 g of it to the weighed evaporating dish. Weigh the evaporating dish containing the zinc and record the total mass to the nearest 0.01 g. Calculate the mass of the zinc.

Slowly, and with constant swirling, add 15 mL of 6 M HCl to the evaporating dish containing the zinc. A vigorous reaction will ensue, and hydrogen gas will be produced. (**CAUTION:** *No flames are permitted in the laboratory while this reaction is taking place, because hydrogen gas is very explosive.*) If any undissolved zinc remains after the reaction ceases, add an additional 5 mL of acid. Continue to add 5-mL portions of acid as needed until all the zinc has dissolved. **CAUTION:** *Zinc chloride is caustic and must be handled carefully in order to avoid any contact with your skin. Should you come in contact with it, immediately wash the area with copious amounts of water.*

Set up a steam bath as illustrated in Figure 1 using a 250-mL beaker, and place the evaporating dish on the steam bath. Heat the evaporating dish very carefully on the steam bath until most of the liquid has disappeared. Then remove the steam bath and heat the dish on the wire gauze. During this last stage of heating, the flame must be carefully controlled or there will be spattering, and some loss of product will occur. (**CAUTION:** *Do not heat to the point that the compound melts, or some will be lost due to sublimation.*) Leave the compound looking somewhat pasty while hot.

Allow the dish to cool to room temperature and weigh it. Record the mass. After this first weighing, heat the dish again very gently. Cool it and

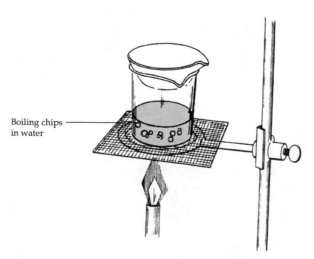

Boiling chips in water

▲ FIGURE 1 Steam bath.

reweigh it. If these weighings do not agree within 0.02 g, repeat the heating and weighing until two successive weighings agree. This is known as *drying to constant mass* and is the only way to be certain that all the moisture is driven off. Zinc chloride is very deliquescent (rapidly absorbs moisture from the air) and so should be weighed as soon as possible after cooling.

Calculate the mass of zinc chloride. The difference in mass between the zinc and zinc chloride is the mass of chlorine. Calculate the mass of chlorine in zinc chloride. From this information, you can readily calculate the empirical formula for zinc chloride and balance the chemical equation for its formation. Perform these operations on the report sheet.

B. Copper Sulfide

Support a clean, dry porcelain crucible and cover on a clay triangle and dry by heating to a dull red in a Bunsen flame, as illustrated in Figure 2. Allow the crucible and cover to cool to room temperature and weigh them. Record the mass to the nearest 0.01 g.

Place 1.5 to 2.0 g of tightly wound copper wire or copper turnings in the crucible and weigh the copper, crucible, and lid to the nearest 0.01 g and record your results. Calculate the mass of copper.

In the hood, add sufficient sulfur to cover the copper, place the crucible with cover in place on the triangle, and heat the crucible gently until sulfur ceases to burn (blue flame) at the end of the cover. Do not remove the cover while the crucible is hot. Finally, heat the crucible to dull redness for about 5 min.

Allow the crucible to cool to room temperature. This will take about 10 min. Then weigh with the cover in place. Record the mass. Again cover the

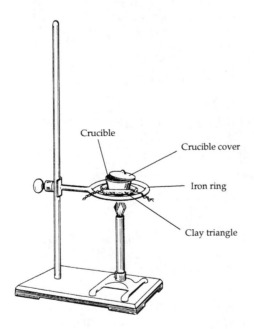

Crucible

Crucible cover

Iron ring

Clay triangle

▲ FIGURE 2 Setup for copper sulfide determination.

contents of the crucible with sulfur and repeat the heating procedure. Allow the crucible to cool and reweigh it. Record the mass. If the last two weighings do not agree to within 0.02 g, the chemical reaction between the copper and sulfur is incomplete. If this is found to be the case, add more sulfur and repeat the heating and weighing until a constant mass is obtained.

Calculate the mass of copper sulfide obtained. The difference in mass between the copper sulfide and copper is the mass of sulfur in copper sulfide. Calculate this mass. From this information the empirical formula for copper sulfide can be obtained, and the chemical equation for its production can be balanced. Perform these operations on your report sheet.

Waste Disposal Instructions All chemicals must be disposed of in the appropriately labeled containers.

PRE LAB QUESTIONS

Before beginning this experiment in the laboratory, you should be able to answer the following questions:

1. Give the chemical symbols for the following elements: (a) carbon, (b) zinc, (c) chlorine, (e) potassium

2. What are the formula weights of: (a) NaCl, (b) $BaCl_2$?

3. Define the term *compound*.

4. Why are atomic weights relative weights?

5. How do formula weights and molecular weights differ?

6. What is the percentage composition of Na_2CO_3?

7. A substance was found by analysis to contain 45.57% tin and 54.43% chlorine. What is the empirical formula for the substance?

8. What is the law of definite proportions?

9. How do empirical and molecular formulas differ?

10. What is the mass in grams of one lead atom?

11. Soda-lime glass is prepared by fusing sodium carbonate, Na_2CO_3; limestone, $CaCO_3$; and sand, SiO_2. The composition of the glass varies, but the commonly accepted reaction for its formation is

    $$Na_2CO_3(s) + CaCO_3(s) + 6\,SiO_2(s) \longrightarrow Na_2CaSi_6O_{14}(s) + 2\,CO_2(g)$$

    Using this equation, how many kilograms of sand would be required to produce enough glass to make 1000 400-g wine bottles?

12. Caffeine, a stimulant found in coffee and tea, contains 49.5% carbon, 5.15% hydrogen, 28.9% nitrogen, and 16.5% oxygen by mass. What is the empirical formula of caffeine? If its molar mass is about 195 g, what is its molecular formula?

13. An analysis of an oxide of nitrogen with a molecular weight of 92.02 amu gave 69.57% oxygen and 30.43% nitrogen. What are the empirical and molecular formulas for this nitrogen oxide? Complete and balance the equation for its formation from the elements nitrogen and oxygen.

14. How many potassium atoms are present in 0.01456 g of potassium?

REPORT SHEET | EXPERIMENT

Chemical Formulas

B. Zinc Chloride

1. Mass of evaporating dish and zinc   _____ g
2. Mass of evaporating dish   _____ g
3. Mass of zinc   _____ g
4. Mass of evaporating dish and zinc chloride:

         first weighing   _____ g

         second weighing   _____ g

         third weighing   _____ g

5. Mass of zinc chloride   _____ g
6. Mass of chlorine in zinc chloride   _____ g

7. Empirical formula for zinc chloride
(show calculations)   _____

8. Balanced chemical equation for the formation of zinc chloride from zinc and HCl

B. Copper Sulfide

1. Mass of crucible, cover, and copper   _____ g
2. Mass of crucible and cover   _____ g
3. Mass of copper   _____ g
4. Mass of crucible, cover, and copper sulfide:

         first weighing   _____ g

         second weighing   _____ g

         third weighing   _____ g

5. Mass of copper sulfide   _____ g

6. Mass of sulfur in copper sulfide   _____ g

7. Empirical formula for copper sulfide   _____
   (show calculations)

8. Balanced chemical equation for the formation of copper sulfide from copper and sulfur

QUESTIONS

1. Can you determine the molecular formula of a substance from its percent composition?

2. Given that zinc chloride has a formula weight of 136.28 amu, what is its formula?

3. Can you determine the atomic weights of zinc or copper by the methods used in this experiment? How? What additional information is necessary in order to do this?

4. How many grams of zinc chloride could be formed from the reaction of 4.96 g of zinc with excess HCl?

5. How many kilograms of copper sulfide could be formed from the reaction of 0.90 mol of copper with excess sulfur?

6. If copper(I) sulfide is partially roasted in air (reaction with O_2), copper(I) sulfite is first formed. Subsequently, upon heating, the copper sulfite thermally decomposes to copper(I) oxide and sulfur dioxide. Write balanced chemical equations for these two reactions.

NOTES AND CALCULATIONS

Answers to Selected
Pre Lab Questions

1. (a) C, (b) Zn, (c) Cl, (d) K.

3. A compound is composed of a definite number of whole atoms in a fixed proportion.

4. We use relative atomic weights because the actual weights of atoms are exceedingly small and are awkward numbers to manipulate.

5. Formula weights are used for ionic compounds that do not exist as discrete molecular entities. Molecular weights are used for covalent compounds that do exist as discrete molecular entities.

6. The formula weight of Na_2CO_3 is:

$$\begin{array}{ccc} Na & C & O \end{array}$$

$$2(23.0 + 12.0 + 3(16.0) = 106 \text{ amu}$$

$$\% \, Na = \frac{46.0 \text{ amu}}{106 \text{ amu}} \times 100 = 43.4\%$$

$$\% \, C = \frac{12.0 \text{ amu}}{106 \text{ amu}} \times 100 = 11.3\%$$

$$\% \, O = \frac{48.0 \text{ amu}}{106 \text{ amu}} \times 100 = 45.3\%$$

7. Assuming 100 g of compound, this would contain 45.57 g of Sn and 54.43 g of Cl. Thus we have

$$\text{moles Sn} = (45.57 \text{ g})\left(\frac{1 \text{ mol Sn}}{118.7 \text{ g}}\right) = 0.3839 \text{ mol}$$

$$\text{moles Cl} = (54.43 \text{ g})\left(\frac{1 \text{ mol Cl}}{35.45 \text{ g}}\right) = 1.535 \text{ mol}$$

or $Sn_{0.384}Cl_{1.54}$, which implies that the smallest whole-number combining ratio of the constituent elements (that is, the empirical formula) is $SnCl_4$.

8. The law of definite proportions states simply that compounds form from elements in definite proportions by weight such that all samples of the same compound will contain the same ratios of the constituent elements.

9. Molecular formulas are always identical to or multiples of the empirical formulas, because the empirical formulas represent the smallest whole-number combining ratios and the molecular formulas the actual numbers of the constituent elements in chemical compounds.

14. $\text{Atoms potassium} = \left(6.022 \times 10^{23} \dfrac{\text{atoms}}{\text{mol}}\right)\left(\dfrac{0.01456 \text{ g}}{39.0983 \text{ g/mL}}\right)$

$$= 2.243 \times 10^{20} \text{ atoms}$$

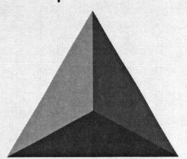

Experiment

Chemical Reactions

To observe some typical chemical reactions, identify some of the products and summarize the chemical changes in terms of balanced chemical equations.

OBJECTIVE

APPARATUS AND CHEMICALS

Apparatus

Bunsen burner	crucible and cover
6-in. test tube	glass tubing
thistle tube or long-stem funnel	ring stand, ring, wire triangle
droppers (2)	tongs

Chemicals

0.1 M sodium oxalate, $Na_2C_2O_4$	0.1 M $KMnO_4$
10 M NaOH	0.1 M $Pb(NO_3)_2$
1 M K_2CrO_4	6 M HCl
mossy zinc	6 M H_2SO_4
6 M $NH_3(aq)$*	3 M $(NH_4)_2CO_3$
conc. HNO_3	$KMnO_4$
0.1 M $NaHSO_3$ (freshly prepared)	Na_2CO_3
2-in. length of copper wire	Na_2SO_3
2 1-in. lengths of copper wire	ZnS
(14, 16, or 18 gauge)	
0.1 M $BaCl_2$	
powdered sulfur	

DISCUSSION

Chemical equations represent what transpires in a chemical reaction. For example, the equation

$$2KClO_3(s) \xrightarrow{\Delta} 2KCl(s) + 3O_2(g)$$

means that potassium chlorate, $KClO_3$, decomposes on heating (Δ is the symbol used for heat) to yield potassium chloride, KCl, and oxygen, O_2. *Before* an equation can be written for a reaction, someone must establish what the products are. How does one decide what these products are? Products are identified by their chemical and physical properties as well as by analyses. That oxygen rather than chlorine gas is produced in the above reaction can be established by the fact that oxygen is a colorless, odorless gas. Chlorine, on the other hand, is a pale yellow-green gas with an irritating odor.

In this experiment, you will observe that in some cases gases are produced, precipitates are formed, or color changes occur during the reactions. These are all indications that a chemical reaction has occurred. To identify some of the products of the reactions, consult Table 1, which lists some of the properties of the substances that could be formed in these reactions.

---

*Reagent bottle may be labeled 6 M NH_4OH.

From *Laboratory Experiments*, Tenth Edition, John H. Nelson and Kenneth C. Kemp. Copyright © 2006 by Pearson Education, Inc. Published by Prentice Hall, Inc. All rights reserved.

TABLE 1 Properties of Reaction Products

Water-soluble solids	Water-insoluble solids	Manganese oxyanions	Gases
KCl: white (colorless solution) NH$_4$Cl: white (colorless solution) KMnO$_4$: purple MnCl$_2$: pink (very pale) Cu(NO$_3$)$_2$: blue	CuS: very dark blue or black Cu$_2$S: black BaCrO$_4$: yellow BaCO$_3$: white PbCl$_2$: white MnO$_2$: black or brown	MnO$_4^-$: purple MnO$_4^{2-}$: dark green MnO$_4^{3-}$: dark blue	H$_2$: colorless; odorless NO$_2$: brown; pungent odor (TOXIC) NO: colorless; slight, pleasant odor CO$_2$: colorless; odorless Cl$_2$: pale yellow-green; pungent odor (TOXIC) SO$_2$: colorless; choking odor (as from matches)(TOXIC) H$_2$S: colorless; rotten-egg odor (TOXIC)

PROCEDURE |
A. A Reaction Between the Elements Copper and Sulfur

PERFORM THIS EXPERIMENT IN THE HOOD WITH A PARTNER. Obtain about a 5-cm (2-in.) length of copper wire and note its properties. Observe that its surface is shiny, that it can be easily bent, and that it has a characteristic color. Make a small coil of the wire by wrapping it around your pencil, and place the wire coil in a crucible. Add sufficient powdered sulfur to the crucible. Cover and place it on a clay triangle on an iron ring for heating. THIS APPARATUS MUST BE SET UP IN THE HOOD, because some sulfur will burn to form noxious sulfur dioxide. Heat the crucible with a Bunsen burner initially with low heat on all sides and then use the hottest flame to heat the bottom of the crucible to red heat. CONTINUE heating until no more smoking occurs, indicating that all the sulfur is burned off. Using the crucible tongs, remove the crucible from the clay triangle without removing the cover, and place it on a heat-resistant pad or wire gauze, *not on the desktop,* to cool. After the crucible has cooled, remove the cover and inspect the substance. Note its properties. Be sure to record your answers on the Report Sheet.

1. Does the substance resemble copper?
2. Is it possible to bend the substance without breaking it?
3. What color is it?
4. Has a reaction occurred?

Copper(II) sulfide, CuS, is insoluble in aqueous ammonia, NH$_3$, (that is, it does not react with NH$_3$), whereas copper(I) sulfide, Cu$_2$S, dissolves (that is, reacts) to give a blue solution with NH$_3$. Place a small portion of your product in a test tube and add 2 mL of 6 M NH$_3$ in the hood. Heat gently with a Bunsen burner.

5. Does your product react with NH$_3$?
6. Suggest a possible formula for the product.
7. Write a reaction showing the formation of your proposed product:

$$Cu(s) + S_8(s) \longrightarrow ?$$

Waste Disposal Instruction   The copper compounds and the acids are toxic and should be handled with care. Avoid spilling any solution, and immediately clean up (using paper towels) any spills that occur. If you spill any solution on your hands, wash them immediately. After completing each series of reactions and before moving on to the next series, dispose of the contents of your test tubes in the designated receptacles. Do not wash the contents down the sink.

B. Oxidation-Reduction Reactions

Many metals react with acids to liberate hydrogen and form the metal salt of the acid. The noble metals do not react with acids to produce hydrogen. Some of the unreactive metals do react with nitric acid, HNO_3; however, in these cases gases that are oxides of nitrogen are formed rather than hydrogen.

Add a small piece of zinc to a test tube containing 2 mL of 6 M HCl, and note what happens.

8.   Record your observations.
9.   Suggest possible products for the observed reaction: $Zn(s) +$ HCl(aq) $\longrightarrow$?

Place a 1-in. piece of copper wire in a clean test tube. Add 2 mL of 6 M HCl, and note if a reaction occurs.

10.   Record your observations.
11.   Is Cu an active or an inactive metal?

WHILE HOLDING A CLEAN TEST TUBE IN THE HOOD, place a 1-in. piece of copper wire in it and add 1 mL of concentrated nitric acid, HNO_3.

12.   Record your observations.
13.   Is the gas colored?
14.   Suggest a formula for the gas.
15.   After the reaction has proceeded for 5 min, carefully add 5 mL of water. Based on the color of the solution, what substance is present in solution?

Potassium permanganate, $KMnO_4$, is an excellent oxidizing agent in acidic media. The permanganate ion is purple and is reduced to the manganous ion, Mn^{2+}, which has a very faint pink color. Place 1 mL of 0.1 M sodium oxalate, $Na_2C_2O_4$, in a clean test tube. Add 10 drops of 6 M sulfuric acid. Mix thoroughly. To the resulting solution add 1 to 2 drops of 0.1 M $KMnO_4$ and stir. If there is no obvious indication that a reaction has occurred, warm the test tube gently in a hot water bath.

16.   Record your observations. Was the $KMnO_4$ reduced to Mn^{2+}?

Place 3 mL of 0.1 M sodium hydrogen sulfite, $NaHSO_3$, solution in a test tube. Add 1 mL of 10 M sodium hydroxide, NaOH, solution and stir. To the mixture in the test tube add 1 drop of 0.1 M $KMnO_4$ solution.

17.   Record your observations. Was the $KMnO_4$ reduced? Identify the manganese compound formed.

Add additional 0.1 M $KMnO_4$ solution, one drop at a time, and observe the effect of each drop until 10 drops have been added.

18. Record your observations.
19. Suggest why the effect of additional potassium permanganate changes as more is added.

WHILE HOLDING A TEST TUBE IN THE FUME HOOD, add one or two crystals of potassium permanganate, $KMnO_4$, to 1 mL of 6 M HCl.

20. Record your observations.
21. Note the color of the gas evolved.
22. Based on the color of the gas, what is the gas?

C. Metathesis Reactions

Additional observations are needed before equations can be written for the reactions above, but we see that we can identify some of the products. The remaining reactions are simple, and you will be able, from available information, not only to identify products but also to write equations. A number of reactions may be represented by equations of the following type:

$$AB + CD \longrightarrow AD + CB$$

These are called double-decomposition, or *metathesis*, reactions. This type of reaction involves the exchange of atoms or groups of atoms between interacting substances. The following is a specific example:

$$NaCl(aq) + AgNO_3(aq) \longrightarrow AgCl(s) + NaNO_3(aq)$$

Place a small sample of sodium carbonate, Na_2CO_3, in a test tube and add several drops of 6 M HCl.

23. Record your observations.
24. Note the odor and color of the gas that forms. (See safety instructions.)
25. What is the evolved gas?
26. Write an equation for the reaction $HCl(aq) + Na_2CO_3(s) \longrightarrow$? (NOTE: In this reaction the products must have H, Cl, Na, and O atoms in some new combinations, but no other elements can be present.)

Note that H_2CO_3 and H_2SO_3 readily decompose as follows:

$$H_2CO_3(aq) \longrightarrow H_2O(l) + CO_2(g)$$

$$H_2SO_3(aq) \longrightarrow H_2O(l) + SO_2(g)$$

IN THE HOOD, repeat the same test with sodium sulfite, Na_2SO_3.

27. Record your observations.
28. What is the gas?
29. Write an equation for the following reaction (note the similarity to the equation above): $HCl(aq) + Na_2SO_3(s) \longrightarrow$?

IN THE HOOD, repeat this test with zinc sulfide, ZnS.

30. Record your observations.
31. What is the gas?
32. Write an equation for the reaction: $HCl(aq) + ZnS(s) \longrightarrow$?

To 1 mL of 0.1 M lead nitrate, $Pb(NO_3)_2$, solution in a clean test tube add a few drops of 6 M HCl.

33. Record your observations.
34. What is the precipitate?
35. Write an equation for the reaction $Pb(NO_3)_2(aq) + HCl(aq) \longrightarrow$?

To 1 mL of 0.1 M barium chloride, $BaCl_2$, solution add 2 drops of 1 M potassium chromate, K_2CrO_4, solution.

36. Record your observations.
37. What is the precipitate?
38. Write an equation for the reaction $BaCl_2(aq) + K_2CrO_4(aq) \longrightarrow$?

To 1 mL of 0.1 M barium chloride, $BaCl_2$, solution add several drops of 3 M ammonium carbonate, $(NH_4)_2CO_3$, solution in a test tube.

39. What is the precipitate?
40. Write an equation for the reaction $(NH_4)_2CO_3(aq) + BaCl_2(aq) \longrightarrow$?

After the precipitate has settled somewhat, carefully decant (that is, pour off) the excess liquid. Add 1 mL of water to the test tube, shake it, allow the precipitate to settle, and again carefully pour off the liquid. To the remaining solid, add several drops of 6 M HCl.

41. Record your observations.
42. Note the odor.
43. What is the evolved gas? (Recall the reaction in step 26 of this experiment.)

Before beginning this experiment in the laboratory, you should be able to answer the following questions:

PRE LAB QUESTIONS

1. Before a chemical equation can be written, what must you know?

2. What observations might you make that suggest that a chemical reaction has occured?

3. How could you distinguish between NO_2 and NO?

4. Define metathesis reactions. Give an example.

5. What is a precipitate?

6. Balance these equations:

$$KBrO_3(s) \xrightarrow{\Delta} KBr(s) + O_2(g)$$

$$MnBr_2(aq) + AgNO_3(aq) \longrightarrow Mn(NO_3)_2(aq) + AgBr(s)$$

7. How could you distinguish between the gases H_2 and H_2S?

8. Using water, how could you distinguish between the white solids KCl and $PbCl_2$?

9. Write equations for the decomposition of $H_2CO_3(aq)$ and $H_2SO_3(aq)$.

REPORT SHEET | EXPERIMENT

Chemical Reactions

A. A Reaction Between the Elements Copper and Sulfur

1. _____

2. _____

3. _____

4. _____

5. _____

6. _____

7. $Cu(s) + S_8(s) \longrightarrow$ _____

B. Oxidation-Reduction Reactions

8. _____

9. $Zn(s) + HCl(aq) \longrightarrow$ _____

10. _____

11. _____

12. _____

13. _____

14. _____

15. _____

16. _____

17. _____

18. _____

19. _____

20. _____

21. _____

22. _____

C. Metathesis Reactions

23. _____

24. _____

25. _____

26. $HCl(aq) + Na_2CO_3(s) \longrightarrow$ _____

27. _____

28. _____

29. $HCl(aq) + Na_2SO_3(s) \longrightarrow$ _____

30. _____

31. _____

32. $HCl(aq) + ZnS(s) \longrightarrow$ _____

33. _____

34. _____

35. $Pb(NO_3)_2(aq) + HCl(aq) \longrightarrow$ _____

36. _____

37. _____

38. $BaCl_2(aq) + K_2CrO_4(aq) \longrightarrow$ _____

39. _____

40. $(NH_4)_2CO_3(aq) + BaCl_2(aq) \longrightarrow$ _____

41. _____

42. _____

43. _____

QUESTIONS:

1. Complete and balance the following chemical reactions

$2HCl(aq) + BaCO_3(s) \longrightarrow$

$2HI(aq) + K_2SO_3(s) \longrightarrow$

$Pb(NO_3)_2(aq) + 2\,KCl(aq) \longrightarrow$

$Ba(NO_3)_2(aq) + Na_2(CrO_4)(aq) \longrightarrow$

$K_2CO_3(aq) + Ba(NO_3)_2(aq) \longrightarrow$

$HCl(aq) + AgNO_3(aq) \longrightarrow$

2. How could you separate gold from a mixture of zinc and gold?

3. How could you determine whether a white powder was zinc sulfide or sodium carbonate using a hydrochloric acid solution. Write balanced equations.

NOTES AND CALCULATIONS

Answers to Selected Pre Lab Questions

1. Before a chemical equation can be written, you must know the reactants and products of the reaction.

2. A color change or formation of a solid or a gas are indicative of a chemical reaction. Also, evolution or absorption of heat.

3. NO_2 is brown in color and has a pungent odor, while NO is colorless and has a slightly pleasant odor.

4. Metathesis reactions are atom (or group) transfer reactions. For example, $AgNO_3(aq) + NaCl(aq) \longrightarrow AgCl(s) + NaNO_3(aq)$ is a metathesis reaction in which chloride transfer occurs.

5. A precipitate is an insoluble substance that separates from a homogeneous chemical reaction as a solid.

6. $2KBrO_3(s) \longrightarrow 2KBr(s) + 3O_2(g)$; $MnBr_2(aq) + 2AgNO_3(aq) \longrightarrow$
$$Mn(NO_3)_2(aq) + 2AgBr(s)$$

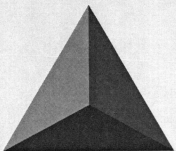

Experiment

Activity Series

To become familiar with the relative activities of metals in chemical reactions.

OBJECTIVE

APPARATUS AND CHEMICALS

Apparatus
small test tubes*(13) test-tube rack

Chemicals
0.2 M Ca(NO$_3$)$_2$ 0.2 M Mg(NO$_3$)$_2$
0.2 M Zn(NO$_3$)$_2$ 0.2 M Fe(NO$_3$)$_3$
0.2 M FeSO$_4$ 0.2 M SnCl$_4$
0.2 M CuSO$_4$ 6 M HCl
7 small pieces each of calcium,
    magnesium, zinc, iron wool,
    tin, copper

DISCUSSION

Chemical elements are usually classified by their properties into three groups: metals, nonmetals, and metalloids. Most of the known elements are metals. Their physical properties include high thermal and electrical conductivity, high luster, malleability (ability to be pounded flat without shattering), and ductility (ability to be drawn out into a fine wire). All common metals are solids at room temperature except mercury, which is a liquid. The periodic table illustrated in Figure 1 shows the three classifications of the elements.

All elements to the left of the shaded area are metals except hydrogen. Those to the right are nonmetals. Those in the shaded area have intermediate

1A																	8A
H	2A											3A	4A	5A	6A	7A	He
Li	Be											B	C	N	O	F	Ne
Na	Mg			Transition elements								Al	Si	P	S	Cl	Ar
K	Ca	Sc	Ti	V	Cr	Mn	Fe	Co	Ni	Cu	Zn	Ga	Ge	As	Se	Br	Kr
Rb	Sr	Y	Zr	Nb	Mo	Tc	Ru	Rh	Pd	Ag	Cd	In	Sn	Sb	Te	L	Xe
Cs	Ba	La	Hf	Ta	W	Re	Os	Ir	Pt	Au	Hg	Tl	Pb	Bi	Po	At	Rn

▲ **FIGURE 1** Partial periodic table of the elements.

*A spot plate may be used in place of test tubes.

From *Laboratory Experiments*, Tenth Edition, John H. Nelson and Kenneth C. Kemp. Copyright © 2006 by Pearson Education, Inc. Published by Prentice Hall, Inc. All rights reserved.

properties and are called semimetals or metalloids. Families or groups of elements consist of elements in vertical columns in the periodic table. Elements within a group or family (called congeners) have similar chemical properties because they have similar valence electronic structures; that is, the number of valence electrons (electrons in the outermost shell) is the same for all members of a family or group. For historical reasons, most of the groups have names, and some are often referred to by them. These are

1. Group 1A, called *alkali metals* because they react with oxygen to form bases
2. Group 2A, called *alkaline earth metals* because their presence makes soils alkaline
3. Group 3A, no common name
4. Group 4A, no common name
5. Group 5A, called *pnictides*, from the Greek word meaning choking suffocation
6. Group 6A, called *chalcogens*, from Greek roots meaning ore former
7. Group 7A, called *halogens*, from Greek roots meaning salt former
8. Group 8A, called *rare, noble*, or *inert gases* because they are rare and were thought to be unreactive

Those most frequently referred to by group name are the alkali metals, the alkaline earth metals, the halogens, and the rare gases.

The three broad categories of the elements also have somewhat similar chemical properties. For example, metals, as compared with the other elements, all have relatively low ionization potentials and enter into chemical combination with nonmetals by *losing* electrons to become cations. This can be symbolized by the following equation:

$$M \longrightarrow M^{n+} + ne^-$$

Nonmetals, as compared with metals, have relatively high electron affinities and enter into chemical combination with metals by *gaining* electrons to become anions. This can be symbolized by the following equation:

$$X + ne^- \longrightarrow X^{n-}$$

Specific examples of these types of reactions can be divided into several useful categories, which will be illustrated by the following examples.

Electron-Transfer Reactions

1 REACTIONS WITH OXYGEN

$$2Mg(s) + O_2(g) \longrightarrow 2MgO(s)$$

In this reaction, magnesium is oxidized by oxygen, which is reduced by magnesium. This can be better illustrated by breaking down the reaction into fictitious although helpful steps:

$$2(Mg \longrightarrow Mg^{2+} + 2e^-) \quad \text{oxidation}$$
$$O_2 + 4e^- \longrightarrow 2O^{2-} \quad \text{reduction}$$
$$2Mg + O_2 \longrightarrow 2MgO \quad \text{oxidation-reduction (redox) reaction}$$

In *oxidation*, the oxidized element loses electrons and becomes more positive. In *reduction*, the reduced element gains electrons and becomes more negative. Oxidation is always associated with a concomitant reduction.

2 REACTIONS WITH WATER

$$2Na(s) + 2H_2O(l) \longrightarrow 2NaOH(aq) + H_2(g)$$
$$Ca(s) + 2H_2O(l) \longrightarrow Ca(OH)_2(aq) + H_2(g)$$

The *ionic* equations for these reactions better illustrate the electron-transfer process:

$$2Na(s) + 2H_2O(l) \longrightarrow 2Na^+(aq) + 2OH^-(aq) + H_2(g)$$

$$Ca(s) + 2H_2O(l) \longrightarrow Ca^{2+}(aq) + 2OH^-(aq) + H_2(g)$$

3 REACTIONS WITH ACIDS

$$Zn(s) + 2HCl(aq) \longrightarrow ZnCl_2(aq) + H_2(g)$$

or

$$Zn(s) + 2H^+(aq) + 2Cl^-(aq) \longrightarrow Zn^{2+}(aq) + 2Cl^-(aq) + H_2(g)$$

Since the chloride ion is merely a spectator—that is, it does not participate in the reaction—it may be omitted, yielding the *net ionic equation:*

$$Zn(s) + 2H^+(aq) \longrightarrow Zn^{2+}(aq) + H_2(g)$$

or simply

$$Zn + 2H^+ \longrightarrow Zn^{2+} + H_2$$

4 ELECTRON TRANSFER AMONG METALS

$$Zn(s) + Cu(NO_3)_2(aq) \longrightarrow Zn(NO_3)_2(aq) + Cu(s)$$

or

$$Zn(s) + Cu^{2+}(aq) \longrightarrow Zn^{2+}(aq) + Cu(s)$$

or simply

$$Zn + Cu^{2+} \longrightarrow Zn^{2+} + Cu$$

Note once again that in the ionic equation the spectator ion (NO_3^-) has been omitted because it takes no active part in the reaction and serves only to provide electrical neutrality. Therefore, any other soluble salt of copper(II), such as chloride, sulfate, or acetate, could perform the same function.

In this game of "musical electrons," there are only enough electrons for one atom of the system. In order to achieve the lowest energy level for the system, the more active metal of a pair will lose electrons to the more passive metal or will react more vigorously with water, acids, or oxygen. In some cases no reaction at all will occur. Without prior knowledge we have no way of predicting these events.

A. Reactions of Metals with Acid

To each of six test tubes containing 0.5 mL of dilute 6 *M* HCl, add a small piece of the metals Ca, Cu, Fe, Mg, Sn, and Zn. Observe the test tubes and note any changes that occur (such as the evolution of a gas, whether it is

PROCEDURE

vigorous or not, and any color changes). Enter your observations on the report sheet, and write both complete and ionic equations for each reaction noted. After completing each series of reactions, dispose of the contents of your test tubes in the designated containers.

B. Reactions of Metals with Solutions of Metal Ions

(WORK IN PAIRS FOR THIS STEP.) Add a small piece of calcium metal to each of seven test tubes containing, respectively, about 0.5 mL of $Ca(NO_3)_2$, $CuSO_4$, $FeSO_4$, $Fe(NO_3)_3$, $Mg(NO_3)_2$, $SnCl_4$, and $Zn(NO_3)_2$ solutions. Note any reaction that occurs by observing whether a color change occurs on the surface of the metal or in the solution or whether a gas is evolved. Record your observations on the report sheet. Write both complete and ionic equations for any reaction that occurs. After completing each series of reactions, dispose of the contents of your test tubes in the designated containers.

Repeat the preceding process by adding a small piece of copper to another 0.5 mL of each of the metal-cation solutions. Do the same for iron, magnesium, tin, and zinc, and record all your observations. Write both complete molecular and ionic equations for all reactions.

C. Relative-Activity Series

From the information contained in the table you constructed in Part B, you can rank these six metals according to their relative chemical reactivities. This can be done in the following manner: One of the metals will replace all others in solution. For example, if calcium metal is oxidized by solutions containing cations of each of the other metals, then it is the most reactive. One of the other metals that will replace all but calcium is the next most reactive. Finally, one of the metals will not replace any of the other metal cations from solution. Therefore, it is the least reactive. List the metals on your report sheet in terms of decreasing reactivity, starting with the most reactive (1) and ending with the least reactive (6).

PRE LAB QUESTIONS

Before beginning this experiment in the laboratory, you should be able to answer the following questions:

1. What distinguishes a metal from a nonmetal?
2. What does ionization potential measure?
3. What does electron affinity measure?
4. Why must oxidation be accompanied by a reduction?
5. How does one determine the relative reactivities of metals?
6. Complete and balance the following:

$$Mg + O_2 \longrightarrow$$
$$Zn + HCl \longrightarrow$$
$$Zn + Cu^{2+} \longrightarrow$$

7. Balance the following reactions and identify the species that have been oxidized and the species that have been reduced.

Reaction	Species oxidized	Species reduced
$Cl_2 + I^- \longrightarrow I_2 + Cl^-$		
$WO_2 + H_2 \longrightarrow W + H_2O$		
$Ca + H_2O \longrightarrow H_2 + Ca(OH)_2$		
$Al + O_2 \longrightarrow Al_2O_3$		

8. If the following redox reactions are found to occur spontaneously, identify the more active metal in each reaction.

Reaction	More-active metal
$2Li + Cu^{2+} \longrightarrow 2Li^+ + Cu$	
$Cr + 3V^{3+} \longrightarrow 3V^{2+} + Cr^{3+}$	
$Cd + 2Ti^{3+} \longrightarrow 2Ti^{2+} + Cd^{2+}$	

NOTES AND CALCULATIONS

REPORT SHEET | EXPERIMENT

Activity Series

A. Reactions of Metals with Acid

Metal	Reaction with HCl	Observation	Equations
Ca	Yes	Fizzing, produces gas, extensive bubbles	
Cu	NO	Nothing	
Mg	Yes, but less reactive than Ca	Extremely fizzy gas, less reactive than Ca	
Fe	NO	Nothing	
Sn	NO	Nothing	
Zn	Yes	Alka seltzer, fizz, gas, but less than Mg	
Example: Co	Yes, slowly	Gas evolved; solution turned blue	

B. Reactions of Metals with Solutions of Metal Ions

Metal ions / Metal	Ca^{2+}	Cu^{2+}	Fe^{3+}	Fe^{2+}	Mg^{2+}	Sn^{4+}	Zn^{2+}	Al^{3+}
Ca								Yes, calcium dissolves
Cu								N.R.
Fe								N.R.
Mg								Yes, magnesium dissolves
Sn								N.R.
Zn								N.R.
Example: Al	N.R.	Yes, aluminum turns brown	Yes, turns aluminum dark	Yes, aluminum turns dark; solution colorless	N.R.	Yes, aluminum turns dark; solution colorless	Yes, aluminum turns dark	

Example:

$$2Al(s) + 3Zn(NO_3)_2(aq) \longrightarrow 2Al(NO_3)_3(aq) + 3Zn(s)$$

$$2Al(s) + 3Zn^{2+}(aq) \longrightarrow 2Al^{3+}(aq) + 3Zn(s)$$

Complete equation	*Net ionic equation*

C. Relative-Activity Series

Most reactive   Least reactive

1. _____ 2. _____ 3. _____ 4. _____ 5. _____ 6. _____

QUESTIONS

1. Which of these six metals should be the most reactive toward oxygen?

2. Which of the oxides would be expected to be thermally unstable and decompose according to the equation?

$$2MO \xrightarrow{\Delta} 2M + O_2$$

3. Sodium is slightly less reactive than calcium. Predict the outcome of the following reactions:

$Na + H_2O \longrightarrow$

$Na + O_2 \longrightarrow$

$Na + HCl \longrightarrow$

$Na + Ca^{2+} \longrightarrow$

4. Which is more reactive, Fe^{2+} or Fe^{3+}, and why?

5. From the data in Table B, rank the activity of aluminum.

6. For each of the following reactions, indicate which substance is oxidized and which is reduced. Which substance is the oxidizing agent and which is the reducing agent?

	Substance oxidized	Substance reduced	Oxidizing agent	Reducing agent
$2Al(s) + 3Cl_2(g) \longrightarrow 2AlCl_3(s)$	_____	_____	_____	_____
$8H^+(aq) + MnO_4^-(aq) + 5Fe^{2+}(aq) \longrightarrow$ $5Fe^{3+}(aq) + Mn^{2+}(aq) + 4H_2O(l)$	_____	_____	_____	_____
$FeS(s) + 3NO_3^-(aq) + 4H^+(aq) \longrightarrow$ $3NO(g) + SO_4^{2-}(aq) + Fe^{3+}(aq) + 2H_2O(l)$	_____	_____	_____	_____

Answers to Selected Pre Lab Questions

1. Most metals have high thermal and electrical conductivities, high luster, malleability, and ductility, whereas nonmetals usually have low thermal and electrical conductivities, low luster, low malleability, and low ductility. In addition, relative to nonmetals, metals have low ionization potentials and low electron affinities.

2. Ionization energy is the energy required to remove an electron from an atom in the gaseous state.

3. Electron affinity is the energy produced when an electron is added to a species in the gas phase and is the inverse of the ionization energy in a physical sense, but the values are not just of opposite sign because you are considering slightly different processes; in each case, they differ by one electron.

4. An oxidation must always be accompanied by a reduction because the species being oxidized must transfer an electron to some other species that is reduced. The electron cannot just be given up to free space.

5. By systematically observing the displacement reactions among metals and their cations, it is possible to determine the relative oxidation potentials of the metals. The metal with the lower reduction potential will reduce a cation of a metal with a higher reduction potential.

6. $2Mg + O_2 \longrightarrow 2MgO$; $Zn + 2HCl \longrightarrow ZnCl_2 + H_2$;
$$Zn + Cu^{2+} \longrightarrow Zn^{2+} + Cu.$$

Gravimetric Determination of Phosphorus in Plant Food

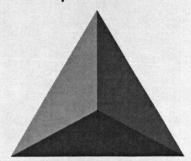

To illustrate an application of gravimetric analysis to a consumer product.

OBJECTIVE

APPARATUS AND CHEMICALS

Apparatus

balance	funnel support
beakers (6), any combination, 250 mL or larger	ring stand
	stirring rods (3) with
filter paper (Whatman No. 40)	rubber policeman
funnels (3)	

Chemicals

75% aqueous isopropyl alcohol*

10% aqueous $MgSO_4 \cdot 7\,H_2O$*

$2\ M\ NH_3(aq)$*

plant food

DISCUSSION

Analytical chemistry is concerned with determining *how much* of one or more constituents is present in a particular sample of material. Two common quantitative methods used in analytical chemistry are *gravimetric* and *volumetric* analysis. Gravimetric analysis derives its name from the fact that the constituent being determined is isolated in some weighable form. Volumetric analysis, on the other hand, derives its name from the fact that the amount of a constituent being determined involves measuring the volume of a reagent. Volumetric analyses are generally less time consuming and less accurate than gravimetric analyses.

Gravimetric analyses may be difficult and time consuming, but they are inherently quite accurate. The accuracy of an analysis is often directly proportional to the time expended in carrying it out. The ultimate use of the analytical result governs how much time and effort the analytical chemist should expend in obtaining it. For example, before building a mill to process gold ore, an accurate analysis of the ore is required. Mills are very expensive to build and operate, and economic factors determine whether or not construction of the mill is worthwhile. Because of the value of gold, the difference of only a few hundredths of a percent of gold in an ore may be the governing factor as to whether or not to construct a mill. On the other hand, the analysis of an inexpensive commodity chemical, such as a plant food, requires much less accuracy; the economic consequences of giving the consumer an extra 0.2% of an active ingredient are usually small even for a large volume of product. Time is too valuable, whether it be the students' or scientists', to be wasted in the pursuit of the ultimate in accuracy when such is not needed.

*Epsom salts, household ammonia (non-sudsy), and rubbing alcohol, respectively, may be substituted for these reagents.

From *Laboratory Experiments*, Tenth Edition, John H. Nelson and Kenneth C. Kemp. Copyright © 2006 by Pearson Education, Inc. Published by Prentice Hall, Inc. All rights reserved.

Consumer chemicals are subject to quality control by the manufacturer and by various consumer protection agencies. Consumer chemicals are usually analyzed both *qualitatively* to determine what substances they contain and *quantitatively* to determine how much of these substances are present. For example, plant foods are analyzed this way.

Plant foods contain three essential nutrients that are likely to be lacking in soils. These are soluble compounds of nitrogen, phosphorus, and potassium. The labels on the plant food usually have a set of numbers such as 15-30-15. These numbers mean that the plant food is guaranteed to contain at least 15% nitrogen, 30% phosphorus (expressed as P_2O_5), and 15% potassium (expressed as K_2O). The rest of the product is other anions or cations necessary to balance charge in the chemical compounds, dyes to provide a pleasing color, and fillers.

EXAMPLE 1

What is the minimum percentage of phosphorus in a plant food whose P_2O_5 percentage is guaranteed to be 15%?

SOLUTION: Assuming 100 g of plant food, we would have 15 g of P_2O_5. Using this quantity, we can calculate the amount of P in the sample:

$$(15 \text{ g } P_2O_5)\left(\frac{1 \text{ mol } P_2O_5}{141.9 \text{ g } P_2O_5}\right)\left(\frac{2 \text{ mol P}}{1 \text{ mol } P_2O_5}\right)\left(\frac{30.97 \text{ g P}}{1 \text{ mol P}}\right) = 6.5 \text{ g P}$$

Thus,

$$\%P = \frac{\text{g P}}{\text{g sample}} \times 100 = \frac{6.5 \text{ g}}{100 \text{ g}} \times 100 = 6.5\%$$

In this experiment we will illustrate one of the quality-control analyses for plant food by gravimetric determination of its phosphorus content. Phosphorus will be determined by precipitation of the sparingly soluble salt magnesium ammonium phosphate hexahydrate according to the reaction

$$5H_2O(l) + HPO_4{}^{2-}(aq) + NH_4{}^{+}(aq) + Mg^{2+}(aq) + OH^-(aq)$$

$$\longrightarrow MgNH_4PO_4 \cdot 6H_2O(s)$$

EXAMPLE 2

If a 10.00-g sample of soluble plant food yields 10.22 g of $MgNH_4PO_4 \cdot 6H_2O$, what are the percentages of P and P_2O_5 in this sample?

SOLUTION: First, solving for the grams of P in the sample

$$(10.22 \text{ g } MgNH_4PO_4 \cdot 6H_2O)\left(\frac{1 \text{ mol } MgNH_4PO_4 \cdot 6H_2O}{245.4 \text{ g } MgNH_4PO_4 \cdot 6H_2O}\right)$$

$$\times \left(\frac{1 \text{ mol P}}{1 \text{ mol } MgNH_4PO_4 \cdot 6H_2O}\right)\left(\frac{30.97 \text{ g P}}{1 \text{ mol P}}\right) = 1.290 \text{ g P}$$

Thus,

$$\%P = \frac{\text{g P}}{\text{g sample}} \times 100 = \frac{1.290 \text{ g P}}{10.00 \text{ g sample}} \times 100 = 12.90\% \text{ P}$$

Similarly, solving for grams of P_2O_5:

$$(10.22 \text{ g MgNH}_4\text{PO}_4 \cdot 6\text{H}_2\text{O})\left(\frac{1 \text{ mol MgNH}_4\text{PO}_4 \cdot 6\text{H}_2\text{O}}{245.4 \text{ g MgNH}_4\text{PO}_4 \cdot 6\text{H}_2\text{O}}\right)$$

$$\times \left(\frac{1 \text{ mol P}}{1 \text{ mol MgNH}_4\text{PO}_4 \cdot 6\text{H}_2\text{O}}\right)\left(\frac{1 \text{ mol P}_2\text{O}_5}{2 \text{ mol P}}\right)\left(\frac{141.9 \text{ g P}_2\text{O}_5}{1 \text{ mol P}_2\text{O}_5}\right) = 2.955 \text{ g P}_2\text{O}_5$$

$$\text{and } \% \text{ P}_2\text{O}_5 = \frac{2.955 \text{ g}}{10.00 \text{ g}} \times 100 = 29.55\% \text{ P}_2\text{O}_5$$

PROCEDURE

Weigh by difference to the nearest hundredth gram 1.5 to 2.5 g of your unknown sample, using weighing paper. Transfer the sample quantitatively to a 250-mL beaker and record the sample mass. Add 35 to 40 mL of distilled water and stir the mixture with a glass stirring rod to dissolve the sample. Although plant foods are all advertised to be water soluble, they may contain a small amount of insoluble residue. If your sample does not completely dissolve, remove the insoluble material by filtration. To the filtrate add about 45 mL of a 10% $MgSO_4 \cdot 7H_2O$ solution. Then add approximately 150 mL of 2 M $NH_3(aq)$ slowly while stirring. A white precipitate of $MgNH_4PO_4 \cdot 6H_2O$ will form. Allow the mixture to sit at room temperature for 15 minutes to complete the precipitation. Collect the precipitate on a preweighed piece of filter paper (Figure 1).

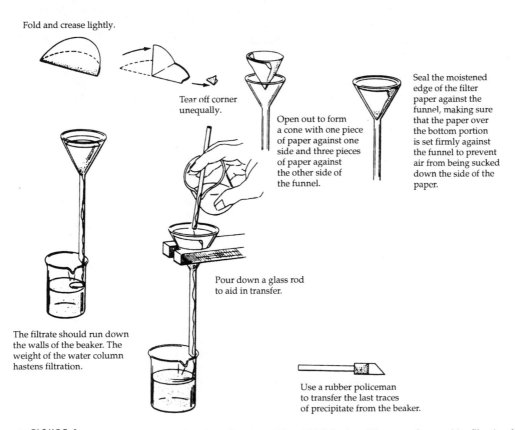

Fold and crease lightly.

Tear off corner unequally.

Open out to form a cone with one piece of paper against one side and three pieces of paper against the other side of the funnel.

Seal the moistened edge of the filter paper against the funnel, making sure that the paper over the bottom portion is set firmly against the funnel to prevent air from being sucked down the side of the paper.

Pour down a glass rod to aid in transfer.

The filtrate should run down the walls of the beaker. The weight of the water column hastens filtration.

Use a rubber policeman to transfer the last traces of precipitate from the beaker.

▲ FIGURE 1 Filter paper use. (*Filtration of $MgNH_4PO_4 \cdot 6H_2O$ is slow. Time may be saved by filtering by suction with a Büchner funnel.*)

Obtain a filter paper (three of these will be needed) and weigh it accurately. (Be certain that you weigh the paper after it has been folded and torn, not before.) Fold the paper as illustrated in Figure 1 and fit it into a glass funnel. Be certain that you open the filter paper in the funnel so that one side has three pieces and one side has one piece of paper against the funnel—not two pieces on each side. *Why?* Your instructor will also demonstrate this for you. Wet the paper with distilled water to hold it in place in the funnel. Completely and quantitatively transfer the precipitate and all of the solution from the beaker onto the filter, using a rubber policeman (your laboratory instructor will show you how to use a rubber policeman). Wash the precipitate with two or three 5-mL portions of distilled water. Do this by adding each portion to the beaker in which you did the precipitation to transfer any remaining precipitate; then pour over the solid on the funnel. Finally, pour two 10 mL portions of 75% isopropyl alcohol through the filter paper. Remove the filter paper, place it on a numbered watch glass, and store it to dry in your locker until the next period.

Repeat the above procedure with two more samples. In the next period, when the $MgNH_4PO_4 \cdot 6H_2O$ is thoroughly dry, weigh the filter papers plus $MgNH_4PO_4 \cdot 6H_2O$. Record the mass and calculate the percentages of phosphorus and P_2O_5 in your original samples.

Standard Deviation

As a means of estimating the precision of your results, it is desirable to calculate the standard deviation. Before we illustrate how to do this, however, we will define some of the terms above as well as some additional ones that are necessary.

Accuracy: correctness of a measurement, closeness to the true result.

Precision: internal consistency among one's own results—that is, reproducibility.

Error: difference between the true result and the determined result.

Determinate errors: errors in method or performance that can be discovered and eliminated.

Indeterminate errors: random errors that are incapable of discovery but which can be treated by statistics.

Mean: arithmetic mean or average (μ), where

$$\mu = \frac{\text{sum of results}}{\text{number of results}}$$

For example, if an experiment's results are 1, 3, and 5, then

$$\mu = \frac{1 + 3 + 5}{3} = 3$$

Median: the midpoint of the results for an odd number of results and the average of the two middle results for an even number of results (m). For example, if an experiment's results are 1, 3, and 5, then $m = 3$. If results are 1.0, 3.0, 4.0, and 5.0, then

$$m = \frac{3.0 + 4.0}{2} = 3.5$$

The scatter about the mean or median—that is, the deviations from the mean or median—are measures of precision. Thus the smaller the deviations, the more precise the measurements.

EXAMPLE 3

If an experiment's results are 1.0, 2.0, 3.0, and 4.0, calculate the mean, the deviations from the mean, the average deviation from the mean, and the relative average deviation from the mean.

SOLUTION: The mean is calculated as follows:

$$\mu = \frac{1.0 + 2.0 + 3.0 + 4.0}{4} = \frac{10.0}{4} = 2.5$$

The deviations from the mean are

$$|2.5 - 1.0| = 1.5$$
$$|2.5 - 2.0| = 0.5$$
$$|2.5 - 3.0| = 0.5$$
$$|2.5 - 4.0| = 1.5$$

The symbol $|\ \ |$ means absolute value, so all differences are positive. The average deviation from the mean is therefore

$$\frac{1.5 + 0.5 + 0.5 + 1.5}{4} = 1.0$$

The relative average deviation from the mean is calculated by dividing the average deviation from the mean by the mean. Thus,

$$\text{Relative deviation} = \frac{1.0}{2.5} = 0.40$$

This can be expressed as 40%, 400 parts/thousand (ppt), or 40,000 parts/million (ppm).

Standard deviation (s) is a better measure of precision and is calculated using the formula

$$s = \sqrt{\frac{\text{sum of the squares of the deviations from the mean}}{\text{number of observations} - 1}}$$

$$= \sqrt{\frac{\Sigma_i \chi_i - \mu^2}{N - 1}}$$

where s = standard deviation from the mean, χ_i = members of the set, μ = mean, and N = number of members in the set of data. The symbol Σ_i means to sum over the members.

EXAMPLE 4

An experiment's results are 1, 3, and 5. Calculate the mean, the deviations from the mean, the standard deviation, and the relative standard deviation for the data.

SOLUTION: The mean is as follows:

$$\mu = \frac{1 + 3 + 5}{3} = 3$$

The deviations from the mean are

$$|\chi_i - \mu| = \text{deviation}$$
$$|1 - 3| = 2$$
$$|3 - 3| = 0$$
$$|5 - 3| = 2$$

$$s = \sqrt{\frac{2^2 + 0^2 + 2^2}{3 - 1}}$$
$$= \sqrt{\frac{4 + 0 + 4}{2}}$$
$$= \sqrt{\frac{8}{2}}$$
$$= \sqrt{4} = 2$$

The results of this experiment would be reported as 3 ± 2. The relative standard deviation is

$$\frac{2}{3} = 0.7, \text{ or } 70\%$$

Calculate the standard deviation of your data and report the results on your report sheet.

The standard deviation may be used to determine whether a result should be retained or discarded. As a rule of thumb, you should discard any result that is more than two standard deviations from the mean. For example, if you had a result of 49.65% and you had determined that your percentage of phosphorus was 49.25 ± 0.09%, this result (49.65%) should be discarded. This is because $s = 0.09$ and $|49.25 - 49.65| = 0.40$, which is greater than 2×0.09. This result is more than two standard deviations from the mean.

PRE LAB QUESTIONS

Before beginning this experiment in the laboratory, you should be able to answer the following questions:

1. Which method of analysis generally is the faster method, gravimetric or volumetric?

2. Why would only three significant figures be required for the analysis of a consumer chemical such as P_2O_5 in plant food?

3. The label on a plant food reads 23-19-17. What does this mean?

4. What is the minimum percentage of phosphorus in the plant food in question 3?

5. What is the minimum percentage of potassium in the plant food in question 3?

6. What is the percent sulfate in $CuSO_4 \cdot 5H_2O$?

7. Does standard deviation give a measure of accuracy or precision?

8. If an experiment's results are 12.1, 12.4 and 12.6, find the mean, the average deviation from the mean, the standard deviation from the mean, and the relative average deviation from the mean.

9. What is meant by the term *indeterminate errors*?

10. Differentiate between qualitative and quantitative analysis.

11. What is meant by the term *accuracy*?

REPORT SHEET | EXPERIMENT

Gravimetric Determination of Phosphorus in Plant Food

Plant Food Name _____   Label Percentage _____

	Trial 1	Trial 2	Trial 3
Mass of sample	_____	_____	_____
Mass of filter paper and $MgNH_4PO_4 \cdot 6H_2O$	_____	_____	_____
Mass of filter paper	_____	_____	_____
Mass of $MgNH_4PO_4 \cdot 6H_2O$	_____	_____	_____
Mass of P in original sample (show calculations)	_____	_____	_____

Percent phosphorus
(show calculations)   _____   _____   _____

Average percent phosphorus
(show calculations)   _____

Standard deviation
(show calculations)   _____

Do any of your results differ from the mean by more than two standard deviations? _____

Reported percent phosphorus _____

Percent P_2O_5 (show calculations) _____

Guaranteed minimum percent P_2O_5 from the bottle label _____

Do the guaranteed and experimental values agree within two standard deviations? _____

QUESTIONS

1. What is the percent phosphorus in $MgKPO_4 \cdot 6H_2O$?

2. $MgNH_4PO_4 \cdot 6H_2O$ has a solubility of 0.023 g/100 mL in water. Suppose a 5.02-g sample were washed with 20 mL of water. What fraction of the $MgNH_4PO_4 \cdot 6H_2O$ would be lost?

3. $MgNH_4PO_4 \cdot 6H_2O$ loses H_2O stepwise as it is heated. Between 40° and 60°C the monohydrate is formed, and above 100°C the anhydrous material is formed. What are the phosphorus percentages of the monohydrate and of the anhydrous material?

4. Ignition of $MgNH_4PO_4 \cdot 6H_2O$ produces NH_3, H_2O, and magnesium pyrophosphate, $Mg_2P_2O_7$. Complete and balance the equation for this reaction. If 2.50 g of $MgNH_4PO_4 \cdot 6H_2O$ are ignited, how many grams of $Mg_2P_2O_7$ would be formed?

5. What is the percentage of P_2O_5 in $Mg_2P_2O_7$?

6. Today sodium content in food is an important health concern. How many milligrams of sodium are present in one ounce of table salt (NaCl)?

NOTES AND CALCULATIONS

Answers to Selected Pre Lab Questions

1. Volumetric analyses are generally faster than gravimetric analyses.

2. Only this level of accuracy is usually required for the analysis of a consumer chemical.

3. $MgSO_4 \cdot 7\,H_2O$ is Epsom salts, NH_3 is household ammonia, and $(CH_3)_2CHOH$ is isopropyl alcohol.

4. The label 23-19-17 means that the plant food is guaranteed to contain at least 23% nitrogen, 19% phosphorus (expressed as P_2O_5), and 17% of potassium (expressed as K_2O).

5. Assuming 100 g of plant food, we would have 19 g of P_2O_5.

$$(19\text{ g P}_2\text{O}_5)\left(\frac{1\text{ mol P}_2\text{O}_5}{141.9\text{ g P}_2\text{O}_5}\right)\left(\frac{2\text{ mol P}}{1\text{ mol P}_2\text{O}_5}\right)\left(\frac{30.97\text{ g P}}{1\text{ mol P}}\right)$$
$$= 8.3\text{ g P} \therefore 8.3\%\text{ P}$$

6. Assuming 100 g of plant food, we would have 17 g of K_2O

$$(17\text{ g K}_2\text{O})\left(\frac{1\text{ mol K}_2\text{O})}{94.2\text{ g K}_2\text{O}}\right)\left(\frac{2\text{ mol K}}{\text{mol K}_2\text{O}}\right)\left(\frac{39.1\text{ g K}}{1\text{ mol K}}\right) = 14\text{ g K}$$

$$\%\text{ K} = \frac{14\text{ g}}{100\text{ g}} \times 100 = 14\%$$

7. The formula weight of $CuSO_4 \cdot 5\,H_2O$ is $63.54 + 32.06 + 9 \times 16.0 + 10 \times 1.0 = 249.6$. So percent sulfate $= \left(\dfrac{96.06\text{ g}}{249.6\text{ g}}\right)(100) = 38.49\%$

8. Standard deviation measures precision.

9. mean $= \dfrac{12.1 + 12.4 + 12.6}{3} = 12.4$

   average deviation from the mean $= \dfrac{0.3 + 0.0 + 0.2}{3} = 0.17$

   $$s = \sqrt{\frac{(0.3)^2 + (0.0)^2 + (0.2)^2}{2}} = 0.3$$

   relative average deviation from the mean $= 0.17/12.4 = 0.014$

10. Indeterminate errors are errors that cannot be detected. They occur randomly and are dealt with statistically.

11. Qualitative analysis determines what substances are present, whereas quantitative analysis tells us how much of the substance is present.

12. Accuracy is the closeness of a result to the true value.

Heat of Neutralization

To measure, using a calorimeter, the energy changes accompanying neutralization reactions.

Apparatus

Bunsen burner	thermometers (2)
Styrofoam cups (2)	50-mL graduated cylinder
cardboard square with hole in center	split one-hole rubber stopper
400-mL beaker	250-mL beaker
wire gauze	ring stand and ring

Chemicals

1 M HCl	1 M NaOH
1 M acetic acid ($HC_2H_3O_2$)	

WORK IN PAIRS, BUT EVALUATE YOUR DATA INDIVIDUALLY.

Every chemical change is accompanied by a change in energy, usually in the form of heat. The energy change of a reaction that occurs at constant pressure is termed the *heat of reaction* or the *enthalpy change*. The symbol ΔH (the symbol Δ means "change in") is used to denote the enthalpy change. If heat is evolved, the reaction is *exothermic* ($\Delta H < 0$); and if heat is absorbed, the reaction is *endothermic* ($\Delta H > 0$). In this experiment, you will measure the heat of neutralization (or the enthalpy of neutralization) when an acid and a base react to form water.

This quantity of heat is measured experimentally by allowing the reaction to take place in a thermally insulated vessel called a *calorimeter*. The heat liberated in the neutralization will cause an increase in the temperature of the solution and of the calorimeter. If the calorimeter were perfect, no heat would be radiated to the laboratory. The calorimeter you will use in this experiment is shown in Figure 1.

Because we are concerned with the heat of the reaction and because some heat is absorbed by the calorimeter itself, we must know the amount of heat absorbed by the calorimeter. This requires that we determine the heat capacity of the calorimeter. By "heat capacity of the calorimeter" we mean the amount of heat (that is, the number of joules) required to raise its temperature 1 kelvin, which is the same as 1°C. In this experiment, the temperature of the calorimeter and its contents is measured before and after the reaction. The change in the enthalpy, ΔH, is equal to the negative

Heat of Neutralization

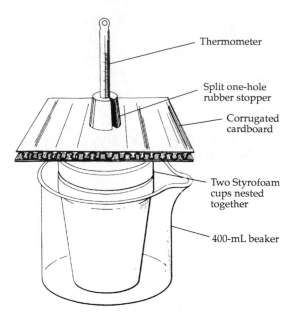

▲ **FIGURE 1** A simple calorimeter.

product of the temperature change, ΔT, times the heat capacity of the calorimeter and its contents:

$$\Delta H = -\Delta T \text{ (heat capacity of calorimeter + heat capacity of contents)} \quad [1]$$

Note that the *numerical difference* on the Celsius scale is the same as the *numerical difference* on the Kelvin scale where ΔT is the difference between the final and initial temperatures: $\Delta T = T_f - T_i$. Because ΔH is negative for an exothermic reaction whereas ΔT is positive, a negative sign is required in Equation [1].

The heat capacity of the calorimeter is determined by measuring the temperature change that occurs when a known amount of hot water is added to a known amount of cold water in the calorimeter. The heat lost by the warm water is equal to the heat gained by the cold water and the calorimeter. (We assume no heat is lost to the laboratory.) For example, if T_1 equals the temperature of a calorimeter and 50 mL of cooler water, if T_2 equals the temperature of 50 mL of warmer water added to it, and if T_f equals the temperature after mixing, then the heat lost by the warmer water is

$$\text{heat lost by warmer water} = (T_2 - T_f) \times 50 \text{ g} \times 4.18 \text{ J/K-g} \quad [2]$$

The specific heat of water is 4.184 J/K-g, and the density of water is 1.00 g/mL. The heat gained by the cooler water is

$$\text{heat gained by cooler water} = (T_f - T_1) \times 50 \text{ g} \times 4.18 \text{ J/K-g} \quad [3]$$

The heat lost to the calorimeter is the difference between heat lost by the warmer water and that gained by the cooler water:

$$\text{(heat lost by warmer water)} - \text{(heat gained by cooler water)}$$

$$= \text{heat gained by the calorimeter}$$

Substituting Equations [2] and [3] we have

$$[(T_2 - T_f) \times 50 \text{ g} \times 4.18 \text{ J/K-g}] - [(T_f - T_1) \times 50 \text{ g} \times 4.18 \text{ J/K-g}]$$
$$= (T_f - T_1) \times \text{heat capacity of calorimeter} \qquad [4]$$

Note that the heat lost to the colorimeter equals its temperature change times its heat capacity. Thus by measuring T_1, T_2, and T_f, the heat capacity of the calorimeter can be calculated from Equation [4]. This is illustrated in Example 1.

EXAMPLE 1

Given the following data, calculate the heat lost by the warmer water, the heat gained by the cooler water, the heat lost to the calorimeter, and the heat capacity of the calorimeter:

> Temperature of 50.0 mL warmer water: 37.92°C = T_2
> Temperature of 50.0 mL cooler water: 20.91°C = T_1
> Temperature after mixing: 29.11°C = T_f

SOLUTION: The heat lost by the warmer water, where $\Delta T = 37.92°C - 29.11°C$, is

$$8.81 \text{ K} \times 50 \text{ g} \times 4.18 \text{ J/K-g} = 1840 \text{ J}$$

The heat gained by the cooler water, where $\Delta T = 29.11°C - 20.91°C$, is

$$8.20 \text{ K} \times 50 \text{ g} \times 4.18 \text{ J/K-g} = 1710 \text{ J}$$

The heat gained by the calorimeter is

$$1840 \text{ J} - 1710 \text{ J} = 130 \text{ J}$$

The heat capacity of the calorimeter is, therefore,

$$130 \text{ J}/8.20 \text{ K} = 16.0 \text{ J/K}$$

Once the heat capacity of the calorimeter is determined, Equation [1] can be used to determine the ΔH for the neutralization reaction. Example 2 illustrates such a calculation.

EXAMPLE 2

Given the following data, calculate the heat gained by the solution, the heat gained by the calorimeter, and the heat of reaction:

> Temperature of 50.0 mL of acid before mixing: 21.02°C
> Temperature of 50.0 mL of base before mixing: 21.02°C
> Temperature of 100.0 mL of solution after mixing: 27.53°C

Assume that the density of these solutions is 1.00 g/mL.

SOLUTION: The heat gained by the solution, where $\Delta T = 27.53°C - 21.02°C$, is

$$6.51 \text{ K} \times 100 \text{ g} \times 4.18 \text{ J/K-g} = 2720 \text{ J}$$

The heat gained by the calorimeter, where $\Delta T = 27.53°C - 21.02°C$, is

$$6.51 \text{ K} \times 16.0 \text{ J/K} = 104 \text{ J}$$

The heat of reaction is therefore

$$2720 \text{ J} + 104 \text{ J} = 2824 \text{ J}$$

or

$$2.82 \text{ kJ}$$

103

PROCEDURE | ## A. Heat Capacity of Calorimeter

Construct a calorimeter similar to the one shown in Figure 1 by nesting two Styrofoam cups together. Use a cork borer to make a hole in the lid just big enough to admit the thermometer and slip the thermometer into a split one-hole rubber stopper to prevent the thermometer from entering too deeply into the calorimeter. The thermometer should not touch the bottom of the cup. Rest the entire apparatus in a 400-mL beaker to provide stability.

Place exactly 50.0 mL of tap water in the calorimeter cup and replace the cover and thermometer. Allow 5 to 10 min for the system to reach thermal equilibrium; then record the temperature to the nearest 0.1°C on the report sheet (1).

Place exactly 50.0 mL of water in a clean, dry 250-mL beaker and heat the water with a low flame until the temperature is approximately 15° to 20°C above room temperature. Do not heat to boiling, or appreciable water will be lost, leading to an erroneous result. Allow the hot water to stand for a minute or two; quickly record its temperature to the nearest 0.1°C on the report sheet (2) and pour it as completely as possible into the calorimeter. Replace the lid with the thermometer and carefully stir the water with the thermometer. Observe the temperature for the next 3 min and record the temperature every 15 s on the temperature vs. time data sheet at the back of the report pages. Plot the temperature as a function of time, as shown in Figure 2. Determine ΔT from your curve and then do the calculations indicated on the report sheet.

B. Heat of Neutralization of HCl—NaOH

Dry the calorimeter and the thermometer with a towel. Carefully measure 50.0 mL of 1.0 M NaOH and add it to the calorimeter. Place the lid on the calorimeter but leave the thermometer out. Measure out exactly 50.0 mL of 1.0 M HCl into a dry beaker. Allow it to stand near the calorimeter for 3 to 4 min. Measure the temperature of the acid, rinse the thermometer with tap water, and wipe dry. Insert the thermometer into the calorimeter and measure the temperature of the NaOH solution.

The temperatures of the NaOH and the HCl should not differ by more than 0.5°C. If the difference is greater than 0.5°C, adjust the temperature of the HCl

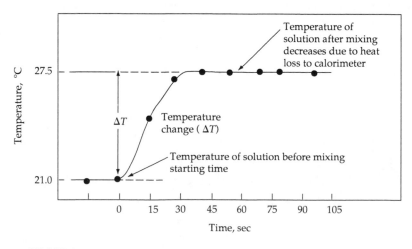

▲ FIGURE 2 Temperature as a function of time.

by *either* warming it by holding the beaker in your hands or cooling the outside of the beaker with tap water until the temperature of the HCl is within 0.5°C of that of the NaOH and record the temperature on the report sheet 1.

Record the temperature of the NaOH solution. Lift the lid and carefully add the 1.0 M HCl all at once. Be careful not to splash any on the upper sides of the cup. Stir the solution gently with the thermometer and record the temperature as a function of time every 15 s for the next 3 min. Construct a temperature-versus-time curve and determine ΔT. Calculate the heat of neutralization per mole of water formed. You may assume that the NaCl solution has the same density and specific heat as water.

C. Heat of Neutralization of $HC_2H_3O_2$—NaOH

Follow the same procedure as in Part B, but substitute 1.0 M $HC_2H_3O_2$ for 1.0 M HCl. Calculate the heat of neutralization per mole of water formed.

Waste Disposal Instructions   Handle the stock solutions carefully. You may use a wet sponge or paper towel to clean up any spills. The reaction mixtures produced in the Styrofoam cups contain harmless salts. They should be disposed of in the designated receptacles.

Before beginning this experiment in the laboratory, you should be able to answer the following questions:

| PRE LAB
| QUESTIONS

1. Define endothermic and exothermic reactions in terms of the sign of ΔH.
2. A 580-mL sample of water was cooled from 60.0°C to 10.0°C. How much heat was lost?
3. Define the term *heat capacity*.
4. How many joules are required to change the temperature of 50.0 g of water from 23.3°C to 47.6°C?
5. Define the term *specific heat*.
6. Calculate the final temperature when 50 mL of water at 60°C are added to 25 mL of water at 25°C.
7. Describe how you could determine the specific heat of a metal by using the apparatus and techniques in this experiment.
8. A piece of metal weighing 5.10 g at a temperature of 48.6°C was placed in a calorimeter into 20.00 mL of water at 22.1°C, and the final equilibrium temperature was found to be 26.8°C. What is the specific heat of the metal?
9. If the specific heat of methanol is 2.51 J/K-g, how many joules are necessary to raise the temperature of 50 g of methanol from 20°C to 60°C?
10. When a 3.25-g sample of solid sodium hydroxide was dissolved in a calorimeter in 100.0 g of water, the temperature rose from 23.9°C to 32.0°C. Calculate ΔH (in kJ/mol NaOH) for the solution process:

$$NaOH(s) \longrightarrow Na^+(aq) + OH(aq)$$

Assume it's a perfect calorimeter and that the specific heat of the solution is the same as that of pure water.

NOTES AND CALCULATIONS

REPORT SHEET | EXPERIMENT

Heat of Neutralization

A. Heat Capacity of Calorimeter

1. Temp. of calorimeter and water before mixing   _____ °C

2. Temp. of warm water   _____ °C

3. Maximum temp. determined from your curve   _____ °C

4. Heat lost by warm water (temp decrease $\times$
   50.0 g $\times$ 4.18 J/K-g) =   _____ J

5. Heat gained by cooler water (temp. increase $\times$
   50.0 g $\times$ 4.18 J/K-g) =   _____ J

6. Heat gained by the calorimeter [(4) − (5)] =   _____ J

7. Heat capacity of calorimeter:

$$\frac{\text{Heat gained by the calorimeter}}{\text{Temperature increase}} =$$ _____ J/K

B. Heat of Neutralization of HCl—NaOH

1. Temp. of calorimeter and NaOH   _____ °C

2. ΔT determined from your curve after adding HCl
   to the NaOH   _____ °C

3. Heat gained by solution (temperature increase $\times$
   100 g $\times$ 4.18 J/K-g)   _____ J

4. Heat gained by calorimeter (temperature increase $\times$
   heat capacity of calorimeter) =   _____ J

5. Total joules released by reaction [(3) + (4)] =   _____ J

6. Complete: $HCl + NaOH \longrightarrow$ _____

7. The number of moles of HCl in 50 mL of 1.0 M HCl
   (show calculations): _____ mol

8. The number of moles of H_2O produced in reaction
   of 50 mL 1.0 M HCl and 50 mL 1.0 M NaOH
   (show calculations): _____ mol

9. Joules released per mole of water formed:

$$\frac{\text{Total joules released (5)}}{\text{Number of moles water produced (8)}} = \quad \text{_____ KJ/mol}$$

C. Heat of Neutralization of $HC_2H_3O_2$—NaOH

1. Temperature of calorimeter and NaOH _____ °C

2. ΔT determined from cooling curve after adding
   $HC_2H_3O_2$ to NaOH _____ °C

3. Heat gained by solution (temp. increase $\times$ 100 g $\times$
   4.18 J/K-g) = _____ J

4. Heat gained by calorimeter (temp. increase $\times$
   heat capacity of calorimeter) = _____ J

5. Total joules released by reaction $[(3) + (4)] =$ _____ J

6. Complete: $HC_2H_3O_2 + NaOH \longrightarrow$ _____

7. The number of moles of H_2O produced in reaction
   of 50 mL 1.0 M $HC_2H_3O_2$ and 50 mL 1.0 M NaOH
   (show calculations): _____ mol

8. Joules released per mole of water formed:

$$\frac{\text{Total joules released (5)}}{\text{Number of moles water produced (7)}} = \quad \text{_____ kJ/mo}$$

Temperature vs Time Data

A. Heat Capacity of Calorimeter		B. Heat of Neutralization of NaOH-HCl		C. Heat of Neutralization of NaOH-HC$_2$H$_3$O$_2$	
Time (s)	Temp (°C)	Time (s)	Temp (°C)	Time (s)	Temp (°C)
0	_____	0	_____	0	_____
15	_____	15	_____	15	_____
30	_____	30	_____	30	_____
45	_____	45	_____	45	_____
60	_____	60	_____	60	_____
75	_____	75	_____	75	_____
90	_____	90	_____	90	_____
105	_____	105	_____	105	_____
120	_____	120	_____	120	_____
135	_____	135	_____	135	_____
150	_____	150	_____	150	_____
165	_____	165	_____	165	_____
180	_____	180	_____	180	_____

QUESTIONS

1. What is the largest source of error in the experiment?

2. How should the two heats of reaction for the neutralization of NaOH and the two acids compare? Why?

3. The experimental procedure has you wash your thermometer and dry it after you measure the temperature of the NaOH solution and before you measure the temperature of the HCl solution. Why?

4. A 50.0-mL sample of a 1.00 M solution of CuSO$_4$ is mixed with 50.0 mL of 2.00 M KOH in a calorimeter. The temperature of both solutions was 20.2°C before mixing and 26.3°C after mixing. The heat capacity of the calorimeter is 12.1 J/K. From these data calculate ΔH for the process

$$CuSO_4(1\ M) + 2KOH(2\ M) \longrightarrow Cu(OH)_2(s) + K_2SO_4(0.5\ M)$$

Assume the specific heat and density of the solution after mixing are the same as those of pure water.

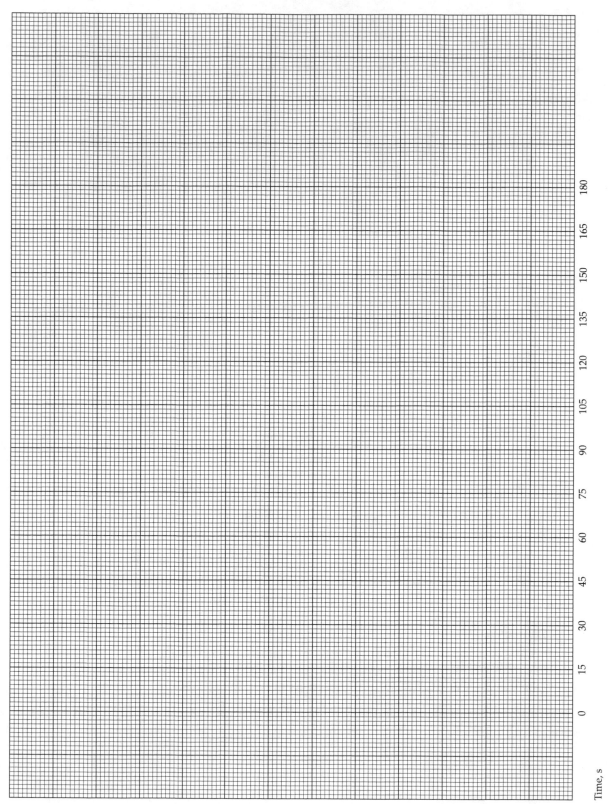

Time, s

Temperature, °C

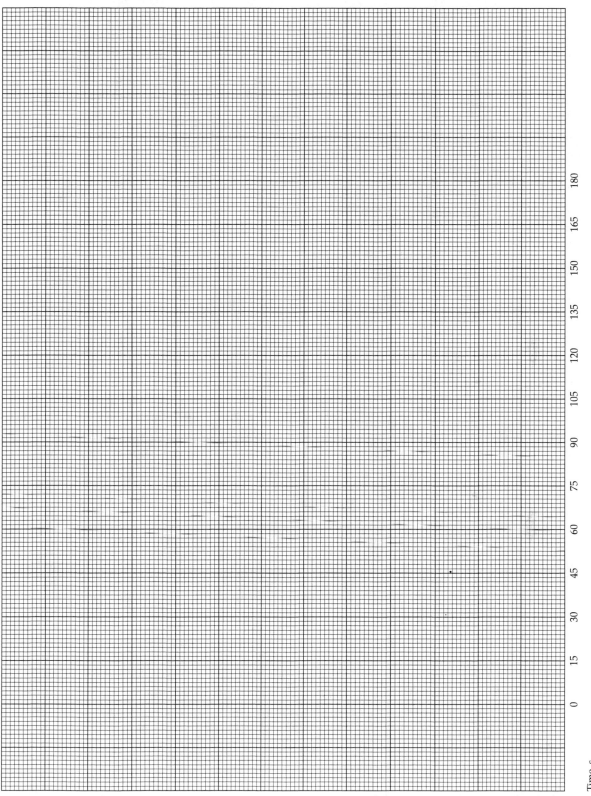

Time, s

Temperature, °C

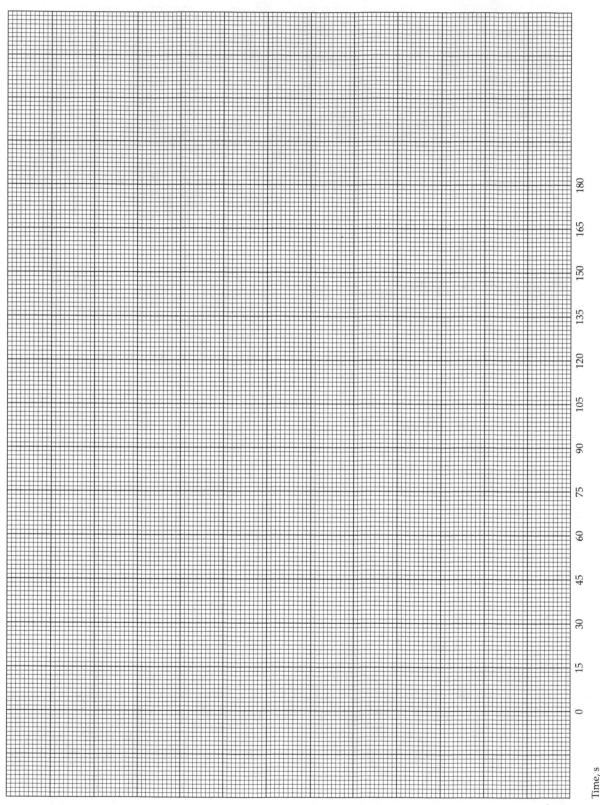

Time, s

Temperature, °C

Answers to Selected
Pre Lab Questions

1. An exothermic reaction is a reaction that produces heat; its ΔH will be less than zero, or negative. An endothermic reaction is a reaction that absorbs heat; its ΔH will be greater than zero, or positive.

2. $(580 \text{ mL})(1.0 \text{ g/mL})(60.0°C - 10.0°C)(4.18 \text{ J/g} - °C) = 119,000 \text{ J}$
    $= 119 \text{ kJ}.$

3. The heat capacity of a substance is the amount of energy, usually in the form of heat, necessary to raise the temperature of a specified amount of the substance (usually 1 g) by 1°C.

4. $\Delta T = 38.8°C - 23.3°C = 15.5°C;$
    heat required $= (60.0 \text{ g})(4.18 \text{ J/g} - °C)(15.5°C) = 3.89 \times 10^3 \text{ J}$

Titration of Acids and Bases

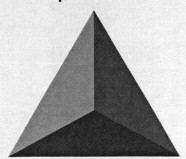

To become familiar with the techniques of titration, a volumetric method of analysis; to determine the amount of acid in an unknown.

OBJECTIVE

Apparatus

50-mL buret	balance
600-mL beaker	Bunsen burner and hose
500-mL Erlenmeyer flask	1-pint bottle with rubber stopper
250-mL Erlenmeyer flasks (3)	wash bottle
weighing bottle	buret clamp and ring stand
ring stand and ring	wire gauze

APPARATUS AND CHEMICALS

Chemicals

19 M NaOH	phenophthalein solution
potassium hydrogen phthalate (KHP, primary standard)	unknown acid

One of the most common and familiar reactions in chemistry is the reaction of an acid with a base. This reaction is termed *neutralization*, and the essential feature of this process in aqueous solution is the combination of hydronium ions with hydroxide ions to form water:

DISCUSSION

$$H_3O^+(aq) + OH^-(aq) \longrightarrow 2H_2O(l)$$

In this experiment, you will use this reaction to determine accurately the concentration of a sodium hydroxide solution that you have prepared. The process of determining the concentration of a solution is called *standardization*. Next you will measure the amount of acid in an unknown. To do this, you will accurately measure, with a buret, the volume of your standard base that is required to exactly neutralize the acid present in the unknown. The technique of accurately measuring the volume of a solution required to react with another reagent is termed *titration*.

An indicator solution is used to determine when an acid has exactly neutralized a base, or vice versa. A suitable indicator changes colors when equivalent amounts of acid and base are present. The color change is termed the *end point* of the titration. Indicators change colors at different pH values. Phenolphthalein, for example, changes from colorless to pink at a pH of about 9. In slightly more acidic solutions it is colorless, whereas, in more alkaline solutions it is pink.

In this experiment your solution of NaOH will be standardized by titrating it against a very pure sample of potassium hydrogen phthalate, $KHC_8H_4O_4$, of known weight. Potassium hydrogen phthalate (often abbreviated as KHP) has

KHP

only one acidic hydrogen. Its structure is shown here. It is a monoprotic acid with the acidic hydrogen bonded to oxygen and has a molar mass of 204.2 g.

The balanced equation for the neutralization of KHP is given in Equation [1]:

$$KHC_8H_4O_4(aq) + NaOH(aq) \longrightarrow H_2O(l) + KNaC_8H_4O_4(aq) \quad [1]$$

In the titration of the base NaOH against KHP, an equal number of moles of KHP and NaOH are present at the equivalence point. In other words, at the equivalence point

$$\text{moles NaOH} = \text{moles KHP} \quad [2]$$

The point at which stoichiometrically equivalent quantities are brought together is known as the *equivalence point* of the titration.

It should be noted that the equivalence point in a titration is a theoretical point. It can be estimated by observing some physical change associated with the condition of equivalence, such as the change in color of an indicator, which is termed the end point.

The most common way of quantifying concentrations is molarity (symbol M), which is defined as the number of moles of solute per liter of solution, or the number of millimoles of solute per milliliter of solution:

$$M = \frac{\text{moles solute}}{\text{volume of solution in liters}}$$
$$= \frac{10^{-3} \text{ mole}}{10^{-3} \text{ liter}} \quad [3]$$
$$= \frac{\text{mmol}}{\text{mL}}$$

From Equation [3] the moles of solute (or mmol solute) are related to the molarity and the volume of the solution as follows:

$$M \times \text{liters} = \text{moles solute and } M \times \text{mL} = \text{mmol solute} \quad [4]$$

Thus, if one measures the volume of base, NaOH, required to neutralize a known weight of KHP, it is possible to calculate the molarity of the NaOH solution.

EXAMPLE 1

Calculate the molarity of a solution that is made by dissolving 16.7 g of sodium sulfate, Na_2SO_4, in enough water to form 125 mL of solution.

SOLUTION:

$$\text{molarity} = \frac{\text{moles } Na_2SO_4}{\text{liters soln}}$$

Using the formula weight of Na_2SO_4, we calculate the number of moles of Na_2SO_4:

$$\text{moles } Na_2SO_4 = (16.7 \text{ g } Na_2SO_4)\left(\frac{1 \text{ mol } Na_2SO_4}{142 \text{ g } Na_2SO_4}\right) = 0.118 \text{ mol } Na_2SO_4$$

Changing the volume of the solution to liters:

$$125 \text{ mL} \times (1 \text{ L}/1000 \text{ mL}) = 0.125 \text{ L}$$

Thus the molarity is:

$$\text{molarity} = \frac{0.118 \text{ mol } Na_2SO_4}{0.125 \text{ L}} = 0.941 \text{ } M \text{ } Na_2SO_4$$

EXAMPLE 2

What is the molarity of a NaOH solution if 35.75 mL of it is required to neutralize 1.070 g of KHP?

SOLUTION: Recall from Equation [2] that at the equivalence point, the number of moles of NaOH equals the number of moles of KHP.

$$\text{moles KHP} = (1.070 \text{ g KHP})\left(\frac{1 \text{ mol KHP}}{204.2 \text{ g KHP}}\right) = 5.240 \times 10^{-3} \text{ mol KHP}$$

Because this is exactly the number of moles of NaOH that is contained in 35.75 mL of solution, its molarity is:

$$\text{molarity} = \frac{5.240 \times 10^{-3} \text{ mol NaOH}}{0.03575 \text{ L}} = 0.1466 \text{ } M \text{ NaOH}$$

Once the molarity of the NaOH solution is accurately known, the base can be used to determine the amount of KHP or any other acid present in a known weight of an impure sample. The percentage of KHP in an impure sample is

$$\% \text{ KHP} = \frac{\text{g KHP}}{\text{mass of sample}} \times 100$$

In this experiment an acid-base indicator, phenolphthalein, is used to signal the end point in the titration. This indicator was chosen because its color change coincides so closely with the equivalence point.

EXAMPLE 3

What is the percentage of KHP in an impure sample of KHP that weighs 2.537 g and requires 32.77 mL of 0.1466 M NaOH to neutralize it?

SOLUTION: The number of grams of KHP in the sample must first be determined. Remember that at the equivalence point, the number of millimoles of NaOH equals the number of millimoles of KHP.

$$\text{mmol NaOH} = (32.77 \text{ mL NaOH})(0.1466 \text{ mmol NaOH/mL NaOH})$$
$$= 4.804 \text{ mmol NaOH}$$

Thus, there are 4.804 mmol of KHP in the sample, which corresponds to the following number of grams of KHP in the sample:

$$\text{grams KHP} = 4.804 \text{ mmol KHP}\left(\frac{1 \text{ mol KHP}}{1000 \text{ mmol KHP}}\right)\left(\frac{204.2 \text{ g KHP}}{1 \text{ mol KHP}}\right)$$
$$= 0.9810 \text{ g KHP}$$

117

Therefore,

$$\% \text{ KHP} = \frac{0.9810 \text{ g}}{2.537 \text{ g}} \times 100 = 38.67\%$$

PROCEDURE | **Preparation of Approximately 0.100 M Sodium Hydroxide (NaOH)** Heat 500 mL of distilled water to boiling in a 600-mL flask,* and *after cooling under the water tap*, transfer to a 1-pint bottle fitted with a rubber stopper.[†] **(CAUTION:** *Do not get any of the 19 M NaOH on yourself. If you do, immediately wash the area with copious amounts of water).* Add 3 mL of stock solution of carbonate-free NaOH (approximately 19 M) and shake vigorously for at least 1 min. The bottle should be stoppered to protect the NaOH solution from CO_2 in the air.

Preparation of a Buret for Use Clean a 50-mL buret with soap solution and a buret brush and thoroughly rinse with tap water. Then rinse with at least five 10-mL portions of distilled water. The water must run freely from the buret without leaving any drops adhering to the sides. Make sure that the buret does not leak and that the stopcock turns freely.

Reading a Buret All liquids, when placed in a buret, form a curved meniscus at their upper surfaces. In the case of water or water solutions, this meniscus is concave (Figure 1), and the most accurate buret readings are obtained by observing the position of the lowest point on the meniscus on the graduated scales.

To avoid parallax errors when taking readings, the eye must be on a level with the meniscus. Wrap a strip of paper around the buret and hold the top edges of the strip evenly together. Adjust the strip so that the front and back edges are in line with the lowest part of the meniscus and take the reading by estimating to the nearest tenth of a marked division (0.01 mL). A simple way of doing this for repeated readings on a buret is illustrated in Figure 1.

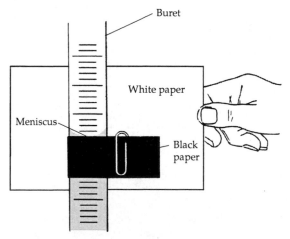

▲ **FIGURE 1** Reading a buret.

---

*The water is boiled to remove carbon dioxide (CO_2), which would react with the NaOH and change its molarity. $NaOH(aq) + CO_2(g) \longrightarrow NaHCO_3(aq)$

[†]A rubber stopper should be used for a bottle containing NaOH solution. A strongly alkaline solution tends to cement a glass stopper so firmly that it is difficult to remove.

A. Standardization of Sodium Hydroxide (NaOH) Solution

Prepare about 400 to 450 mL of CO_2-free water by boiling for about 5 min. To save time, make an additional 400 mL of CO_2-free water for Part B by boiling it now. Weigh from a weighing bottle (your lab instructor will show you how to use a weighing bottle if you don't already know) triplicate samples of between 0.4 and 0.6 g each of pure potassium hydrogen phthalate (KHP) into three separate 250-mL Erlenmeyer flasks; accurately weigh to four significant figures.* Do not weigh the flasks. Record the masses and label the three flasks in order to distinguish among them. Add to each sample about 100 mL of distilled water that has been freed from CO_2 by boiling, and warm gently with swirling until the salt is completely dissolved. Add to each flask two drops of phenolphthalein indicator solution.

Rinse the previously cleaned buret with at least four 5-mL portions of the approximately 0.100 M NaOH solution that you have prepared. Discard each portion into the designated receptacle. *Do not return any of the washings to the bottle.* Completely fill the buret with the solution and remove the air from the tip by running out some of the liquid into an empty beaker. Make sure that the lower part of the meniscus is at the zero mark or slightly lower. Allow the buret to stand for at least 30 sec before reading the exact position of the meniscus. Remove any hanging drop from the buret tip by touching it to the side of the beaker used for the washings. Record the initial buret reading on your report sheet.

Slowly add the NaOH solution to one of your flasks of KHP solution while gently swirling the contents of the flask, as illustrated in Figure 2. As the NaOH solution is added, a pink color appears where the drops of the base come in contact with the solution. This coloration disappears with swirling. As the end point is approached, the color disappears more slowly, at which time the NaOH should be added drop by drop. It is most important

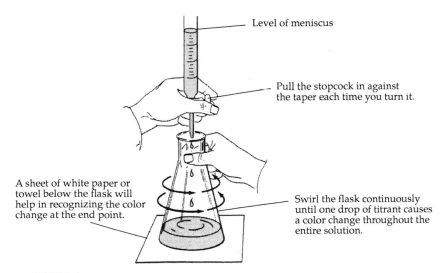

Level of meniscus

Pull the stopcock in against the taper each time you turn it.

A sheet of white paper or towel below the flask will help in recognizing the color change at the end point.

Swirl the flask continuously until one drop of titrant causes a color change throughout the entire solution.

▲ FIGURE 2 Titration procedure.

---

*In cases where the mass of a sample is larger than 1 g, it is necessary to weigh only to the nearest milligram to obtain four significant figures. Buret readings can be read only to the nearest 0.02 mL, and for readings greater than 10 mL, this represents four significant figures.

that the flask be swirled constantly throughout the entire titration. The end point is reached when one drop of the NaOH solution turns the entire solution in the flask from colorless to pink. The solution should remain pink when it is swirled. Allow the titrated solution to stand for at least 1 min so the buret will drain properly. Remove any hanging drop from the buret tip by touching it to the side of the flask and wash down the sides of the flask with a stream of water from the wash bottle. Record the buret reading on your report sheet. Repeat this procedure with the other two samples. Dispose of the neutralized solutions as instructed.

From the data you obtain in the three titrations, calculate the molarity of the NaOH solution to four significant figures as in Example 2.

The three determinations should agree within 1.0%. If they do not, the standardization should be repeated until agreement is reached. The average of the three acceptable determinations is taken as the molarity of the NaOH. Calculate the standard deviation of your results. SAVE your standardized solution for the unknown determination.

B. Analysis of an Unknown Acid

Calculate the approximate mass of unknown that should be taken to require about 20 mL of your standardized NaOH, assuming that your unknown sample is 75% KHP.

From a weighing bottle, weigh by difference triplicate portions of the sample to four significant figures and place them in three separate 250-mL flasks. The sample size should be about the amount determined by the above computation. Dissolve the sample in 100 mL of CO_2-free distilled water (prepared by boiling) and add two drops of phenolphthalein indicator solution. Titrate with your standard NaOH solution to the faintest visible shade of pink (not red) as described above in the standardization procedure. Calculate the percentage of KHP in the samples as in Example 3. For good results, the three determinations should agree within 1.0%. Your answers should have four significant figures. Compute the standard deviation of your results.

Test your results by computing the average deviation from the mean. If one result is noticeably different from the others, perform an additional titration. If any result is more than two standard deviations away from the mean, discard it and titrate another sample.

PRE LAB QUESTIONS

Before beginning this experiment in the laboratory, you should be able to answer the following questions:

1. Define *standardization* and state how you would go about doing it.
2. Define the term *titration*.
3. Define the term *molarity*.
4. Why do you weigh by difference?
5. What are equivalence points and end points, and how do they differ?
6. Why should the standarized NaOH solution be kept in a stoppered bottle? Why use a rubber stopper?

7. What is parallax, and why should you avoid it?

8. Why is it necessary to rid the distilled water of CO_2?

9. What is the molarity of a solution that contains 2.38 g of $H_2C_2O_4 \cdot 2H_2O$ in 200 mL of solution?

10. If 50.0 mL of NaOH solution is required to react completely with 0.47 g KHP, what is the molarity of the NaOH solution?

11. In the titration of an impure sample of KHP, it was found that 36.0 mL of 0.100 M NaOH was required to react completely with 0.765 g of sample. What is the percentage of KHP in this sample?

REPORT SHEET | EXPERIMENT

Titration of Acids and Bases

A. Standardization of Sodium Hydroxide (NaOH) Solution

	Trial 1	Trial 2	Trial 3
Mass of bottle + KHP	_____	_____	_____
Mass of bottle	_____	_____	_____
Mass of KHP used	_____	_____	_____
Final buret reading	_____	_____	_____
Initial buret reading	_____	_____	_____
mL of NaOH used	_____	_____	_____
Molarity of NaOH	_____	_____	_____

Average molarity _____ Standard deviation _____

Show your calculations for molarity and standard deviation:

B. Analysis of an Unknown Acid

	Trial 1	Trial 2	Trial 3
Mass of bottle + unknown	_____	_____	_____
Mass of bottle	_____	_____	_____
Mass of unknown used	_____	_____	_____
Final buret reading	_____	_____	_____
Initial buret reading	_____	_____	_____
mL of NaOH used	_____	_____	_____
Mass of KHP in unknown	_____	_____	_____
Percent of KHP in unknown	_____	_____	_____

Average percent of KHP_____ Standard deviation _____

Calculations of percent KHP and standard deviation (show using equations with units):

QUESTIONS

1. Write the balanced chemical equation for the reaction of KHP with NaOH.

2. Suppose your laboratory instructor inadvertently gave you a sample of KHP contaminated with NaCl to standardize your NaOH. How would this affect the molarity you calculated for your NaOH solution? Justify your answer.

3. How many grams of NaOH are needed to prepare 250 mL of 0.205 M NaOH?

4. A solution of malonic acid, $H_2C_3H_2O_4$, was standardized by titration with 0.1000 M NaOH solution. If 20.76 mL of the NaOH solution were required to neutralize completely 13.15 mL of the malonic acid solution, what is the molarity of the malonic acid solution?

$$H_2C_3H_2O_4 + 2NaOH \longrightarrow Na_2C_3H_2O_4 + 2H_2O$$

5. Sodium carbonate is a reagent that may be used to standardize acids in the same way that you have used KHP in this experiment. In such a standardization it was found that a 0.498-g sample of sodium carbonate required 23.5 mL of a sulfuric acid solution to reach the end point for the reaction.

$$Na_2CO_3(aq) + H_2SO_4(aq) \longrightarrow H_2O(l) + CO_2(g) + Na_2SO_4(qq)$$

What is the molarity of the H_2SO_4?

6. A solution contains 0.063 g of oxalic acid, $H_2C_2O_4 \cdot 2\,H_2O$, in 250 mL. What is the molarity of this solution?

NOTES AND CALCULATIONS

Answers to Selected
Pre Lab Questions

1. Standardization is the process of determining the concentration of a solution. It is usually achieved by titrating the solution to be standardized against a known amount of a primary standard substance according to a known reaction.

2. Titration is the technique of accurately measuring the volume of a solution that is required to react with a known amount of another reagent.

3. Molarity is the number of moles of solute in a liter of solution.

4. You weigh by difference because this is in general more accurate than weighing directly.

5. An equivalence point is the point in a titration at which stoichiometrically equivalent amounts of the two reactants are brought together. An end point is the point in a titration where some indicator (such as a dye or electrode) undergoes a discernible change. Ideally, one hopes that these two points coincide, but in practice they differ slightly. It becomes of primary importance to minimize the difference if accuracy is desired.

7. Parallax is the apparent displacement or the difference in apparent direction of an object as seen from two different points not on a straight line with the object. It should be avoided because it introduces an error in the measurement.

8. Carbon dioxide should be removed from the water because it is an acid anhydride and reacts with water to produce carbonic acid according to the reaction $CO_2 + H_2O \rightleftharpoons H_2CO_3$. Its presence would lead to an erroneous determination of the amount of a particular acid or base in solution. It is particularly detrimental to sodium hydroxide solutions as these absorb carbon dioxide to produce sodium carbonate.

9. $$\text{Molarity} = \frac{\text{moles solute}}{\text{liter solution}}$$
$$= \frac{(2.38 \text{ g})}{(126 \text{ g/mol})(0.200 \text{ L})} = 0.0944 \text{ } M$$

Chemicals in Everyday Life: What Are They and How Do We Know?

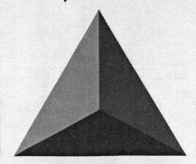

OBJECTIVE

To observe some reactions of common substances found around the home and to learn how to identify them.

APPARATUS AND CHEMICALS

Apparatus

150-mL beaker	3-in. test tubes (6)
medicine droppers (3)	red and blue litmus paper

Chemicals

household ammonia	chemical fertilizer
household bleach (chlorine)	table salt
baking soda	vinegar
chalk	Epsom salts
mineral oil	NaI
$1\ M\ NH_4Cl$	$8\ M\ NaOH$
$(NH_4)_2CO_3$	$18\ M\ H_2SO_4$
$Ba(OH)_2$ (sat. soln.)	$0.1\ M\ AgNO_3$
$3\ M\ HNO_3$	solid unknown containing
$0.2\ M\ BaCl_2$	CO_3^{2-}, Cl^-, SO_4^{2-}, or I^-

DISCUSSION

One important aspect of chemistry is the identification of substances. The identification of minerals—for example, "fool's gold" as opposed to genuine gold—was and still is of great importance to prospectors. The rapid identification of a toxic substance ingested by an infant may expedite the child's rapid recovery, or in fact it may be the determining factor in saving a life. Substances are identified either by the use of instruments or by reactions characteristic of the substance, or both. Reactions that are characteristic of a substance are frequently referred to as a *test*. For example, one may test for oxygen with a glowing splint; if the splint bursts into flame, oxygen is probably present. One tests for chloride ions by adding silver nitrate to an acidified solution. The formation of a white precipitate suggests the presence of chloride ions. Since other substances may yield a white precipitate under these conditions, one "confirms" the presence of chloride ions by observing that this precipitate dissolves in ammonium hydroxide. The area of chemistry concerned with identification of substances is termed *qualitative analysis*.

In this experiment, you will perform tests on or with substances that you are apt to encounter in everyday life, such as table salt, bleach, smelling salts, and baking soda. You probably don't think of these as "chemicals," and yet they are, even though we don't refer to them around the home by their chemical names (which are sodium chloride, chlorine, ammonium carbonate, and sodium bicarbonate, respectively), but rather by a trade name. After observing some reactions of these household chemicals, you will partially identify an unknown. Your task will be to determine whether the substance contains the carbonate (CO_3^{2-}), chloride (Cl^-), sulfate (SO_4^{2-}), or iodide (I^-) ion.

(**CAUTION:** *Even though household chemicals may appear innocuous, NEVER mix them unless you are absolutely certain you know what you are doing. Innocuous chemicals, when combined, can sometimes produce severe explosions or other hazardous reactions.*)

PROCEDURE | **A. Household Ammonia**

Obtain 1 mL of household ammonia in a 150-mL beaker. Hold a dry piece of red litmus paper over the beaker, being careful not to touch the sides of the beaker or the solution with the paper. Record your observations on the report sheet (1). Repeat the operation using a piece of red litmus paper that has been moistened with tap water. Do you note any difference in the time required for the litmus to change colors or the intensity of the color change? Record your observations on the report sheet (2).

Ammonium salts are converted to ammonia, NH_3, by the action of strong bases. Hence, one can test for the ammonium ion, NH_4^+, by adding sodium hydroxide, NaOH, and noting the familiar odor of NH_3 or by the use of red litmus. The *net* reaction is as follows:

$$NH_4^+(aq) + OH^-(aq) \rightleftharpoons NH_3(aq) + H_2O(l)$$

Place about 1 mL of 1 M NH_4Cl, ammonium chloride, in a test tube and hold a moist piece of red litmus in the mouth of the tube. Record your observations (3). Now add about 1 mL of 8 M NaOH and repeat the test. (Do not allow the litmus to touch the sides of the tube, because it may come in contact with NaOH, which will turn it blue.) If the litmus does not change color, gently warm the test tube, but do not boil the solution. Record your observations (4).

You may suspect that ordinary garden fertilizer contains ammonium compounds. Confirm your suspicions by placing some solid fertilizer, an amount about the size of a pea, in a test tube; add 1 mL of 8 M NaOH and test as above with moist litmus paper. Does the fertilizer contain ammonium salts (5)?

What is the active ingredient in "smelling salts"? Hold a moist piece of red litmus over the mouth of an open jar of ammonium carbonate, $(NH_4)_2CO_3$. Carefully fan your hand over the jar and see if you can detect a familiar odor. Record your observations on the report sheet (6). Most ammonium salts are stable; for example, the ammonium chloride solution that you tested above should not have had any effect on litmus *before* you added the sodium hydroxide. However, $(NH_4)_2CO_3$ is quite unstable and decomposes to ammonia and carbon dioxide:

$$(NH_4)_2CO_3(s) \xrightarrow{\Delta} 2NH_3(g) + CO_2(g) + H_2O(g)$$

Smelling salts contain ammonium carbonate that has been moistened with ammonium hydroxide.

Dispose of the chemicals used in this part, as well as those used in parts B, C, D, and E in the designated receptacles.

B. Baking Soda, $NaHCO_3$

Substances that contain the carbonate ion, CO_3^{2-}, react with acids to liberate carbon dioxide, CO_2, which is a colorless and odorless gas. Carbon dioxide, when released from baking soda by acids (for example, those present in lemon juice or sour milk), helps to "raise" the cake:

$$NaHCO_3(s) + H^+(aq) \longrightarrow CO_2(g) + H_2O(l) + Na^+(aq)$$

Place in a small, dry test tube an amount of solid baking soda about the size of a small pea. (**CAUTION:** *Concentrated H_2SO_4 causes severe burns. Do not get it on your skin. If you come in contact with it, immediately wash the area with copious amounts of water.*) Then add 1 or 2 drops of 18 M H_2SO_4 and notice what happens. Record your observations on the report sheet (7). Repeat this procedure, but use vinegar in place of the sulfuric acid. Record your observations on the report sheet (8).

A confirmatory test for CO_2 is to allow it to react with $Ba(OH)_2$, barium hydroxide, solution. A white precipitate of $BaCO_3$, barium carbonate, is produced:

$$CO_2(g) + Ba(OH)_2(aq) \longrightarrow BaCO_3(s) + H_2O(l)$$

Many substances, such as eggshells, oyster shells, and limestone, contain the carbonate ion. To determine whether common blackboard chalk contains the carbonate ion, place a small piece of chalk in a dry test tube and then add a few drops of 2 M HCl. Test the escaping gas for CO_2 by carefully holding a drop of $Ba(OH)_2$, suspended from the tip of a medicine dropper or a wire loop, a short distance down into the mouth of the test tube. Clouding of the drop is due to the formation of $BaCO_3$ and proves the presence of carbonate. (**NOTE:** *Breathing on the drop will cause it to cloud, since your breath contains CO_2!*) Record your observations on the report sheet (9).

C. Table Salt, NaCl

Chloride salts react with sulfuric acid to liberate hydrogen chloride, which is a pungent and colorless gas that turns moist blue litmus red:

$$2Cl^-(s) + H_2SO_4(aq) \longrightarrow 2HCl(g) + SO_4^{2-}(aq)$$

This reaction will occur independently of whether the substance is $BaCl_2$, KCl, or $ZnCl_2$; the only requirement is that the salt be a chloride. For KCl, the complete equation is

$$2KCl(s) + H_2SO_4(aq) \longrightarrow 2HCl(g) + K_2SO_4(aq)$$

Another reaction characteristic of the chloride ion is its reaction with silver nitrate to form silver chloride, AgCl, a white, insoluble substance:

$$Cl^-(aq) + AgNO_3(aq) \longrightarrow AgCl(s) + NO_3^-(aq)$$

Place in a small, dry test tube an amount of sodium chloride about the size of a small pea and add 1 or 2 drops of 18 M H_2SO_4.

(**CAUTION:** *Concentrated H_2SO_4 causes severe burns. Do not get it on your skin. If you come in contact with it, immediately wash the area with copious amounts of water.*) Very carefully note the color and odor of the escaping gas by fanning the gas with your hand toward your nose. DO NOT PLACE YOUR NOSE DIRECTLY OVER THE MOUTH OF THE TEST TUBE. Record your observations on the report sheet (10). Complete the equation NaCl + H_2SO_4 $\longrightarrow$? on the report sheet (11).

Place a small amount (about the size of a pea) of NaCl in a small test tube and add 15 drops of distilled water and one drop of 3 M HNO_3. Then add

3 or 4 drops of 0.1 M $AgNO_3$ and mix the contents. Record your observations on the report sheet (12). Why should you use distilled water for this test (13)? Confirm your answer by testing tap water for chloride ions: Add 1 drop of 3 M HNO_3 to about 2 mL of tap water and then add 3 drops of 0.1 M $AgNO_3$. Does this test indicate the presence of chloride ions in tap water? Record your answer on the report sheet (14).

Sodium ions impart a yellow color to a flame. When potatoes boil over on the gas stove or the campfire, a burst of yellow flames appears because of the presence of sodium ions. Simply handling a utensil will contaminate it sufficiently with sodium ions from the skin so that when the utensil is placed in a hot flame, a yellow color will appear. Obtain a few crystals of table salt on the tip of a clean spatula and place the tip in the flame of your burner for a brief moment. Record your observations on the report sheet (15).

D. Epsom Salts, $MgSO_4 \cdot 7 H_2O$

Epsom salts are used as a purgative, and solutions of this salt are used to soak "tired, aching feet." The following tests are characteristic of the sulfate ion, SO_4^{2-}. Place a small quantity of Epsom salts in a small, dry test tube. Add 1 or 2 drops of 18 M H_2SO_4. (**CAUTION: *Concentrated H_2SO_4 causes severe burns. Do not get it on your skin. If you come in contact with it, immediately wash the area with copious amounts of water.*) Record your observations on the report sheet (16). Note the difference in the behavior of this substance toward sulfuric acid compared with the behavior of baking soda toward sulfuric acid.

Place some Epsom salts (an amount the size of a small pea) in a small test tube and dissolve it in 1 mL of distilled water. Add 1 drop of 3 M HNO_3 and then 1 or 2 drops of 0.2 M $BaCl_2$. Record your observations on the report sheet (17). Barium sulfate is a white, insoluble substance that forms when barium chloride is added to a solution of any soluble sulfate salt, such as Epsom salts, as follows:

$$SO_4^{2-}(aq) + BaCl_2(aq) \longrightarrow BaSO_4(s) + 2 Cl^-(aq)$$

E. Bleach

Commercial bleach is usually a 5% solution of sodium hypochlorite, NaOCl. This solution behaves as though only chlorine, Cl_2, were dissolved in it. Since this solution is fairly concentrated, direct contact with the skin or eyes must be avoided! The element chlorine, Cl_2, behaves very differently from the chloride ion. Chlorine is a pale yellow-green gas with an irritating odor, is slightly soluble in water, and is toxic. It is capable of liberating the element iodine, I_2, from iodide salts:

$$Cl_2(aq) + 2 I^-(aq) \longrightarrow I_2(aq) + 2 Cl^-(aq)$$

Iodine gives a reddish-brown color to water; it is more soluble in mineral oil than in water, and it imparts a violet color to mineral oil. Thus, chlorine can be used to identify iodide salts.

In a small test tube, dissolve a small amount (about the size of a pea) of sodium iodide, NaI, in 1 mL of distilled water; add 5 drops of bleach. Note the color, then add several drops of mineral oil, shake, and allow to separate, which takes about 20 sec. Note that the mineral oil is the top layer. Record your observations on the report sheet (18).

TABLE 1 Reaction of Solid Salts with H_2SO_4

Ion	Reaction
CO_3^{2-}	Colorless, odorless gas, CO_2, evolved
Cl^-	Colorless, pungent gas, HCl, evolved, which turns blue litmus red
SO_4^{2-}	No observable reaction
I^-	Violet vapors of I_2 formed

Another reaction characteristic of iodides is that they form a pale yellow precipitate when treated with silver nitrate solution:

$$I^-(aq) + AgNO_3(aq) \longrightarrow AgI(s) + NO_3^-(aq)$$

Dissolve a small amount of sodium iodide in 1 mL of distilled water and add a drop of 3 M HNO_3, then add 3 or 4 drops of 0.1 M $AgNO_3$ solution. Record your observations on the report sheet (19).

Solid iodide salts react with concentrated sulfuric acid by instantly turning dark brown, with the slight evolution of a gas that fumes in moist air and with the appearance of violet fumes of iodine. (**CAUTION:** *Concentrated H_2SO_4 causes severe burns. Do not get it on your skin. If you come in contact with it, immediately wash the area with copious amounts of water.*) Place a small amount (about the size of a pea) of sodium iodide in a small, dry test tube and add, IN THE HOOD, 1 or 2 drops of 18 M H_2SO_4. Record your observations on the report sheet (20).

F. Unknown

Your solid unknown will contain only one of the following ions: carbonate, chloride, sulfate, or iodide. Table 1 summarizes the behavior of these ions toward H_2SO_4.

Place a small amount of your unknown (save some for further tests) in a small, dry test tube and add a drop of 18 M H_2SO_4. Record your observations and the formula for the unknown ion on the report sheet (21). What additional test might you perform to help identify the ion? Consult with your instructor *before* doing the test. Record your answer on the report sheet.

Before beginning this experiment in the laboratory, you should be able to answer the following questions:

PRE LAB QUESTIONS

1. Why is it unwise to haphazardly mix household chemicals or other chemicals?
2. How could you detect the presence of the NH_4^+ ion?
3. How could you detect the presence of the CO_3^{2-} ion?
4. How could you detect the presence of the Cl^- ion?
5. How could you detect the presence of the SO_4^{2-} ion?
6. How could you detect the presence of the I^- ion?
7. How could you detect the presence of the Ag^+ ion?

8. Complete and balance the following equations:

$$LiCl(s) + H_2SO_4(aq) \longrightarrow$$
$$NH_4^+(aq) + OH^-(aq) \rightleftharpoons$$
$$AgNO_3(aq) + I^-(aq) \longrightarrow$$
$$NaHCO_3(s) + H^+(aq) \longrightarrow$$

9. Why should distilled water be used when making chemical tests?

10. Assume you had a mixture of solid Na_2CO_3 and NaCl. Could you use only H_2SO_4 to determine whether or not Na_2CO_3 was present? Explain.

11. Assume you had a mixture of solid Na_2CO_3 and NaCl. How could you show the presence of both carbonate and chloride in this mixture?

12. How could you show the presence of both iodide and sulfate in a mixture?

Name _____ Desk _____

Date _____ Laboratory Instructor _____

Unknown no. or letter _____

REPORT SHEET | EXPERIMENT

Chemicals in Everyday Life: What Are They and How Do We Know?

A. Household Ammonia

1. Effect of household ammonia on dry litmus _____

2. Effect of household ammonia on moist litmus _____

3. Effect of NH_4Cl on litmus _____

4. Effect of NH_4Cl + NaOH on litmus _____

5. Fertilizers contain ammonium salts: Yes _____ No _____

6. Smelling salt _____

B. Baking Soda, NaHCO$_3$

7. Baking soda + H_2SO_4 _____

8. Baking soda + vinegar _____

9. Chalk contains carbonate ion: Yes _____ No _____

C. Table Salt, NaCl

10. Effect of H_2SO_4 on table salt _____

11. $H_2SO_4(l) + 2NaCl(s) \longrightarrow$ _____

12. Effect of $AgNO_3$ on table salt _____

13. Why use distilled water? _____

14. Chloride ions in tap water: Yes _____ No _____

15. Salt in flame _____

D. Epsom Salts, MgSO$_4 \cdot$ 7H$_2$O

16. Effect of H_2SO_4 on Epsom salts _____

17. $BaCl_2$ + Epsom salts _____

E. Bleach, Cl$_2$ Water

18. Bleach + NaI _____

19. Silver nitrate + NaI _____

20. Effect of H_2SO_4 on NaI _____

_____

F. Unknown

21. Unknown ion _____

22. Confirmatory test _____

_____

QUESTIONS

1. How could you distinguish sodium chloride (table salt) from sodium iodide (a poison)? Show reactions.

2. How could you distinguish solid barium chloride from solid barium sulfate?

3. Do you think that washing soda, Na_2CO_3, could be used for the same purpose as baking soda, $NaHCO_3$? Would Na_2CO_3 react with HCl? Write the chemical equation. Write the chemical equation for the reaction of $NaHCO_3$ with HCl.

4. Sodium benzoate is a food preservative. What are its formula and its solubility in water? (Consult a handbook or the Internet.) Source: *Handbook of Chemistry & Physics*

5. Citric acid is often found in soft drinks. What is its melting point? (Consult a handbook or the Internet). Source: *Handbook of Chemistry & Physics*

6. p-Phenylenediamine (also named 1,4-diaminobenzene) dyes hair black. Is this substance a liquid or solid at room temperature? (Consult a handbook or the Internet.) Source: *Handbook of Chemistry and Physics*

7. Household vinegar is a 5% solution of acetic acid. Give the formula for acetic acid.

8. Consult the label on a can of Drano (not liquid) and write the chemical formula for the contents. (There are also small pieces of aluminum inside the can.)

NOTES AND CALCULATIONS

Answers to Selected Pre Lab Questions

1. Many chemicals are hazardous, and the haphazard mixing of chemicals could lead to the production of species with very dangerous properties.

2. Addition of a strong base to a solution containing NH_4^+ will release gaseous NH_3, which will cause a piece of moist, red litmus held above the reaction solution to turn blue.

3. Addition of an acid to a solution containing CO_3^{2-} will release gaseous CO_2, which will react with $Ba(OH)_2$ to precipitate $BaCO_3$.

4. Solid chloride salts will release gaseous HCl when heated with concentrated H_2SO_4, and solutions of chloride salts will precipitate AgCl if treated with $AgNO_3$ solution.

5. Solutions of sulfate salts will precipitate $BaSO_4$ when treated with $BaCl_2$.

6. Solutions of iodide salts will react with Cl_2 to liberate I_2, which will appear brown in H_2O and purple in mineral oil.

8. $2LiCl(s) + H_2SO_4(aq) \longrightarrow 2HCl(g) + Li_2SO_4(aq)$

    $NH_4^+(aq) + OH^-(aq) \longrightarrow NH_3(g) + H_2O(l)$
    $AgNO_3(aq) + I^-(aq) \longrightarrow AgI(s) + NO_3^-(aq)$
    $NaHCO_3(s) + H^+(aq) \longrightarrow CO_2(g) + H_2O(l) + Na^+(aq)$

Molecular Geometries of Covalent Molecules: Lewis Structures and the VSEPR Model

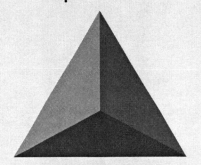

OBJECTIVE

To become familiar with Lewis structures, the principles of the VSEPR model, and the three-dimensional structures of covalent molecules.

APPARATUS

Prentice-Hall Molecular Model Set for General and Organic Chemistry or Styrofoam balls* and pipe cleaners

DISCUSSION

Types of Bonding Interactions

Whenever atoms or ions are strongly attached to one another, we say that there is a *chemical bond* between them. There are three types of chemical bonds: ionic, covalent, and metallic. The term *ionic bond* refers to electrostatic forces that exist between ions of opposite charge. Ions may be formed by the transfer of one or more electrons from an atom with a low ionization energy to an atom with a high electron affinity. Thus, ionic substances generally result from the interaction of metals on the far left side of the periodic table with nonmetals on the far right side of the periodic table (excluding the noble gases, group 8A). A *covalent bond* results from the sharing of electrons between two atoms. The more familiar examples of covalent bonding are found among nonmetallic elements interacting with one another. This experiment illustrates the geometric (three-dimensional) shapes of molecules and ions resulting from covalent bonding among various numbers of elements, and two of the consequences of geometric structure—isomers and polarity. *Metallic bonds* are found in metals such as gold, iron, and magnesium. In the metals, each atom is bonded to several neighboring atoms. The bonding electrons are relatively free to move throughout the three-dimensional structure of the metal. Metallic bonds give rise to such typical metallic properties as high electrical and thermal conductivity and luster.

Lewis Symbols

The electrons involved in chemical bonding are the *valence electrons,* those residing in the incomplete outer shell of an atom. The American chemist G. N. Lewis suggested a simple way of showing these valence electrons, which we now call Lewis electron-dot symbols or simply Lewis symbols. The **Lewis symbol** for an element consists of the chemical abbreviation for the element plus a dot for each valence electron. For example, oxygen has the electron configuration $[He]2s^22p^4$; its Lewis symbol therefore shows six valence electrons. The dots are placed on the four sides of the atomic abbreviation.

*Available from Snow Foam Products, Inc., 9917 W. Gidley St., El Monte, CA 91731.

Each side can accommodate up to two electrons. All four sides are equivalent; the placement of two electrons versus one electron is arbitrary. The number of valence electrons of any representative element is the same as the group number of the element in the periodic table.

The Octet Rule

Atoms often gain, lose, or share electrons so as to achieve the same number of electrons as the noble gas closest to them in the periodic table. Because all noble gases (except He) have eight valence electrons, many atoms undergoing reactions also end up with eight valence electrons. This observation has led to the **octet rule:** *Atoms tend to gain, lose, or share electrons until they are surrounded by eight valence electrons.* An octet of electrons consists of full *s* and *p* subshells on an atom. In terms of Lewis symbols, an octet can be thought of as four pairs of valence electrons arranged around the atom as in the configuration for Ne, which is :N̈e: There are many exceptions to the octet rule, but it provides a useful framework for many important concepts of bonding.

Covalent Bonding

Ionic substances have several characteristic properties. They are usually brittle, have high melting points, and are crystalline solids with well-formed faces that can often be cleaved along smooth, flat surfaces. These characteristics result from electrostatic forces that maintain the ions in a rigid, well-defined, three-dimensional arrangement.

The vast majority of chemical substances do not have the characteristics of ionic materials. Most of the substances with which we come in daily contact, such as water, gasoline, oxygen, and sugar, tend to be either liquids, gases, or low-melting solids. Many of them, such as charcoal lighter fluid, vaporize readily. Many are pliable in their solid form, for example, plastic bags and paraffin wax.

For the very large class of substances that do not behave like ionic substances, we need a different model for the bonding between atoms. Lewis reasoned that atoms might acquire a noble-gas electron configuration by sharing electrons with other atoms to form *covalent bonds*. The hydrogen molecule, H_2, provides the simplest possible example of a covalent bond. When two hydrogen atoms are close to each other, electrostatic interactions occur between them. The two positively charged nuclei and the two negatively charged electrons repel each other, whereas the nuclei and electrons attract each other. The attraction between the nuclei and the electrons cause electron density to concentrate between the nuclei. As a result, the overall electrostatic interactions are attractive in nature.

In essence, the shared pair of electrons in any covalent bond acts as a kind of "glue" to bind the two hydrogen atoms together in the H_2 molecule.

Lewis Structures

The formation of covalent bonds can be represented using Lewis symbols as shown below for H_2:

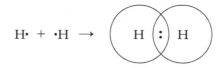

The formation of a bond between two F atoms to give a F_2 molecule can be represented in a similar way.

$$:\!\ddot{F}\!\cdot \;+\; \cdot\ddot{F}\!: \;\longrightarrow\; \left(\; :\!\ddot{F} \;(\;:\;)\; \ddot{F}\!: \;\right)$$

By sharing the bonding electron pair, each fluorine atom acquires eight electrons (an octet) in its valence shell. It thus achieves the noble-gas electron configuration of neon. The structures shown here for H_2 and F_2 are called *Lewis structures* (or Lewis electron-dot structures). In writing Lewis structures, we usually show each electron pair shared between atoms as a line, to emphasize it is a bond, and the unshared electron pairs as dots. Writing them this way, the Lewis structures for H_2 and F_2 are shown as follows:

$$H\!-\!H \qquad\qquad :\!\ddot{F}\!-\!\ddot{F}\!:$$

The number of valence electrons for the nonmetal is the same as the group number. Therefore, one might predict that 7A elements, such as F, would form one covalent bond to achieve an octet; 6A elements, such as O, would form two covalent bonds; 5A elements, such as N, would form three covalent bonds; and 4A elements, such as C, would form four covalent bonds. For example, consider the simple hydrogen compounds of the nonmetals of the second row of the periodic table.

$$
H\!-\!\ddot{\underset{\ddot{}}{F}}\!: \qquad
H\!-\!\overset{\cdot\cdot}{\underset{\underset{H}{|}}{O}}\!: \qquad
H\!-\!\overset{\cdot\cdot}{\underset{\underset{H}{|}}{N}}\!-\!H \qquad
H\!-\!\overset{\overset{H}{|}}{\underset{\underset{H}{|}}{C}}\!-\!H
$$

Thus, the Lewis model succeeds in accounting for the compounds of nonmetals, in which covalent bonding predominates.

Multiple Bonds

The sharing of a pair of electrons constitutes a single covalent bond, generally referred to simply as a *single bond*. In many molecules, atoms attain complete octets by sharing more than one pair of electrons between them. When two electron pairs are shared, two lines (representing a *double bond*) are drawn. A *triple bond* corresponds to the sharing of three pairs of electrons. Such multiple bonding is found in CO_2 and N_2.

$$\ddot{O}\!=\!C\!=\!\ddot{O}\!: \qquad\qquad :\!N\!\equiv\!N\!:$$

Drawing Lewis Structures

Lewis structures are useful in understanding the bonding in many compounds and are frequently used when discussing the properties of molecules. To draw Lewis structures, we follow a regular procedure.

1. *Sum the valence electrons from all atoms.* Use the periodic table as necessary to help determine the number of valence electrons on each atom. For an anion, add an electron to the total for each negative charge. For a cation, subtract an electron for each positive charge.

2. *Write the symbols for the atoms to show which atoms are attached to which, and connect them with a single bond* (a dash, representing two electrons). Chemical formulas are often written in the order in which the atoms are connected in the molecule or ion, as in HCN. When a central atom has a group of other atoms bonded to it, the central atom is usually written first, as in CO_3^{2-} or BF_3. In other cases you may need more information before you can draw the Lewis structure.
3. *Complete the octets of the atoms bonded to the central atom.* (Remember, however, that hydrogen can have only two electrons.)
4. *Place any leftover electrons on the central atom,* even if doing so results in more than an octet.
5. *If there are not enough electrons to give the central atom an octet, try multiple bonds.* Use one or more of the unshared pairs of electrons on the atoms bonded to the central atom to form double or triple bonds.

Formal Charge

When we draw a Lewis structure, we are describing how the electrons are distributed in a molecule (or ion). In some instances we can draw several different Lewis structures that all obey the octet rule. How do we decide which one is the most reasonable? One approach is to do some "bookkeeping" of the valence electrons to determine the *formal charge* of each atom in each Lewis structure. The formal charge of an atom is the charge that an atom in a molecule or ion would have if all atoms had the same electronegativity. To calculate the formal charge on any atom in a Lewis structure, we assign the electrons to the atoms as follows:

1. All of the unshared (nonbonding) electrons are assigned to the atom on which they are found.
2. Half of the bonding electrons are assigned to each atom in the bond.
3. Check atom formal charges for reasonableness (zero formal charges are preferred, otherwise more electronegative atoms should have negative formal charges).

EXAMPLE 1

Draw the Lewis structures for SCN^-. Calculate formal charges, and designate the preferred structure.

SOLUTION: The total number of valence electrons is 6(S) + 4(C) + 5(N) + 1 (minus charge) = 16 electrons. There are three possible Lewis structures:

$$[:\overset{..}{\underset{..}{S}}-C\equiv N:]^{-} \qquad [:\overset{..}{\underset{..}{S}}=C=\overset{..}{N}:]^{-} \qquad [:S\equiv C-\overset{..}{\underset{..}{N}}:]^{-}$$

$$\quad\;\; -1 \quad\; 0 \quad\; 0 \qquad\qquad\;\; 0 \quad\; 0 \quad -1 \qquad\qquad\; +1 \quad\; 0 \quad -2$$

$$\qquad\quad\; I \qquad\qquad\qquad\qquad\quad II \qquad\qquad\qquad\qquad\quad III$$

All the atoms have octets in each structure. Because nitrogen is more electronegative than sulfur, structure II is preferred on the basis of formal charges. Structure III is not favored, because of the large charge separation.

Bond Polarity and Dipole Moments

A covalent bond between two different kinds of atoms is usually a polar bond. This is because the two different atoms have different electronegativities and the electrons in the bond are then not shared equally by the two bound atoms. This creates a bond dipole moment, μ, which is a charge separation, Q, over a distance, r:

$$\mu = Qr$$

The bonding electrons have an increased attraction to the more electronegative atom, thus creating an excess of electron density (δ^-) near it and a deficiency of electron density (δ^+) near the less electronegative atom. We symbolize the bond dipole (a vector) with an arrow and a cross, $\mapsto$, with the point of the arrow representing the negative and the cross the positive end of the dipole. Thus, in the polar covalent molecule H—Cl, because chlorine is more electronegative than hydrogen, the bond dipole is as illustrated below:

$$\delta^+ \quad \delta^-$$
$$H \mapsto Cl$$

The bond dipole is a vector (it has magnitude and direction), and the dipole moments of polyatomic molecules are the vector sums of the individual bond dipoles as illustrated in Figure 1.

Because H_2O has a molecular dipole and CCl_4 does not, H_2O is a polar molecule and CCl_4 is a nonpolar molecule.

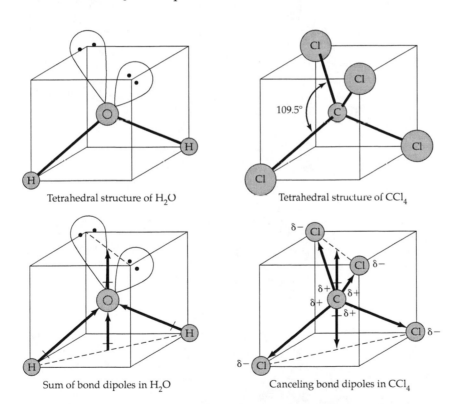

Tetrahedral structure of H_2O

Tetrahedral structure of CCl_4

Sum of bond dipoles in H_2O

Canceling bond dipoles in CCl_4

▲ **FIGURE 1** The bond dipoles in H_2O add to give a net molecular dipole that bisects the HOH angle and points upward in this drawing. In contrast, because of the symmetry of CCl_4, the bond dipoles cancel and the CCl_4 molecule has no molecular dipole moment.

The VSEPR Model

In covalent molecules, atoms are bonded together by sharing pairs of valence-shell electrons. Electron pairs repel one another and try to stay out of each other's way. *The best arrangement of a given number of electron pairs is the one that minimizes the repulsions among them.* This simple idea is the basis of valence-shell electron pair repulsion, or the **VSEPR** model. Thus, as illustrated in Table 1, two electron pairs are arranged *linearly*, three pairs are arranged in a *trigonal*

TABLE 1 Electron-Pair Geometries as a Function of the Number of Electron Pairs

Number of electron pairs	Arrangement of electron pairs	Electron-pair geometry	Predicted bond angles
2	180°	Linear	180°
3	120°	Trigonal planar	120°
4	109.5°	Tetrahedral	109.5°
5	90° / 120°	Trigonal bipyramidal	120° / 90°
6	90° / 90°	Octahedral	90° / 180°

planar fashion, four are arranged *tetrahedrally*, five are arranged in a *trigonal bipyramidal* geometry, and six are arranged *octahedrally*. The shape of a molecule or ion can be related to these five basic arrangements of electron pairs.

Predicting Molecular Geometries   When we draw Lewis structures, we encounter two types of valence-shell electron pairs: **bonding pairs**, which are shared by atoms in bonds, and nonbonding pairs (or *lone pairs*) such as in the Lewis structure for NH_3.

Nonbonding or lone pair

H — $\overset{..}{N}$ — H

H

Bonding pairs

Because there are four electron pairs around the N atom, the electron-pair repulsions will be minimized when the electron pairs point toward the vertices of a tetrahedron (see Table 1). The arrangement of electron pairs about the central atom of an AB_n molecule is called its **electron-pair geometry**. However, when we use experiments to determine the structure of a molecule, we locate atoms, not electron pairs. The **molecular geometry** of a molecule (or ion) is the arrangement of the *atoms* in space. We can predict the molecular geometry of a molecule from its electron-pair geometry. In NH_3, the three bonding pairs point toward three vertices of a tetrahedron. The hydrogen atoms are therefore located at the three vertices of a tetrahedron and the lone pair is located at a fourth vertex. The arrangement of the atoms in NH_3 is thus a *trigonal pyramid*, and the sequence of steps to arrive at this prediction are illustrated in Figure 2. We see that the trigonal-pyramidal molecular geometry of NH_3 is a consequence of its tetrahedral electron-pair geometry. When describing the shapes of molecules, we always give the molecular geometry rather than the electron-pair geometry.

Following are the steps used to predict molecular geometries with the VSEPR model:

1.   Sketch the Lewis structure of the molecule or ion.
2.   Count the total number of electron pairs around the central atom, and arrange them in a way that minimizes electron-pair repulsions (see Table 1)
3.   Describe the molecular geometry in terms of the angular arrangement of the bonding pairs, which corresponds with the arrangement of bound atoms.

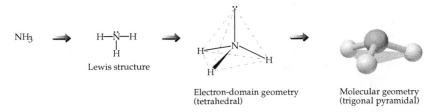

NH_3 → H — $\overset{..}{N}$ — H →
   H
Lewis structure

Electron-domain geometry
(tetrahedral)

Molecular geometry
(trigonal pyramidal)

▲ FIGURE 2

Application of the VSEPR model to molecules that contain multiple bonds reveals that a double or triple bond has essentially the same effect on bond angles as does a single bond. This observation leads to one further rule:

4. A double or triple bond is counted as one bonding pair when predicting geometry.

EXAMPLE 2

Using the VSEPR model, predict the molecular geometries of (a) SCl_2 and (b) NO_2^-.

SOLUTION:

a. The Lewis structure for SCl_2 is: $:\ddot{C}l—\ddot{S}—\ddot{C}l:$ The central S atom is surrounded by two nonbonding electron pairs and two single bonds. Thus, the electron pair geometry is tetrahedral, and the molecular geometry is bent.

b. For NO_2^- we can draw two equivalent resonance structures.

Because of resonance, the bonds between N and the two O atoms are of equal length. Both resonance structures show one nonbonding electron pair, one single bond, and one double bond about the central N atom. When we predict geometry, a double bond is counted as one electron pair (rule 4). Thus, the arrangement of valence-shell electrons is trigonal planar. Two of these positions are occupied by O atoms, so the ion has a bent shape.

Valence-Bond (VB) Theory: Covalent Bonding and Orbital Overlap

Although the VSEPR model provides a simple means for predicting molecular shapes, it does not explain why bonds exist between atoms. In 1931 Linus Pauling developed a bonding model called **valence-bond theory,** based on the marriage of Lewis's notion of electron-pair bonds to the idea of atomic orbitals. By extending this approach to include the ways in which atomic orbitals can mix with one another, we obtain a picture that corresponds nicely to the VSEPR model.

In the Lewis theory, covalent bonding occurs when atoms share electrons. Such sharing concentrates electron density between the nuclei. In the

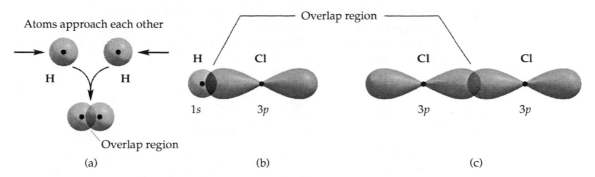

Atoms approach each other

Overlap region

H Cl

$1s$ $3p$

Cl   Cl

$3p$ $3p$

Overlap region

(a)   (b)   (c)

▲ **FIGURE 3** The overlap of orbitals to form covalent bonds. (a) The bond in H_2 results from the overlap of two $1s$ orbitals from two H atoms. (b) The bond in HCl results from the overlap of a $1s$ orbital of H and one of the lobes of a $3p$ orbital of Cl. (c) The bond in Cl_2 results from the overlap of two $3p$ orbitals from two Cl atoms.

valence-bond theory, the buildup of electron density between two nuclei is visualized as occurring when a valence atomic orbital of one atom merges with that of another atom. The orbitals are then said to share a region of space, or to overlap. The overlap of orbitals allows two electrons of opposite spin to share the common space between the nuclei, forming a covalent bond as shown for the H_2, HCl, and Cl_2 molecules in Figure 3.

Hybrid Orbitals

Although the idea of orbital overlap allows us to understand the formation of covalent bonds, it is not always easy to extend these ideas to polyatomic molecules. We need to explain both the formation of electron-pair bonds and the observed geometry. Consider the molecule BeF_2:

$$:\ddot{F}-Be-\ddot{F}:$$

The VSEPR model predicts, correctly, that this molecule is linear. Beryllium has a $1s^2 2s^2$ electron configuration with no unpaired electrons. Which orbitals on Be overlap with orbitals on F to form bonds? If the electron configuration of Be were promoted to $1s^2 2s^1 2p^1$, then a Be s and a p orbital could be used for bonding. We can also answer the former question by "mixing" the $2s$ orbital with one of the $2p$ orbitals on Be to generate two new orbitals as shown in Figure 4.

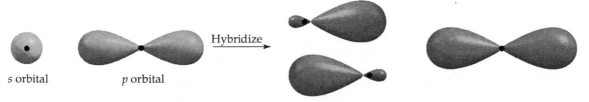

s orbital p orbital

Hybridize

Two sp hybrid orbitals sp hybrid orbitals shown together (large lobes only)

▲ **FIGURE 4** One s orbital and one p orbital can hybridize to form two equivalent sp hybrid orbitals. The two hybrid orbitals have their large lobes pointing in opposite directions, 180° apart.

Like p orbitals, each of the new sp orbitals has two lobes. The two new orbitals are identical in shape, but their large lobes point in opposite directions. We have created two **hybrid orbitals,** orbitals formed by mixing two or more atomic orbitals on an atom, a procedure called hybridization. Other types of hybrid orbitals and their geometric arrangements are shown in Table 2.

TABLE 2 Geometrical Arrangements Characteristic of Hybrid Orbital Sets

Atomic orbital set	Hybrid orbital set	Geometry	Examples
s,p	Two sp	180° — Linear	BeF_2, $HgCl_2$
s,p,p	Three sp^2	120° — Trigonal planar	BF_3, SO_3
s,p,p,p	Four sp^3	109.5° — Tetrahedral	CH_4, NH_3, H_2O, NH_4^+
s,p,p,p,d	Five sp^3d	90° 120° — Trigonal bipyramidal	PF_5, SF_4, BrF_3, $SbCl_5$
s,p,p,p,d,d	Six sp^3d^2	90° 90° — Octahedral	SF_6, ClF_5, XeF_4, PF_6^-

In this experiment, you will draw Lewis structures for molecules and ions, predict their geometric structures from the VSEPR model and valence-bond theory, and predict some of their properties, based on molecular models.

Before beginning this experiment in the laboratory, you should be able to answer the following questions:

PRE LAB QUESTIONS

1. Distinguish among ionic, covalent, and metallic bonding.
2. Which of the following molecules possess polar covalent bonds: H_2, N_2, HCl, HCN, CO_2?
3. Which of the molecules in question 2 have molecular dipole moments?
4. What are the favored geometrical arrangements for AB_n molecules for which the A atom has 2, 3, 4, 5, and 6 pairs of electrons in its valence shell?
5. How many equivalent orbitals are involved in each of the following sets of hybrid orbitals: sp, sp^2, sp^3d, sp^3d^2?
6. Define the term *formal charge*.
7. Calculate the formal charges of the atoms in CO, CO_2, and CO_3^{2-}.

NOTES AND CALCULATIONS

REPORT SHEET | EXPERIMENT

Molecular Geometries of Covalent Molecules: Lewis Structures and the VSEPR Model

1. Using an appropriate set of models, make molecular models of the compounds listed below and complete the table.

Molecular formula	No. of bond pairs	No. of lone pairs on central atom	Hybridization of central atoms	Molecular geometry	Bond angle(s)	Dipole moment (yes or no)
$BeCl_2$						
BF_3						
$SnCl_2$						
CH_4						
NH_3						
H_2O						
PCl_5						
SF_4						
BrF_3						
XeF_2						
SF_6						
IF_5						
XeF_4						

2. From your models of SF_4, BrF_3, and XeF_4, deduce whether different atom arrangements, called geometrical isomers, are possible, and, if so, sketch them below. Indicate the preferred geometry for each case and suggest a reason for your choice. Indicate which structures have dipole moments, and show their direction.

	Molecule	*Dipole moment*	*Preferred geometry*	*Reason*

(a) SF_4

(b) BrF_3

(c) XeF_4

3. Predict the structures of the fo   and state the hybridization of the central atom.

	Ion	*Structure*	*Central atom hybridization*

N_3^-

Ion	Structure	Central atom hybridization
$CO_3{}^{2-}$		
$NO_3{}^-$		
$BF_4{}^-$		

4. Because lone pairs are larger than bonding pairs, lone pair–lone pair interactions are greater than lone pair–bonding pair interactions, which are in turn larger than bonding pair–bonding pair interactions. Using this notion, suggest how the following species would distort from regular geometries.

(a) OF_2

(b) SCl_2

(c) PF_3

5. There are several families of hydrocarbons, among which are alkanes, alkenes, and alkynes. The parents of each family are CH_4 (methane), $H_2C{=}CH_2$ (ethene), and $H{-}C{\equiv}C{-}H$ (ethyne), respectively. Predict the geometries of these molecules, give the hybridization of carbon in each molecule, and suggest whether they are polar or nonpolar molecules.

Molecule	C-hybridization	Polar (yes or no)
CH_4		

Molecule	*C-hybridization*	*Polar (yes or no)*
C_2H_4		
C_2H_2		

6. Calculate the formal charges of all atoms in NH_3, NO_2^-, and NO_3^-.

Answers to Selected Pre Lab Questions

1. Ionic bonding involves the transfer of one or more electrons from an atom with a low ionization potential to an atom with a high electron affinity. Covalent bonding results from the sharing of electrons between two atoms. Metallic bonding is a type of covalent bonding, but it involves the sharing of electron density among several neighboring atoms in three dimensions.

2. HCl, HCN, and CO_2 possess polar covalent bonds.

3. HCl and HCN have molecular dipole moments.

4. AB_n molecules wherein the A atom is surrounded by 2, 3, 4, 5, and 6 electron pairs have linear, trigonal-planar, tetrahedral, trigonal-bipyramidal, and octahedral geometries, respectively.

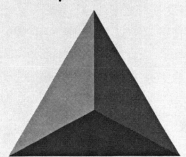

Determination of R: The Gas-Law Constant

To gain a feeling for how well real gases obey the ideal-gas law and to determine the ideal-gas-law constant, R.

Apparatus

balance	barometer
Bunsen burner and hose	glass tubing with 60-degree bends (2)
test tube	and straight pieces (2)
250-mL beaker	125-mL Erlenmeyer flask
8-oz wide-mouth bottle	rubber tubing
rubber stoppers (2)	thermometer
pinch clamp	Styrofoam cups
clamp	ring stand

Chemicals

$KClO_3$	MnO_2

Most gases obey the ideal-gas equation, $PV = nRT$, quite well under ordinary conditions, that is, at room temperature and atmospheric pressure. Small deviations from this law are observed, however, because real-gas molecules are finite in size and exhibit mutual attractive forces. The van der Waals equation,

$$\left(P + \frac{n^2 a}{V^2}\right)(V - nb) = nRT$$

where a and b are constants characteristic of a given gas, takes into account these two causes for deviation and is applicable over a much wider range of temperatures and pressures than the ideal-gas equation. The term nb in the expression $(V - nb)$ is a correction for the finite volume of the molecules; the correction to the pressure by the term $n^2 a/V^2$ takes into account the intermolecular attractions.

In this experiment you will determine the numerical value of the gas-law constant R, in its common units of L-atm/mol-K. This will be done using both the ideal-gas law and the van der Waals equation together with measured values of pressure, P, temperature, T, volume, V, and number of moles, n, of an enclosed sample of oxygen. Then you will perform an error analysis on the experimentally determined constant.

The oxygen will be prepared by the decomposition of potassium chlorate, using manganese dioxide as a catalyst:

$$2KClO_3(s) \xrightarrow[\Delta]{MnO_2(s)} 2KCl(s) + 3O_2(g)$$

Determination of R: The Gas-Law Constant

If the $KClO_3$ is accurately weighed before and after the oxygen has been driven off, the weight of the oxygen can be obtained by difference. The oxygen can be collected by displacing water from a bottle, and the volume of gas can be determined from the volume of water displaced. The pressure of the gas may be obtained through use of Dalton's law of partial pressures, the vapor pressure of water, and atmospheric pressure. Dalton's law states that the pressure of a mixture of gases in a container is equal to the sum of the pressures that each gas would exert if it were present alone:

$$P_{total} = \sum_i P_i$$

Because this experiment is conducted at atmospheric pressure, $P_{total} = P_{atmospheric}$. Hence,

$$P_{atmospheric} = P_{O_2} + P_{H_2O \ vapor}$$

PROCEDURE | Add a small amount of MnO_2 (about 0.02 g) and approximately 0.3 g of $KClO_3$ to a test tube and accurately weigh to the nearest 0.0001 g. Your instructor will demonstrate how to insert the glass tubing into the rubber stoppers. Be extremely careful to follow his or her instructions. Assemble the apparatus illustrated in Figure 1, but do not attach the test tube. Be sure that tube B does not extend below the water level in the bottle. Fill glass tube A and the rubber tubing with water by loosening the pinch clamp and attaching a rubber bulb to tube B and applying pressure through it. Close the clamp when the tube is filled.

Mix the solids in the test tube by rotating the tube, being certain that none of the mixture is lost from the tube, and attach tube B as shown in Figure 1. (**CAUTION:** *When you attach the test tube, be certain that none of the $KClO_3$ and MnO_2 comes into contact with the rubber stopper, or a se-*

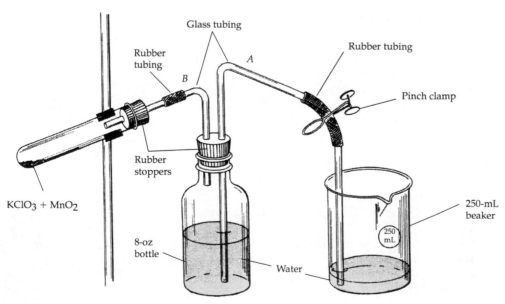

▲ **FIGURE 1** Apparatus for determination of R.

vere explosion may result. Make certain that the clamp holding the test tube is secure so that the test tube cannot move).

Fill the beaker about half full of water, insert glass tube *A* in it, open the pinch clamp, and lift the beaker until the levels of water in the bottle and beaker are identical. Then close the clamp, discard the water in the beaker, and dry the beaker. The purpose of equalizing the levels is to produce atmospheric pressure inside the bottle and test tube.

Set the beaker with tube *A* in it on the desk and open the pinch clamp. A little water will flow into the beaker, but if the system is airtight and has no leaks, the flow will soon stop and tube *A* will remain filled with water. If this is not the case, check the apparatus for leaks and start over. Leave in the beaker the water that has flowed into it; at the end of the experiment, the water levels will be adjusted and this water will flow back into the bottle.

Heat the lower part of the test tube gently (be certain that the pinch clamp is open) so that a slow but steady stream of gas is produced, as evidenced by the flow of water into the beaker. When the rate of gas evolution slows considerably, increase the rate of heating, and heat until no more oxygen is evolved. Allow the apparatus to cool to room temperature, making certain that the end of the glass tube in the beaker is always below the surface of the water. Equalize the water levels in the beaker and the bottle as before and close the clamp. Weigh a 125-mL Erlenmeyer flask[*] to the nearest 0.01 g and empty the water from the beaker into the flask.[*] Weigh the flask[*] with the water in it. Measure the temperature of the water and, using the density of water in Table 1, calculate the volume of the water displaced. This is equal to the volume of oxygen produced. Remove the test tube from the apparatus and accurately weigh the tube plus the contents. The difference in mass between this and the original mass of the tube plus MnO_2 and $KClO_3$ is the mass of the oxygen produced.

Record the barometric pressure. The vapor pressure of water at various temperatures is also given in Table 1.

TABLE 1 Density and Vapor Pressure of Pure Water at Various Temperatures

Temperature (°C)	Density (*d*) (g/mL)	Temperature (°C)	H_2O vapor pressure (mm Hg)
15	0.999099	15	12.8
16	0.998943	16	13.6
17	0.998774	17	14.5
18	0.998595	18	15.5
19	0.998405	19	16.5
20	0.998203	20	17.5
21	0.997992	21	18.6
22	0.997770	22	19.8
23	0.997538	23	21.1
24	0.997296	24	22.4
25	0.997044	25	23.8
26	0.996783		
27	0.996512		
28	0.996232		

[*]Or Styrofoam cup. The volume of water may also be measured directly, but less accurately, with a graduated cylinder.

Waste Disposal Instructions $KClO_3$ is a powerful oxidizing agent and must not be disposed of in a waste basket! Do not attempt to clean out the residue that remains in the test tube. Return the test tube to the instructor or follow his instructions for disposal of its contents.

Calculate the gas-law constant, *R*, from your data, using the ideal-gas equation. Calculate *R* using the van der Waals equation $(P + n^2a/V^2)(V - nb) = nRT$ (for O_2, $a = 1.360 \text{ L}^2 \text{ atm/mol}^2$), and $b = 31.83 \text{ cm}^3/\text{mol}$). Be sure to keep your units straight.

Error Analysis

Determine the maximum and the minimum value of *R* consistent with the experimental reliability of your data from the ideal-gas law:

$$R = \frac{PV}{nT} = \frac{(32.00 \text{ g/mol})PV}{mT}$$

Assume that the reliabilities for the various measured quantities in this experiment are as follows:

$$P = \pm 0.1 \text{ mm Hg} \qquad T = \pm 1°C$$
$$V = \pm 0.0001 \text{ L} \qquad m = \pm 0.0001 \text{ g}$$

To determine the maximum value of *R*, use the maximum values that the pressure and volume may have and the minimum values that the mass and temperature may have. Similarly, calculate the minimum value of *R* from the minimum values of *P* and *V* and the maximum values for *m* and *T*. Determine the average value of *R* and assign an uncertainty range to this average value.

EXAMPLE 1

Assume that the measured quantities were as follows: $P = 705.5 \text{ mm Hg}$; $T = 20°C$; $V = 242.9 \text{ mL}$; and $m = 0.3002 \text{ g}$. What would be the maximum and minimum values of *R*, the average value of *R*, and the uncertainty range to be assigned to this average value?

SOLUTION: First put the measured quantities into proper units as follows:

$$P = \frac{705.5 \text{ mm Hg}}{760 \text{ mm Hg/atm}} = 0.928 \text{ atm}$$

$$V = 242.9 \text{ mL} = 0.2429 \text{ L}$$

$$m = 0.3002 \text{ g}$$

$$T = (20°C + 273) \text{ K} = 293 \text{ K}$$

Therefore,

$$\text{Maximum } R = \frac{[705.6 \text{ mm Hg}/(760 \text{ mm Hg/atm})](0.2430 \text{ L})(32.00 \text{ g/mol})}{(0.3001 \text{ g})(292 \text{ K})}$$

$$= 0.0823 \text{ L-atm/mol-K}$$

$$\text{Minimum } R = \frac{[705.4 \text{ mm Hg}/(760 \text{ mm Hg/atm})](0.2428 \text{ L})(32.00 \text{ g/mol})}{(0.3003 \text{ g})(294 \text{ K})}$$

$$= 0.0816 \text{ L-atm/mol-K}$$

The average value for R is, therefore,

$$\text{Average } R = \frac{0.0823 + 0.0816}{2} \text{ L-atm/mol-K}$$

$$= 0.0820 \text{ L-atm/mol-K}$$

Note that the minimum and maximum values of R differ from the average by 0.0004. Consequently, the uncertainty in R can be written as ±0.0004 L-atm/mol-K and the data would be reported as

$$R = 0.0820 \pm 0.0004 \text{ L-atm/mol-K}$$

Before beginning this experiment in the laboratory, you should be able to answer the following questions:

PRE LAB QUESTIONS

1. Under what conditions of temperature and pressure would you expect gases to obey the ideal-gas equation?

2. Calculate the value of R in L-atm/mol-K by assuming that an ideal gas occupies 22.4 L/mol at STP.

3. Why do you equalize the water levels in the bottle and the beaker?

4. Why does the vapor pressure of water contribute to the total pressure in the bottle?

5. What is the value of an error analysis?

6. Suggest reasons why real gases might deviate from the ideal-gas law on the molecular level.

7. At present, automobile batteries are sealed. When lead storage batteries discharge, they produce hydrogen. Suppose the void volume in the battery is 100 mL at 1 atm of pressure and 25°C. What would be the pressure increase if 0.05 g H_2 were produced by the discharge of the battery? Does this present a problem? Do you know why sealed lead storage batteries were not used in the past?

8. Why is the corrective term to the volume subtracted and not added to the volume in the van der Waals equation?

9. A sample of pure gas at 20°C and 670 mm Hg occupied a volume of 562 cm^3. How many moles of gas does this represent? (HINT: Use the value of R that you found in question 2.)

10. A certain compound containing only carbon and hydrogen was found to have a vapor density of 2.550 g/L at 100°C and 760 mm Hg. If the empirical formula of this compound is CH, what is the molecular formula of this compound?

11. Which gas would you expect to behave more like an ideal gas, Ne or HBr? Why?

NOTES AND CALCULATIONS

REPORT SHEET | EXPERIMENT

Determination of R:
The Gas-Law Constant

1. Mass of test tube $+ KClO_3 + MnO_2$ _____ g

2. Mass of test tube $+$ contents after reaction   _____ g

3. Mass of oxygen produced   _____ g

4. Mass of 125-mL flask* $+$ water   _____ g

5. Mass of 125-mL flask*   _____ g

6. Mass of water   _____ g

7. Temperature of water _____

8. Density of water _____

9. Volume of water _____ = volume of O_2 gas _____

10. Barometric pressure _____

11. Vapor pressure of water _____

12. Pressure of O_2 gas (show calculations) _____

13. Gas-law constant, R, from ideal-gas law (show calculations) _____

14. R from the van der Waals equation (show calculations) _____

15. Accepted value of R _____ (source of R value) _____

_____

*Or Styrofoam cup.

16. Uncertainty in *R* (show calculations) _____

QUESTIONS

1. Does your value of *R* agree with the accepted value within your uncertainty limits?

2. Discuss possible sources of error in the experiment. Indicate the ones that you feel are most important.

3. Which gas would you expect to deviate more from ideality, H_2 or HBr? Explain your answer.

4. How does the solubility of oxygen in water affect the value of *R* you determined? Explain your answer.

5a. Use the van der Waals equation to calculate the pressure exerted by 1.000 mol of Cl_2 in 22.41L at 0.0°C. The van der Waals constants for Cl_2 are: $a = 6.49$ L^2 atm/mol^2 and $b = 0.0562$ L/mol.

5b. Which factor is the major cause for deviation from ideal behavior, the volume of the Cl_2 molecules or the attractive forces between them?

6. How much potassium chlorate is needed to produce 20.0 mL of oxygen gas at 670 mm Hg and 20°C?

7. If oxygen gas were collected over water at 20°C and the total pressure of the wet gas were 670 mm Hg, what would be the partial pressure of the oxygen?

8. An oxide of nitrogen was found by elemental analysis to contain 30.4% nitrogen and 69.6% oxygen. If 23.0 g of this gas were found to occupy 5.6 L at STP, what are the empirical and molecular formulas for this oxide of nitrogen?

9. The gauge pressure in an automobile tire reads 32 pounds per square inch (psi) in the winter at 32°F. The gauge reads the difference between the tire pressure and the atmospheric pressure (14.7 psi). In other words, the tire pressure is the gauge reading plus 14.7 psi. If the same tire were used in the summer at 110°F and no air had leaked from the tire, what would be the tire gauge reading in the summer? (HINT: Recall that $°C = \frac{5}{9}(°F - 32)$.)

NOTES AND CALCULATIONS

Answers to Selected Pre Lab Questions

1. Gases obey the ideal-gas law at relatively high temperatures and low pressures.

2. From $PV = nRT$, $R = PV/nT$ and STP is 1 atm and 0°C, or 273 K, so that

$$R = \frac{(1 \text{ atm})(22.4 \text{ L})}{(1 \text{ mol})(273 \text{ K})} = 0.082 \frac{\text{L-atm}}{\text{mol-K}}$$

3. Equalizing the water levels equalizes the pressures and ensures that the total pressure in the bottle is atmospheric and does not contain a contribution from the pressure due to the height of the water column.

4. Since gaseous and liquid water are in dynamic equilibrium, there will always be some water vapor above a sample of liquid water. Since the vapor pressure of water is reasonably high at ambient temperature, it makes a significant contribution to the total pressure.

5. An error analysis allows you to judge the reliability of your data and gives an indication of the potential sources of error.

6. The ideal-gas law assumes that there are no forces of attraction between the individual gaseous molecules. Whenever this isn't so, real molecules will not obey the ideal-gas law. This would be expected to occur at very high pressures and at very low temperatures where molecules are so close to one another that they necessarily interact.

   The ideal-gas law also assumes that the gas particles have no volume. At high pressures their volume may become appreciable relative to the volume of the container.

7. $PV = nRT$

$$P = \frac{nRT}{V} = \frac{\left(\dfrac{0.05 \text{ g}}{2 \text{ g/mol}}\right)\left(\dfrac{0.082 \text{ L-atm}}{\text{mol-K}}\right)(298 \text{ K})}{0.100 \text{ L}}$$

$$= 6 \text{ atm}$$

assuming no gas in the void volume. Clearly this does present a problem, as H_2 gas is extremely explosive. Because lead-storage batteries produce H_2, sealing them would be dangerous.

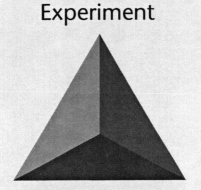

Chemical Reactions of Copper and Percent Yield

To gain some familiarity with basic laboratory procedures, some chemistry of a typical transition element, and the concept of percent yield.

Apparatus

balance	Bunsen burner and hose
250-mL beakers (2)	100-mL graduated cylinder
evaporating dish	weighing paper
stirring rod	boiling chips
towel	ring stand and iron ring
wire gauze	

Chemicals

0.5-g piece of copper wire (16 or 18 gauge)	conc. HNO_3
6 M H_2SO_4	3.0 M NaOH
methanol	granular zinc
aluminum foil cut in 1-in. squares	acetone
	conc. HCl

Most chemical syntheses involve the separation and purification of the desired product from unwanted contaminants. Common methods of separation are filtration, sedimentation, decantation, extraction, and sublimation. This experiment is designed to be a quantitative evaluation of your individual laboratory skills in carrying out some of these operations. At the same time, you will become acquainted with two fundamental types of chemical reactions, called redox reactions and metathesis reactions. By means of these reactions, you will carry out several chemical transformations involving copper and its compounds, and finally you will recover the copper sample with maximum efficiency. The chemical reactions involved are the following:

$$Cu(s) + 4HNO_3(aq) \longrightarrow Cu(NO_3)_2(aq) + 2NO_2(g) + 2H_2O(l) \qquad \text{Redox} \qquad [1]$$

$$Cu(NO_3)_2(aq) + 2NaOH(aq) \longrightarrow Cu(OH)_2(s) + 2NaNO_3(aq) \qquad \text{Metathesis} \qquad [2]$$

$$Cu(OH)_2(s) \xrightarrow{\Delta} CuO(s) + H_2O(g) \qquad \text{Dehydration} \qquad [3]$$

$$CuO(s) + H_2SO_4(aq) \longrightarrow CuSO_4(aq) + H_2O(l) \qquad \text{Metathesis} \qquad [4]$$

$$CuSO_4(aq) + Zn(s) \longrightarrow ZnSO_4(aq) + Cu(s) \qquad \text{Redox} \qquad [5]$$

$$3CuSO_4(aq) + 2Al(s) \longrightarrow Al_2(SO_4)_3(aq) + 3Cu(s) \qquad \text{Redox} \qquad [6]$$

Each of these reactions proceeds to completion. Metathesis reactions proceed to completion whenever one of the products is removed from the solution, such as in the formation of a gas or an insoluble substance.

This is the case for reactions [1], [2], and [3], where in reactions [1] and [3] a gas and in reaction [2] an insoluble precipitate are formed. (Reactions [5] and [6] proceed to completion because copper is more difficult to oxidize than either zinc or aluminum.)

The object of this experiment is to recover all of the copper with which you began. This is the test of your laboratory skills.

The percent yield of the copper can be expressed as the ratio of the recovered mass to initial mass, multiplied by 100:

$$\% \text{ yield} = \frac{\text{recovered mass of Cu}}{\text{initial mass of Cu}} \times 100$$

PROCEDURE | Weigh approximately 0.500 g of no. 16 or no. 18 copper wire to the nearest 0.0001 g and record its mass (1). Place it in a 250-mL beaker. IN THE HOOD add 4 or 5 mL of concentrated HNO_3 to the beaker. (**CAUTION:** *Be careful not to get any of the nitric acid on yourself. If you do, wash it off immediately with copious amounts of water. The gas produced in this reaction is toxic, and the reaction must be performed in the hood.*) After the reaction is complete, add 100 mL of distilled H_2O. Describe the reaction as to color change, evolution of a gas, and change in temperature (exothermic or endothermic) on the report sheet (6).

Add 30 mL of 3.0 M NaOH to the solution in your beaker and describe the reaction on the report sheet (7). Add two or three boiling chips and carefully heat the solution—while stirring with a stirring rod—just to the boiling point. Describe the reaction on your report sheet (8).

Allow the black CuO to settle, then decant the supernatant liquid. Add about 200 mL of very hot distilled water, stir, and then allow the CuO to settle. Decant once more. What are you removing by the washing and decantation (9)?

Add 15 mL of 6.0 M H_2SO_4. What copper compound is present in the beaker now (10)?

Your instructor will tell you whether you should use zinc or aluminum for the reduction of Cu(II) in the following step.

A. Reduction with Zinc

In the hood, add 2.0 g of 30-mesh zinc metal all at once and stir until the supernatant liquid is colorless. Describe the reaction on your report sheet (11). What is present in solution (12)? When gas evolution has become *very* slow, heat the solution gently (but do not boil) and allow it to cool. What gas is formed in this reaction (13)? How do you know (14)?

B. Reduction with Aluminum

In the hood, add several 1-in. squares of aluminum foil and a few drops of concentrated HCl. Continue to add pieces of aluminum until the supernatant liquid is colorless. Describe the reaction on your report sheet (11). What is present in solution (12)? What gas is formed in this reaction (13)? How do you know (14)?

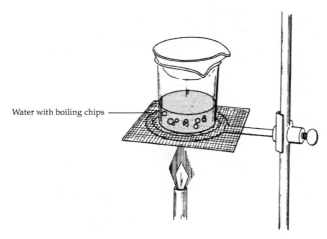

▲ **FIGURE 1** Steam bath.

For Either Reduction Method When gas evolution has ceased, decant the solution and transfer the precipitate to a preweighed porcelain evaporating dish and record its mass on the report sheet (3). Wash the precipitated copper with about 5 mL of distilled water, allow it to settle, decant the solution, and repeat the process. What are you removing by washing (15)? Wash the precipitate with about 5 mL of methanol. **(CAUTION:** *Keep the methanol away from flames—it is flammable!! Methanol is also extremely toxic. Avoid breathing the vapors as much as possible.***)** Allow the precipitate to settle, and decant the methanol. Finally, wash the precipitate with about 5 mL of acetone. **(CAUTION:** *Keep the acetone away from flames—it is extremely flammable!!***)** Allow the precipitate to settle, and decant the acetone from the precipitate. Prepare a steam bath as illustrated in Figure 1 and dry the product on your steam bath for at least 5 min. Wipe the bottom of the evaporating dish with a towel, remove the boiling chips, weigh the evaporating dish plus copper, and record its mass (2). Calculate the final mass of copper (4). Compare the mass with your initial mass and calculate the percent yield (5). What color is your copper sample (16)? Is it uniform in appearance (17)? Suggest possible sources of error in this experiment (18).

Dispose of the chemicals in the designated receptacles.

Before beginning this experiment in the laboratory, you should be able to answer the following questions:

PRE LAB QUESTIONS

1. Give an example, other than the ones listed in this experiment, of redox and methathesis reactions.
2. When will reactions proceed to completion?
3. Define *percent yield* in general terms.
4. Name six methods of separating materials.
5. Give criteria in terms of temperature changes for exothermic and endothermic reactions.
6. If 3.35 g of $Cu(NO_3)_2$ are obtained from allowing 2.25 g of Cu to react with excess HNO_3, what is the percent yield of the reaction?

7. What is the maximum percent yield in any reaction?
8. What is meant by the terms *decantation* and *filtration*?
9. When $Cu(OH)_2(s)$ is heated, copper(II) oxide and water are formed. Write a balanced equation for the reaction.
10. When sulfuric acid and copper(II) oxide are allowed to react, copper(II) sulfate and water are formed. Write a balanced equation for this reaction.

REPORT SHEET | EXPERIMENT

Chemical Reactions of Copper and Percent Yield

1. Initial mass of copper   _____
2. Mass of copper and evaporating dish   _____
3. Mass of evaporating dish   _____
4. Mass of recovered copper   _____
5. Percent yield (show calculations)   _____

6. Describe the reaction $Cu(s) + HNO_3(aq) \longrightarrow$

7. Describe the reaction $Cu(NO_3)_2(aq) + NaOH(aq) \longrightarrow$

8. Describe the reaction $Cu(OH)_2(s) \overset{\Delta}{\longrightarrow}$

9. What are you removing by this washing? _____

10. What copper compound is present in the beaker? _____

11. Describe the reaction $CuSO_4(aq) + Zn(s)$, or $CuSO_4(aq) + Al(s)$ _____

12. What is present in solution? _____

13. What is the gas? _____

14. How do you know? _____

15. What are you removing by washing? _____

16. What color is your copper sample? _____

17. Is it uniform in appearance? _____

18. Suggest possible sources of error in this experiment.

QUESTIONS

1. If your percent yield of copper were greater than 100%, what are two plausible errors you may have made?

2. Consider the combustion of methane, CH_4:

$$CH_4(g) + 2O_2(g) \longrightarrow CO_2(g) + 2H_2O(g)$$

Suppose 2.8 moles of methane are allowed to react with 3 moles of oxygen.

(a) What is the limiting reagent?

(b) How many moles of CO_2 can be made from this mixture? How many grams of CO_2?

3. Suppose 8.00 g of CH_4 is allowed to burn in the presence of 6.00 g of oxygen. How much (in grams) CH_4, O_2, CO_2, and H_2O remain after the reaction is complete?

4. Define molarity.

5. How many milliliters of 6.0 M H_2SO_4 are required to react with 0.80 g of CuO according to Equation [4]?

6. If 2.00 g of Zn is allowed to react with 1.75 g of $CuSO_4$ according to Equation [5], how many grams of Zn will remain after the reaction is complete?

7. What is meant by the term *limiting reagent*?

NOTES AND CALCULATIONS

Answers to Selected Pre Lab Questions

1. Numerous examples of redox and metathesis reactions could be cited. Two are $CuO + H_2 \longrightarrow Cu + H_2O$ (redox) and $AgNO_3 + NaI \longrightarrow AgI + NaNO_3$ (metathesis).

2. Reactions will proceed to completion whenever one of the products is physically removed from the reaction medium. This often occurs when a gas or a solid is formed.

3. Percent yield = (actual yield/theoretical yield)(100).

4. Materials can be separated from one another by distillation, sublimation, filtration, decantation, sedimentation, chromatography, and extraction.

5. Exothermic reactions are usually accompanied by a temperature increase, while endothermic reactions are usually accompanied by a temperature decrease.

6. The balanced chemical equation is $Cu + 4HNO_3 \longrightarrow Cu(NO_3)_2 + 2H_2O + 2NO_2$. From this equation we have moles $Cu(NO_3)_2$ = moles Cu and

$$\text{moles Cu} = \frac{2.25 \text{ g}}{63.5 \text{ g/mol}} = 0.0354 \text{ mol}$$

The theoretical yield is $Cu(NO_3)_2$ = (0.0354 mol)(188 g/mol) = 6.66 g

$$\% \text{ yield} = \frac{3.35 \text{ g} \times 100}{6.66 \text{ g}} = 50.3\%$$

7. The maximum percent yield in any reaction is 100%.

Reactions in Aqueous Solutions: Metathesis Reactions and Net Ionic Equations

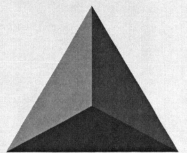

To become familiar with writing equations for metathesis reactions, including net ionic equations.

OBJECTIVE

Apparatus

small test tubes (12)	100-mL beaker (2)
evaporating dish	600-mL beaker
thermometer	funnels (2)
filter paper	short-stem funnel
Bunsen burner and hose	funnel support
magnifying glass	ring stand and ring

APPARATUS AND CHEMICALS

Chemicals

sodium nitrate	0.1 M sodium acetate
potassium chloride	0.1 M lead nitrate
0.1 M potassium chloride	0.1 M copper(II) sulfate
0.1 M barium chloride	0.1 M sodium nitrate
0.1 M sodium phosphate	1.0 M sulfuric acid
0.1 M silver nitrate	1.0 M ammonium chloride
0.1 M nickel chloride	1.0 M sodium hydroxide
0.1 M sodium sulfide	1.0 M hydrochloric acid
0.1 M cadmium chloride	1.0 M sodium carbonate
ice	

ALL SOLUTIONS SHOULD BE PROVIDED IN DROPPER BOTTLES.

In molecular equations for many aqueous reactions, cations and anions appear to exchange partners. These reactions conform to the following general equation:

DISCUSSION

$$AX + BY \longrightarrow AY + BX \qquad [1]$$

Such reactions are known as *metathesis reactions*. For a metathesis reaction to lead to a net change in solution, ions must be removed from the solution. In general, three chemical processes can lead to the removal of ions from solution, thus serving as a *driving force* for metathesis to occur:

1. The formation of a precipitate
2. The formation of a weak electrolyte or nonelectrolyte
3. The formation of a gas that escapes from solution

FORMATION OF A PRECIPITATE

The reaction of barium chloride with silver nitrate is a typical example:

$$BaCl_2(aq) + 2AgNO_3(aq) \longrightarrow Ba(NO_3)_2(aq) + 2AgCl(s) \qquad [2]$$

This form of the equation for this reaction is referred to as the *molecular equation*. Because we know that the salts $BaCl_2$, $AgNO_3$, and $Ba(NO_3)_2$ are strong electrolytes and are completely dissociated in solution, we can more realistically write the equation as follows:

$$Ba^{2+}(aq) + 2Cl^-(aq) + 2Ag^+(aq) + 2NO_3^-(aq) \longrightarrow Ba^{2+}(aq) + 2NO_3^-(aq) + 2AgCl(s)$$

$$[3]$$

This form, in which all ions are shown, is known as the *complete ionic equation*. Reaction [2] occurs because the insoluble substance AgCl precipitates out of solution. The other product, barium nitrate, is soluble in water and remains in solution. We see that Ba^{2+} and NO_3^- ions appear on both sides of the equation and thus do not enter into the reaction. Such ions are called *spectator ions*. If we eliminate or omit them from both sides, we obtain the *net ionic equation*:

$$Ag^+(aq) + Cl^-(aq) \longrightarrow AgCl(s) \qquad [4]$$

This equation focuses our attention on the salient feature of the reaction: the formation of the precipitate AgCl. It tells us that solutions of any soluble Ag^+ salt and any soluble Cl^- salt, when mixed, will form insoluble AgCl. When writing net ionic equations, remember that only *strong electrolytes* are written in the ionic form. Solids, gases, nonelectrolytes, and weak electrolytes are written in the molecular form. Frequently the symbol (aq) is omitted from ionic equations. The symbols (g) for gas and (s) for solid should not be omitted. Thus, Equation [4] can be written as

$$Ag^+ + Cl^- \longrightarrow AgCl(s) \qquad [5]$$

Consider mixing solutions of KCl and $NaNO_3$. The ionic equation for the reaction is

$$K^+(aq) + Cl^-(aq) + Na^+(aq) + NO_3^-(aq)$$
$$\longrightarrow K^+(aq) + NO_3^-(aq) + Na^+(aq) + Cl^-(aq) \qquad [6]$$

Because all the compounds are water-soluble and are strong electrolytes, they have been written in the ionic form. They completely dissolve in water. If we eliminate spectator ions from the equation, nothing remains. Hence, there is no reaction:

$$K^+(aq) + Cl^-(aq) + Na^+(aq) + NO_3^-(aq) \longrightarrow \text{no reaction} \qquad [7]$$

Metathesis reactions occur when a precipitate, a gas, a weak electrolyte, or a nonelectrolyte is formed. The following equations are further illustrations of such processes.

FORMATION OF A GAS

Molecular equation:

$$2HCl(aq) + Na_2S(aq) \longrightarrow 2NaCl(aq) + H_2S(g)$$

Complete ionic equation:

$$2H^+(aq) + 2Cl^-(aq) + 2Na^+(aq) + S^{2-}(aq) \longrightarrow 2Na^+(aq) + 2Cl^-(aq) + H_2S(g)$$

Net ionic equation:

$$2H^+(aq) + S^{2-}(aq) \longrightarrow H_2S(g)$$

or

$$2H^+ + S^{2-} \longrightarrow H_2S(g)$$

FORMATION OF A WEAK ELECTROLYTE

Molecular equation:

$$HNO_3(aq) + NaOH(aq) \longrightarrow H_2O(l) + NaNO_3(aq)$$

Complete ionic equation:

$$H^+(aq) + NO_3^-(aq) + Na^+(aq) + OH^-(aq) \longrightarrow H_2O(l) + Na^+(aq) + NO_3^-(aq)$$

Net ionic equation:

$$H^+(aq) + OH^-(aq) \longrightarrow H_2O(l)$$

In order to decide if a reaction occurs, we need to be able to determine whether or not a precipitate, a gas, a nonelectrolyte, or a weak electrolyte will be formed. The following brief discussion is intended to aid you in this regard. Table 1 summarizes solubility rules and should be consulted while performing this experiment.

TABLE 1 Solubility Rules

Water-soluble salts

Na^+, K^+, NH_4^+	All sodium, potassium, and ammonium salts are soluble.
$NO_3^-, ClO_3^-, C_2H_3O_2^-$	All nitrates, chlorates, and acetates are soluble.
Cl^-	All chlorides are soluble except AgCl, Hg_2Cl_2, and $PbCl_2$*.
Br^-	All bromides are soluble except AgBr, Hg_2Br_2, $PbBr_2$,* and $HgBr_2$*.
I^-	All iodides are soluble except AgI, Hg_2I_2, PbI_2, and HgI_2.
SO_4^{2-}	All sulfates are soluble except $CaSO_4$,* $SrSO_4$, $BaSO_4$, Hg_2SO_4, $PbSO_4$, and Ag_2SO_4.

Water-insoluble salts

$CO_3^{2-}, SO_3^{2-}, PO_4^{3-}, CrO_4^{2-}$	All carbonates, sulfites, phosphates, and chromates are insoluble except those of alkali metals and NH_4^+.
OH^-	All hydroxides are insoluble except those of alkali metals and $Ca(OH)_2$,* $Sr(OH)_2$,* and $Ba(OH)_2$.
S^{2-}	All sulfides are insoluble except those of the alkali metals, alkaline earths, and NH_4^+.

*Slightly soluble.

183

The common gases are CO_2, SO_2, H_2S, and NH_3. Carbon dioxide and sulfur dioxide may be regarded as resulting from the decomposition of their corresponding weak acids, which are initially formed when carbonate and sulfite salts are treated with acid:

$$H_2CO_3(aq) \longrightarrow H_2O(l) + CO_2(g)$$

and

$$H_2SO_3(aq) \longrightarrow H_2O(l) + SO_2(g)$$

Ammonium salts form NH_3 when they are treated with strong bases:

$$NH_4^+(aq) + OH^- \longrightarrow NH_3(g) + H_2O(l)$$

Which are the weak electrolytes? The easiest way of answering this question is to identify all of the strong electrolytes, and if the substance does not fall in that category it is a weak electrolyte. Note, water is a nonelectrolyte. Strong electrolytes are summarized in Table 2.

In the first part of this experiment, you will study some metathesis reactions. In some instances it will be very evident that a reaction has occurred, whereas in others it will not be so apparent. In the doubtful case, use the guidelines above to decide whether or not a reaction has taken place. You will be given the names of the compounds to use but not their formulas. This is being done deliberately to give practice in writing formulas from names.

In the second part of this experiment, you will study the effect of temperature on solubility. The effect that temperature has on solubility varies from salt to salt. We conclude that mixing solutions of KCl and $NaNO_3$ resulted in no reaction (see Equations [6] and [7]). What would happen if we cooled such a mixture? The solution would eventually become saturated with respect to one of the salts, and crystals of that salt would begin to appear as its solubility was exceeded. Examination of Equation [6] reveals that crystals of any of the following salts could appear initially: KNO_3, KCl, $NaNO_3$, or NaCl.

Consequently, if a solution containing Na^+, K^+, Cl^-, and NO_3^- ions is evaporated at a given temperature, the solution becomes more and more concentrated and will eventually become saturated with respect to one of the four compounds. If evaporation is continued, that compound will crystallize out, removing its ions from solution. The other ions will remain in solution and increase in concentration. Before beginning this laboratory exercise you are to plot the solubilities of the four salts given in Table 3 on the graph on your report sheet.

TABLE 2 Strong Electrolytes

Salts	All common soluble salts
Acids	$HClO_4$, HCl, HBr, HI, HNO_3, and H_2SO_4 are strong electrolytes; all others are weak.
Bases	Alkali metal hydroxides, $Ca(OH)_2$, $Sr(OH)_2$, and $Ba(OH)_2$ are strong electrolytes; all others are weak.

TABLE 3 Molar Solubilities of NaCl, NaNO₃, KCl, and KNO₃ (mol/L)

Compound	0°C	20°C	40°C	60°C	80°C	100°C
NaCl	5.4	5.4	5.5	5.5	5.5	5.6
NaNO₃	6.7	7.6	8.5	9.4	10.4	11.3
KCl	3.4	4.0	4.6	5.1	5.5	5.8
KNO₃	1.3	3.2	5.2	7.0	9.0	11.0

A. Metathesis Reactions

The report sheet lists 16 pairs of chemicals that are to be mixed. Use about 15 drops of the reagents to be combined as indicated on the report sheet. Mix the solutions in small test tubes and record your observations on the report sheet. If there is no reaction, write N.R. (The reactions need not be carried out in the order listed. Congestion at the reagent shelf can be avoided if everyone does not start with reagents for reaction 1.) Dispose of the contents of your test tubes in the designated receptacles.

B. Solubility, Temperature, and Crystallization

Place 8.5 g of sodium nitrate and 7.5 g of potassium chloride in a 100-mL beaker and add 25 mL of water. Warm the mixture, stirring, until the solids completely dissolve. Assuming a volume of 25 mL for the solution, calculate the molarity of the solution with respect to NaNO₃, KCl, NaCl, and KNO₃, and record these molarities (1).

Cool the solution to about 10°C by dipping the beaker in ice water in a 600-mL beaker and stir the solution carefully with a thermometer, being careful not to break it. (SHOULD THE THERMOMETER BREAK, IMMEDIATELY CONSULT YOUR INSTRUCTOR.) When no more crystals form, at approximately 10C, filter the cold solution quickly and allow the filtrate to drain thoroughly into an evaporating dish. Dry the crystals between two dry pieces of filter paper or paper towels. Examine the crystals with a magnifying glass (or fill a Florence flask with water and look at the crystals through it). Describe the shape of the crystals—that is, needles, cubes, plates, rhombs, and so forth (2). Based upon your solubility graph, which compound crystallized out of solution (3)?

Evaporate the filtrate to about half of its volume using a Bunsen burner and ring stand. A second crop of crystals should form. Record the temperature (4) and rapidly filter the hot solution, collecting the filtrate in a clean 100-mL beaker. Dry the second batch of crystals between two pieces of filter paper and examine their shape. Compare their shape with the first batch of crystals (5). Based upon your solubility graph, what is this substance (6)?

Finally, cool the filtrate to 10°C while stirring carefully with a thermometer to obtain a third crop of crystals. Carefully observe their shapes and compare them with those of the first and second batches (7). What compound is the third batch of crystals (8)? Dispose of the chemicals in the designated receptacles.

Before beginning this experiment in the laboratory, you should be able to answer the following questions:

1. Write molecular, complete ionic, and net ionic equations for the reactions that occur, if any, when solutions of the following substances are mixed:
   (a) nitric acid and barium carbonate
   (b) zinc chloride and lead nitrate

PROCEDURE

PRE LAB
QUESTIONS

(c) acetic acid and sodium hydroxide
(d) calcium nitrate and sodium carbonate
(e) ammonium chloride and potassium hydroxide

2. Which of the following are not water-soluble: $Ba(NO_3)_2$, $FeCl_3$, $CuCO_3$, $CuSO_4$, ZnS, $ZnSO_4$?

3. Write equations for the decomposition of H_2CO_3 and H_2SO_3.

4. At what temperature (from your graph) do KNO_3 and $NaCl$ have the same molar solubility?

5. Which of the following are strong electrolytes: $BaCl_2$, $AgNO_3$, HCl, HNO_3, $HC_2H_3O_2$?

6. Which of the following are weak electrolytes: HNO_3, HF, HCl, $NH_3(aq)$, $NaOH$?

7. For each of the following water-soluble compounds, indicate the ions present in an aqueous solution: NaI, K_2SO_4, $NaCN$, $Ba(OH)_2$, $(NH_4)_2SO_4$.

8. Write a balanced chemical equation showing how you could prepare each of the following salts from an acid-base reaction: $NaNO_3$, KCl, $BaSO_4$.

REPORT SHEET | EXPERIMENT

Reactions in Aqueous Solutions: Metathesis Reactions and Net Ionic Equations

A. Metathesis Reactions

1. Copper(II) sulfate + sodium carbonate

   Observations _____

   Molecular equation _____

   Complete ionic equation _____

   Net ionic equation _____

2. Copper(II) sulfate + barium chloride

   Observations _____

   Molecular equation _____

   Complete ionic equation _____

   Net ionic equation _____

3. Copper(II) sulfate + sodium phosphate

   Observations _____

   Molecular equation _____

   Complete ionic equation _____

   Net ionic equation _____

4. Sodium carbonate + sulfuric acid

   Observations _____

   Molecular equation _____

   Complete ionic equation _____

   Net ionic equation _____

5. Sodium carbonate + hydrochloric acid

   Observations _____

   Molecular equation _____

   Complete ionic equation _____

   Net ionic equation _____

6. Cadmium chloride + sodium sulfide

   Observations _____

   Molecular equation _____

   Complete ionic equation _____

   Net ionic equation _____

7. Cadmium chloride + sodium hydroxide
   Observations _____
   Molecular equation _____
   Complete ionic equation _____
   Net ionic equation _____

8. Nickel chloride + silver nitrate
   Observations _____
   Molecular equation _____
   Complete ionic equation _____
   Net ionic equation _____

9. Nickel chloride + sodium carbonate
   Observations _____
   Molecular equation _____
   Complete ionic equation _____
   Net ionic equation _____

10. Hydrochloric acid + sodium hydroxide
    Observations _____
    Molecular equation _____
    Complete ionic equation _____
    Net ionic equation _____

11. Ammonium chloride + sodium hydroxide
    Observations _____
    Molecular equation _____
    Complete ionic equation _____
    Net ionic equation _____

12. Sodium acetate + hydrochloric acid
    Observations _____
    Molecular equation _____
    Complete ionic equation _____
    Net ionic equation _____

13. Sodium sulfide + hydrochloric acid
    Observations _____
    Molecular equation _____
    Complete ionic equation _____
    Net ionic equation _____

14. Lead nitrate + sodium sulfide
    Observations _____
    Molecular equation _____
    Complete ionic equation _____
    Net ionic equation _____

15. Lead nitrate + sulfuric acid
    Observations _____
    Molecular equation _____
    Complete ionic equation _____
    Net ionic equation _____
16. Potassium chloride + sodium nitrate
    Observations _____
    Molecular equation _____
    Complete ionic equation _____
    Net ionic equation _____

B. Solubility, Temperature, and Crystallization

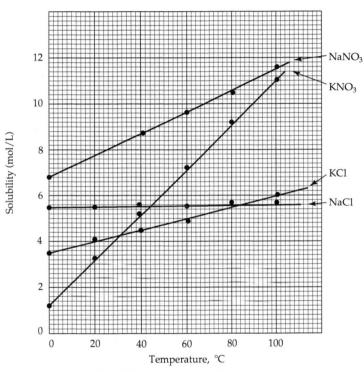

Solubilities as a function of temperature

1. Molarities
   _____ M NaNO₃, _____ M KCl, _____ M NaCl, _____ M KNO₃
2. Crystal shape _____
3. Identity of crystals _____
4. Temperature of filtrate _____
5. Crystal shape of second batch _____
6. Identity of second batch of crystals _____

7. Crystal shape of third batch _____

8. Identity of third batch of crystals _____

QUESTIONS

1. Which of the following reactions are metathesis reactions?

   (a) $2KClO_3 \longrightarrow 2KCl + 3O_2$

   (b) $Cu(NO_3)_2 + Zn \longrightarrow Cu + Zn(NO_3)_2$

   (c) $BaCO_3 + 2HCl \longrightarrow BaCl_2 + H_2O + CO_2$

   (d) $Na_2CO_3 + CuSO_4 \longrightarrow Na_2SO_4 + CuCO_3$

2. How many grams of each of the following substances will dissolve in 100 mL of cold water? Consult a handbook, or the Internet and cite your source.

   $Ce(IO_3)_4$, $RaSO_4$, $Pb(NO_3)_2$, $(NH_4)_2SeO_4$

3. Suppose you have a solution that might contain any or all of the following cations: Cu^{2+}, Ag^+, Ba^{2+}, and Mn^{2+}. Addition of HCl causes a precipitate to form. After the precipitate is filtered off, H_2SO_4 is added to the supernate and another precipitate forms. This precipitate is filtered off, and a solution of NaOH is added to the supernatant liquid until it is strongly alkaline. No precipitate is formed. Which ions are present in each of the precipitates? Which cations are not present in the original solution?

4. Write balanced net ionic equations for the reactions, if any, that occur between (a) FeS(s) and HBr(aq); (b) K_2CO_3(aq) and $CuCl_2$(aq); (c) $Fe(NO_3)_2$(aq) and HCl(aq); (d) $Bi(OH)_3$(s) and HNO_3(aq).

Answers to Selected
Pre Lab Questions

1. (a) Molecular: $2HNO_3(aq) + BaCO_3(s) \longrightarrow Ba(NO_3)_2(aq) + CO_2(g) + H_2O(l)$;
    ionic: $2H^+(aq) + 2NO_3^-(aq) + BaCO_3(s) \longrightarrow$
    $Ba^{2+}(aq) + 2NO_3^-(aq) + CO_2(g) + H_2O(l)$;
    net ionic: $BaCO_3(s) + 2H^+(aq) \longrightarrow Ba^{2+}(aq) + H_2O(l) + CO_2(g)$
    (b) As above; insoluble product $PbCl_2(s)$ is formed; net ionic:
    $Pb^{2+}(aq) + 2Cl^-(aq) \longrightarrow PbCl_2(s)$
    (c) Net ionic: $HC_2H_3O_2(aq) + OH^-(aq) \longrightarrow H_2O(l) + C_2H_3O_2^-(aq)$.
    (d) Net ionic: $Ca^{2+}(aq) + CO_3^{2-}(aq) \longrightarrow CaCO_3(s)$
    (e) Net ionic: $NH_4^+(aq) + OH^-(aq) \longrightarrow NH_3(g) + H_2O(l)$

2. The following are not water soluble: $CuCO_3$, ZnS.

5. $BaCl_2$, $AgNO_3$, HCl, and HNO_3 are strong electrolytes.

6. HF and NH_3 are weak electrolytes.

Colligative Properties: Freezing-Point Depression and Molar Mass

Experiment

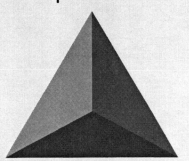

To become familiar with colligative properties and to use them to determine the molar mass of a substance.

OBJECTIVE

Apparatus

APPARATUS AND CHEMICALS

800-mL beaker	balance
400-mL beaker	wire stirrer
15 × 150 mm test tube	weighing paper
20 × 150 mm test tube	ring stand
clamp	watch

Chemicals

unknown solid	cyclohexane
acetone	sodium chloride
ice	

WORK IN PAIRS, BUT EVALUATE YOUR DATA INDEPENDENTLY.

Solutions are homogeneous mixtures that contain two or more substances. The major component is called the *solvent*, and the minor component is called the *solute*. Since the solution is primarily composed of solvent, physical properties of a solution resemble those of the solvent. Some of these physical properties, called *colligative properties,* are independent of the nature of the solute and depend only upon the solute concentration. The colligative properties include vapor-pressure lowering, boiling-point elevation, freezing-point lowering, and osmotic pressure. The *vapor pressure* is just the escaping tendency of the solvent molecules. When the vapor pressure of a solvent is equal to atmospheric pressure, the solvent boils. At this temperature the gaseous and liquid states of the solvent are in dynamic equilibrium, and the rate of molecules going from the liquid to the gaseous state is equal to the rate of molecules going from the gaseous state to the liquid state. It has been found experimentally that the dissolution of a nonvolatile solute (one with very low vapor pressure) in a solvent lowers the vapor pressure of the solvent, which in turn raises the boiling point and lowers the freezing point. This is shown graphically by the phase diagram given in Figure 1.

You are probably familiar with some common uses of these effects: Antifreeze is used to lower the freezing point and raise the boiling point of coolant (water) in an automobile radiator, and salt is used to melt ice. These effects are expressed quantitatively by the *colligative-property law*, which states that the freezing point and boiling point of a solution differ from those of the pure solvent by amounts that are directly proportional to the molal

DISCUSSION

From *Laboratory Experiments*, Tenth Edition, John H. Nelson and Kenneth C. Kemp. Copyright © 2006 by Pearson Education, Inc. Published by Prentice Hall, Inc. All rights reserved.

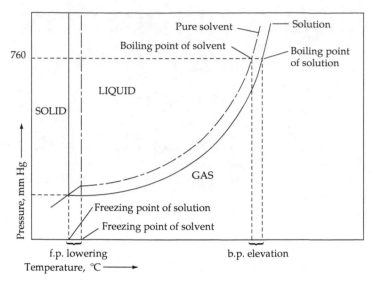

▲ **FIGURE 1** Phase diagram for a solvent and a solution.

concentration of the solute. This relationship is expressed by Equation [1] for the freezing-point lowering and boiling-point elevation

$$\Delta T = Km \qquad [1]$$

where ΔT is the freezing-point lowering or boiling-point elevation, K is a constant that is specific for each solvent, and m is the molality of the solution (number of moles solute per kg solvent). Some representative constants, boiling points, and freezing points are given in Table 1. For cyclohexane, the solvent used in this experiment, the molal freezing-point depression constant (K_{fp}) has a value of 20.4°C/m.

EXAMPLE 1

What would be the freezing point of a solution containing 1.95 g of biphenyl ($C_{12}H_{10}$) dissolved in 100 g of cyclohexane if the normal freezing point of cyclohexane is 6.6°C?

TABLE 1 Molal Freezing-Point and Boiling-Point Constants

Solvent	Freezing point (°C)	K_{fp}(°C/m)	Boiling point (°C)	K_{bp}(°C/m)
CH_3COOH (acetic acid)	16.6	3.90	118.1	2.93
C_6H_6 (benzene)	5.5	5.12	80.1	2.53
$CHCl_3$ (chloroform)	−63.5	4.68	61.2	3.63
C_2H_5OH (ethyl alcohol)	−114.6	1.99	78.4	1.22
H_2O (water)	0.0	1.86	100.0	0.51
$C_{10}H_8$ (naphthalene)	80.6	6.9	218	—
C_6H_{12} (cyclohexane)	6.6	20.4	80.7	2.79

SOLUTION:

$$\text{moles } C_{12}H_{10} = \frac{1.95 \text{ g}}{154 \text{ g/mol}} = 0.0127 \text{ mol}$$

$$\frac{\text{moles } C_{12}H_{10}}{1 \text{ kg cyclohexane}} = \left(\frac{0.0127 \text{ mol}}{100 \text{ g}}\right)\left(\frac{1000 \text{ g}}{1 \text{ kg}}\right)$$

$$= 0.127 \text{ m}$$

$$\Delta T = (20.4°C/m)(1.27 \text{ m})$$

$$= 2.6°C$$

Since the freezing point is lowered, the observed freezing point of this solution will be

$$6.6°C - 2.6°C = 4.0°C$$

Since the molal freezing-point-depression constant is known, it is possible to obtain the molar mass of a solute by measuring the freezing point of a solution and the mass of both the solute and solvent.

EXAMPLE 2

What is the molar mass of urea if the freezing point of a solution containing 15 g of urea in 100 g of naphthalene is 63.3°C?

SOLUTION: The freezing point of pure naphthalene is 80.6°C. Therefore, the freezing-point lowering (ΔT) is:

$$\Delta T = 80.6°C - 63.3°C = 17.3°C$$

From Equation [1] above,

$$17.3°C = K_{fp}m$$

$$m = \frac{17.3°C}{K_{fp}}$$

We know that K_{fp} for naphthalene is 6.9°C/m. Therefore, the molality of this solution is

$$m = \frac{17.3°C}{6.9°C/m} = 2.5 \text{ m}$$

Remember that molality is the number of moles of solute per kg of solvent. In our solution there are 15 g urea in 100 g of naphthalene, or 150 g of urea in 1000 g of naphthalene. Thus

$$150 \text{ g} = 2.5 \text{ mol}$$

$$1 \text{ mol} = 60 \text{ g}$$

The molar mass of urea is, therefore, 60 g/mol.

In this experiment you will determine the molar mass of an unknown. You will do this by determining the freezing-point depression of a cyclohexane solution having a known concentration of your unknown. The freezing temperature is difficult to ascertain by direct visual observation because of a phenomenon called supercooling and also because solidification of solutions usually occurs over a broad temperature range. Temperature-time graphs, called *cooling curves*, reveal freezing temperatures rather clearly. Similarly, warming curves

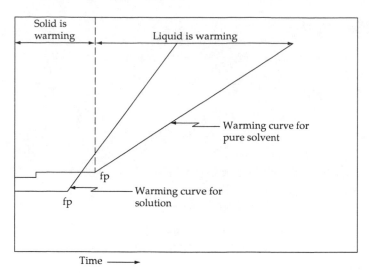

▲ FIGURE 2 Warming curves for a solvent and a solution.

may be used for the same purpose and often avoid the problem of supercooling. Therefore, you will study the rate at which frozen cyclohenane and a frozen cyclohexane solution warm and you will construct warming curves similar to those shown in Figure 2.

PROCEDURE | ## A. Warming Curve for Pure Cyclohexane

(Caution: No flames are permitted in the laboratory during this experiment as cyclohexane is very flammable)

Prepare an ice/salt/water bath by placing about 50 g of solid NaCl in a 400 mL beaker and adding just enough water to dissolve it (about 200 to 300 mL). Fill a 800 mL beaker about 2/3 full with ice, then pour the salt water mixture into it, leaving about 2 inches of the beaker empty. Stir the mixture in the beaker. Into the inner of two nested test tubes add about 10 mL of cyclohexane from a buret in the hood. Measure the initial and final buret readings and record them on your report sheet. Measure the volume of the cyclohexane to the nearest 0.05 mL and from the density of cyclohexane (0.7726 g/mL) calculate the mass of the cyclohexane. Place a −10 to +110°C thermometer in the cyclohexane with a wire stirrer around the thermometer. Clamp the nested test tubes containing the cyclohexane, thermometer, and wire stirrer to a ring stand and lower them into the ice/salt/water bath as illustrated in Figure 3. Gently stir the cyclohexane with the wire stirrer until crystals form in the bottom of the test tube. Raise the test tube assembly out of the ice/salt/water bath and clamp it to the ring stand. Measure and record the temperature, to the nearest 0.2 °C, every 30 s until the temperature reaches about 12 to 15 °C. Place the assembly back into the ice/salt/water bath and repeat the process. Plot the temperature/time data on the graph paper provided. From the inflection point in the graph determine the freezing point of cyclohexane.

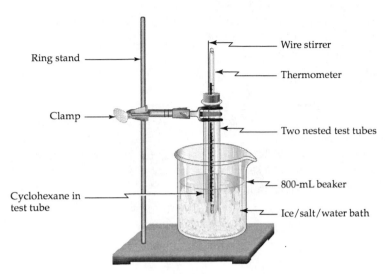

▲ **FIGURE 3** Apparatus for determination of warming curve.

B. Determination of the Molar Mass of an Unknown

Using weighing paper, weigh about 0.3 to 0.4 g of your unknown to the near-est 0.001 g. Add your unknown to the cyclohexane in the test tube and stir gently with the wire stirrer until *all* of the unknown has dissolved. Place the test tube assembly into the ice/salt/water bath (adding more ice if neces-sary) and stir the cyclohexane solution gently with the wire stirrer until it be-comes slushy. Raise the test tube assembly out of the bath and clamp it to the ring stand. Measure and record the temperature of the solution to the nearest 0.2 °C until the temperature reaches 10 to 15 °C. Then lower the test tube assembly into the bath once again and repeat the process.

C. Cleanup

Pour your cyclohexane solution into the appropriate waste container in the hood. Rinse the test tube out with a few mL of acetone and add the acetone rinse to the waste container. *(Caution: Acetone is quite flammable. Do this rinsing in the hood.)* The test tube should then be placed in your locker to air dry.

Before beginning this experiment in the laboratory, you should be able to answer the following questions:

| PRE LAB QUESTIONS

1. Distinguish between *solute* and *solvent*.
2. List three colligative properties and suggest a rationale for the choice of the word *colligative* to describe these properties.
3. Distinguish between volatile and nonvolatile substances.
4. What effect does the presence of a nonvolatile solute have upon (a) the vapor pressure of a solution, (b) the freezing point, and (c) the boiling point?

5. What is the molality of a solution that contains 2.6 g urea (molecular weight = 60 amu) in 100 g of benzene?

6. What is supercooling? How can it be minimized?

7. Calculate the freezing point of a solution containing 2.50 g of benzene in 120 g of chloroform.

8. A solution containing 0.200 g of an unknown substance in 2.50 g of cyclohexane was found to freeze at 5.1°C. What is the molar mass of the unknown substance?

9. How many grams of $NaNO_3$ would you add to 500 g of H_2O in order to prepare a solution that is 0.500 molal in $NaNO_3$?

10. Define the terms *molality* and *molarity*.

Name _____ Desk _____

Date _____ Laboratory Instructor _____

Unknown no. _____

REPORT SHEET | EXPERIMENT

Colligative Properties: Freezing-Point Depression and Molar Mass

1. Final buret reading _____ mL

2. Initial buret reading _____ mL

3. Volume of cyclohexane _____ mL

4. Mass of cyclohexane _____ g

   Show calculation _____

5. Mass of paper plus unknown _____ g

6. Mass of paper _____ g

7. Mass of unknown _____ g

A. Warming Curve Data–Pure Cyclohehane

Trial 1

Temp °C	Time (min)	Temp °C	Time (min)
_____	_____	_____	_____
_____	_____	_____	_____
_____	_____	_____	_____
_____	_____	_____	_____
_____	_____	_____	_____
_____	_____	_____	_____
_____	_____	_____	_____
_____	_____	_____	_____
_____	_____	_____	_____
_____	_____	_____	_____
_____	_____	_____	_____
_____	_____	_____	_____
_____	_____	_____	_____
		_____	_____
		_____	_____

Trial 2

Temp °C	Time (min)	Temp °C	Time (min)
_____	_____	_____	_____
_____	_____	_____	_____
_____	_____	_____	_____
_____	_____	_____	_____
_____	_____	_____	_____
_____	_____	_____	_____
_____	_____	_____	_____
_____	_____	_____	_____
_____	_____	_____	_____
_____	_____	_____	_____
_____	_____	_____	_____
_____	_____	_____	_____
_____	_____	_____	_____

8. Freezing point of pure cyclohexane, from warming curves _____   _____°C

9. Average freezing point _____

B. Warming Curve Data–Solution Containing Unknown

Trial 1

Temp °C	Time (min)	Temp °C	Time (min)
_____	_____	_____	_____
_____	_____	_____	_____
_____	_____	_____	_____
_____	_____	_____	_____
_____	_____	_____	_____
_____	_____	_____	_____
_____	_____	_____	_____
_____	_____	_____	_____
_____	_____	_____	_____
_____	_____	_____	_____
_____	_____	_____	_____
_____	_____	_____	_____
_____	_____	_____	_____

Trial 2

Temp °C	Time (min)	Temp °C	Time (min)
_____	_____	_____	_____
_____	_____	_____	_____
_____	_____	_____	_____

Trial 2

Temp °C	Time (min)	Temp °C	Time (min)
_____	_____	_____	_____
_____	_____	_____	_____
_____	_____	_____	_____
_____	_____	_____	_____
_____	_____	_____	_____
_____	_____	_____	_____
_____	_____	_____	_____
_____	_____	_____	_____
_____	_____	_____	_____
_____	_____	_____	_____
_____	_____	_____	_____
_____	_____	_____	_____
_____	_____	_____	_____
_____	_____	_____	_____
_____	_____	_____	_____
_____	_____	_____	_____

10. Freezing point of solution (trial 1) _____°C-(trial 2) _____°C

11. Average freezing point of solution _____

12. Δt _____ °C

13. Molality of unknown (show calculations) _____ m

14. Molar mass of unknown (show calculations) _____

HAND IN YOUR WARMING CURVES WITH YOUR REPORT SHEET.

QUESTIONS

1. What are the major sources of error in this experiment?

2. Suppose your thermometer consistently read a temperature 1.2° lower than the correct temperature throughout the experiment. How would this have affected the molar mass you found?

3. If the freezing point of the solution had been incorrectly read 0.3° lower than the true freezing point, would the calculated molar mass of the solute be too high or too low? Explain your answer.

4. Arrange the following aqueous solutions in order of increasing freezing points (lowest to highest temperature): 0.10 m glucose, 0.10 m $BaCl_2$, 0.20 m NaCl, and 0.20 m Na_2SO_4.

5. What mass of NaCl is dissolved in 150 g of water in a 0.050 m solution?

6. Calculate the molalities of some commercial reagents from the following data:

	HCl	$HC_2H_3O_2$	$NH_3(aq)$
Formula weight (amu)	36.465	60.05	17.03
Density of solution (g/mL)	1.19	1.05	0.90
Weight %	37.2	99.8	28.0
Molarity	12.1	17.4	14.8

7. A solution of 2.00 g of para-dichlorobenzene (a clothes moth repellant) in 50.0 g of cyclohexane freezes at 1.05°C. What is the molar mass of this substance?

Warming Curve for Pure Cyclohexane

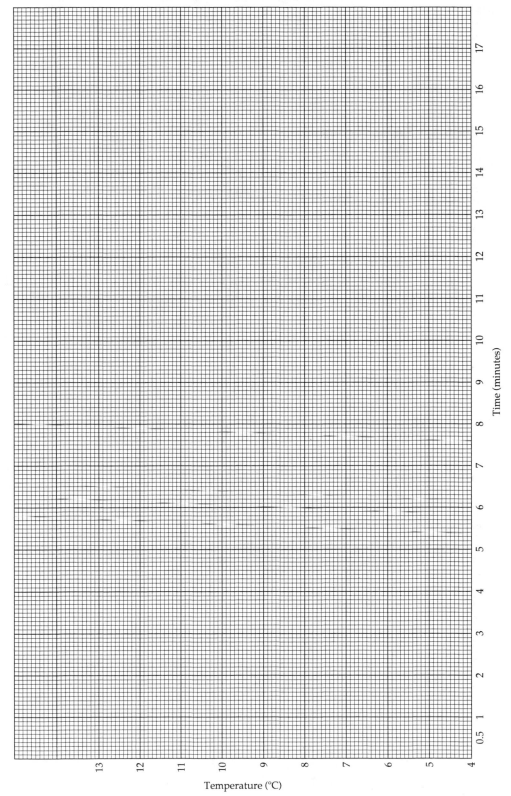

Time (minutes)

Temperature (°C)

Warming Curve for Cyclohexane +1, 4-dibromobenzene

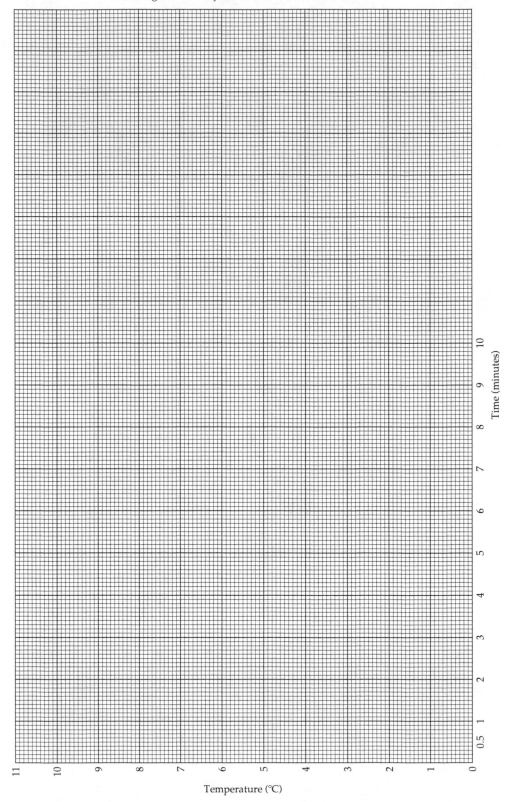

Time (minutes)

Temperature (°C)

Answers to Selected Pre Lab Questions

1. Solute is the lesser component and solvent the greater component in a solution.

2. Three colligative properties are boiling point, freezing point, and vapor pressure. They are called colligative properties because they are related to the number and energy of collisions between particles and not to what the particles are.

3. A volatile substance has a high vapor pressure, and a nonvolatile substance has a low vapor pressure at room temperature. Obviously, volatility is a relative term and depends upon temperature and pressure. Volatility increases with increasing temperature and decreases with increasing pressure.

6. Supercooling involves the lowering of the temperature of a substance below its normal freezing point without the solidification of the substance. Supercooling can be minimized by cooling slowly with rapid stirring.

7. Mol of benzene is 2.50 g/(78 g/mol) = 0.032 mol. Consequently, a solution of 2.50 g of benzene in 120 g of $CHCl_3$ is 0.032 mol/0.120 kg or 0.267 molal. The freezing-point lowering is thus $\Delta T = K_{fp}m$, or $\Delta T = (4.68°C/m)(0.267\ m) = 1.25°C$, and the freezing point is $-63.5°C - 1.25°C = -64.8°C$.

8. $\Delta T = 6.6°C - 5.1°C = 1.5°C$; $m = \Delta T/K_{fp} = 1.5°C/(20.4°C/m) = 0.074\ m$; m = moles solute/1000 g solvent, so that 0.200 g/2.50 g = x g/1000 g, x = 80 g, and 80 g = 0.074 mol, or molar mass = 80 g/0.074 mol = 1081 g/mol = 1.1×10^2 g/mol.

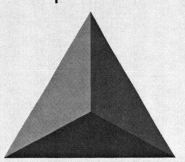

Experiment

Rates of Chemical Reactions I: A Clock Reaction

To measure the effect of concentration upon the rate of the reaction of peroxydisulfate ion with iodide ion; to determine the order of the reaction with respect to the reactant concentrations; and to obtain the rate law for the chemical reaction.

OBJECTIVE

Apparatus

burets (2)	25-mL pipet
1-mL pipets (2)	50-mL pipet
clock or watch with second hand	test tubes (8)
pipet bulb	250-mL Erlenmeyer flasks (4)
buret clamp	100-mL beakers (4)
ring stand	

APPARATUS AND CHEMICALS

Chemicals

0.2 M KI	0.4 M $Na_2S_2O_3$ (freshly prepared)
1% starch solution, boiled	0.1 M solution of Na_2H_2EDTA
0.2 M $(NH_4)_2S_2O_8$ (freshly prepared)	0.2 M KNO_3

WORK IN PAIRS, BUT EVALUATE YOUR DATA INDIVIDUALLY.

Factors Affecting Rates of Reactions

DISCUSSION

On the basis of the experiments you've performed, you probably have already noticed that reactions occur at varying speeds. There is an entire spectrum of speeds of reactions, ranging from very slow to extremely fast. For example, the rusting of iron is reasonably slow, whereas the decomposition of TNT is extremely fast. The branch of chemistry that is concerned with the rates of reactions is called *chemical kinetics*. Experiments show that rates of homogeneous reactions in solution depend upon:

1. The nature of the reactants
2. The concentration of the reactants
3. The temperature
4. Catalysis

Before a reaction can occur, the reactants must come into direct contact via collisions of the reacting particles. However, even then, the reacting particles (ions or molecules) must collide with sufficient energy to result in a reaction. If they do not, their collisions are ineffective and analogous to collisions of billiard balls. With these considerations in mind, we can qualitatively explain how the various factors influence the rates of reactions.

Concentration   Changing the concentration of a solution alters the number of particles per unit volume. The more particles present in a given volume, the greater the probability of their colliding. Hence, increasing the concentration of a solution increases the number of collisions per unit time and therefore the rate of reaction.

Temperature   Since temperature is a measure of the average kinetic energy, an increase in temperature increases the kinetic energy of the particles. An increase in kinetic energy increases the velocity of the particles and therefore the number of collisions between them in a *given period of time*. Thus, the rate of reaction increases. Also, an increase in kinetic energy results in a greater proportion of the collisions having the required energy for reaction. As a rule of thumb, for each 10°C increase in temperature, the rate of reaction doubles.

Catalyst   Catalysts, in some cases, are believed to increase reaction rates by bringing particles into close juxtaposition in the correct geometrical arrangement for reaction to occur. In other instances, catalysts offer an alternative route to the reaction, one that requires less energetic collisions between reactant particles. If less energy is required for a successful collision, a larger percentage of the collisions will have the requisite energy, and the reaction will occur faster. Actually, the catalyst may take an active part in the reaction, but at the end of the reaction, the catalyst can be recovered chemically unchanged.

Order of Reaction Defined

Let's examine precisely what is meant by the expression *rate of reaction*. Consider the hypothetical reaction

$$A + B \longrightarrow C + D \qquad [1]$$

The rate of this reaction may be measured by observing the rate of disappearance of either of the reactants A and B or the rate of appearance of either of the products C and D. In practice, then, one measures the change of concentration with time of either A, B, C, or D. Which species you choose to observe is a matter of convenience. For example, if A, B, and D are colorless and C is colored, you could conveniently measure the rate of appearance of C by observing an increase in the intensity of the color of the solution as a function of time. Mathematically, the rate of reaction may be expressed as follows:

$$\text{rate of disappearance of A} = \frac{\text{change in concentration of A}}{\text{time required for change}} = \frac{-\Delta[A]}{\Delta t}$$

$$\text{rate of appearance of C} = \frac{\text{change in concentration of C}}{\text{time required for change}} = \frac{\Delta[C]}{\Delta t}$$

In general, the rate of the reaction will depend on the concentrations of the reactants. Thus, the rate of our hypothetical reaction may be expressed as

$$\text{rate} = k[A]^x[B]^y \qquad [2]$$

where [A] and [B] are the molar concentrations of A and B, x and y are the powers to which the respective concentrations must be raised to describe the rate, and k is the *specific rate constant*. One of the objectives of chemical kinetics is to determine the rate law. Stated slightly differently, one goal of measuring the rate of the reaction is to determine the numerical values of x and y in Equation 2. Suppose that we found $x = 2$ and $y = 1$ for this reaction. Then,

$$\text{rate} = k[A]^2[B] \qquad [3]$$

would be the rate law. It should be evident from Equation [3] that doubling the concentration of B (keeping [A] the same) would cause the reaction rate to double. On the other hand, doubling the concentration of A (keeping [B] the same) would cause the rate to increase by a factor of 4, because the rate of the reaction is proportional to the *square* of the concentration of A. The powers to which the concentrations in the rate law are raised are termed the *order of the reaction*. In this case, the reaction is said to be second order in A and first order in B. The *overall order* of the reaction is the sum of the exponents, $2 + 1 = 3$, or a third-order reaction. It is possible to determine the order of the reaction by noting the effects of changing reagent concentrations on the rate of the reaction. Note that the order of a reaction may be (and frequently is) different from the stoichiometry of the reaction.

It should be emphasized that k, the specific rate constant, has a definite value that is independent of the concentration. It is characteristic of a given reaction and depends only on temperature. Once the rate is known, the value of k can be calculated.

Reaction of Peroxydisulfate Ion with Iodide Ion

In this experiment you will measure the rate of the reaction

$$S_2O_8^{2-} + 2I^- \longrightarrow I_2 + 2SO_4^{2-} \qquad [4]$$

and you will determine the rate law by measuring the amount of peroxydisulfate, $S_2O_8^{2-}$, that reacts as a function of time. The rate law to be determined is of the form

$$\text{Rate of disappearance of } S_2O_8^{2-} = k[S_2O_8^{2-}]^x[I^-]^y \qquad [5]$$

or

$$\frac{\Delta[S_2O_8^{2-}]}{\Delta t} = k[S_2O_8^{2-}]^x[I^-]^y$$

Your goal will be to determine the values of x and y as well as the specific rate constant, k.

You will add to the solution a small amount of another reagent (sodium thiosulfate, $Na_2S_2O_3$), which will cause a change in the color of the solution. The amount is such that the color change will occur when 2×10^{-4} mol of $S_2O_8^{2-}$ has reacted. For reasons to be explained shortly, the solution will turn blue-black when 2×10^{-4} mol of $S_2O_8^{2-}$ has reacted. You will quickly add another portion of $Na_2S_2O_3$ after the appearance of the color, and the blue-black color will disappear. When the blue-black color reappears the second time, *another* 2×10^{-4} mol of $S_2O_8^{2-}$ has reacted, making a total of $2(2 \times 10^{-4})$ mol of $S_2O_8^{2-}$ that has reacted. You will repeat this procedure several times, keeping *careful* note of the time for the appearance of the blue-black colors. By graphing the amount of $S_2O_8^{2-}$ consumed versus time, you will be able to determine the rate of the reaction. By changing the initial concentrations of $S_2O_8^{2-}$ and I^- and observing the effects upon the rate of the reaction, you will determine the order of the reaction with respect to $S_2O_8^{2-}$ and I^-.

The blue-black color that will appear in the reaction is due to the presence of a starch-iodine complex that is formed from iodine, I_2, and starch in the solution. The color therefore will not appear until a detectable amount of I_2 is formed according to Equation [4]. The thiosulfate that is added to the solution reacts *extremely rapidly* with the iodine, as follows:

$$I_2 + 2S_2O_3^{2-} \longrightarrow 2I^- + S_4O_6^{2-} \qquad [6]$$

Consequently, until the same amount of $S_2O_3^{2-}$ that is added is all consumed, there will not be a sufficient amount of I_2 in the solution to yield the blue-black color. You will add 4×10^{-4} mol of $S_2O_3^{2-}$ each time (these equal portions are termed *aliquots*). From the stoichiometry of Equations [4] and [6] you can verify that when this quantity of $S_2O_3^{2-}$ has reacted, 2×10^{-4} mol of $S_2O_8^{2-}$ has reacted. Note also that although iodide, I^-, is consumed according to Equation [4], it is rapidly regenerated according to Equation [6] and therefore its concentration does not change during a given experiment.

Graphical Determination of Rate

The more rapidly the 2×10^{-4} mol of $S_2O_8^{2-}$ is consumed, the faster is the reaction. To determine the rate of the reaction, a plot of moles of $S_2O_8^{2-}$ that have reacted versus the time required for the reaction is made, as shown in Figure 1. The best straight line passing through the origin is drawn, and the slope is determined. The slope, $\Delta S_2O_8^{2-}/\Delta t$, corresponds to the moles of $S_2O_8^{2-}$ that have been consumed per second and is proportional to the rate. Since the rate corresponds to the change in the concentration of $S_2O_8^{2-}$ per second, dividing the slope by the volume of the solution yields the rate of

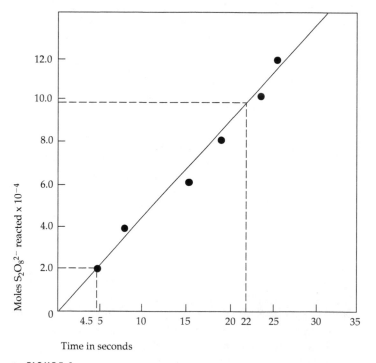

$$\text{Slope} = \frac{\Delta S_2O_8^{2-}}{\Delta t}$$

$$= \frac{(9.8 - 2.0) \times 10^{-4}\,\text{mol}}{(22.0 - 4.5)\,\text{s}}$$

$$= \frac{7.8 \times 10^{-4}\,\text{mol}}{17.5\,\text{s}}$$

$$= 4.5 \times 10^{-5}\,\text{mol/s}$$

▲ **FIGURE 1** Graphical determination of rate.

disappearance of $S_2O_8^{2-}$, that is, $\Delta[S_2O_8^{2-}]\Delta t$. If the total volume of the solution in this example were 75 mL, the rate would be as follows:

$$\frac{4.5 \times 10^{-5} \text{mol/s}}{0.075 \text{ L}} = 6.0 \times 10^{-4} \text{ mol/L-s}$$

If we obtain a rate of 6.0×10^{-4} mol/L-s when $[S_2O_8^{2-}] = 2.0\ M$ and $[I^-] = 2.0\ M$, and a rate of 3.0×10^{-4} mol/L-s mol/L-s when $[S_2O_8^{2-}] = 1.0\ M$ and $[I^-] = 2.0\ M$, we then know that doubling the concentration of $S_2O_8^{2-}$ doubles the rate of the reaction and the reaction is first order in $S_2O_8^{2-}$. By varying the initial concentrations of $S_2O_8^{2-}$ and I^-, you can, via the above analysis, determine the order of the reaction with respect to both of these species.

Helpful Comments

1. According to the procedure of this experiment, the solution will turn blue-black when exactly 2×10^{-4} mol mol of $S_2O_8^{-2}$ has reacted.
2. The purpose of the KNO_3 solution in this reaction is to keep the *reaction medium* the same in each run in terms of the concentration of ions; it does not enter into the reaction in any way.
3. The reaction studied in this experiment is catalyzed by metal ions. The purpose of the drop of the EDTA solution is to minimize the effects of trace quantities of metal ion impurities that would cause spurious effects on the reaction.
4. You will perform a few preliminary experiments to become acquainted with the observations in this experiment so that you will know what to expect in the reactions.
5. The initial concentrations of the reactants have been provided for you on the report sheet.

A. Preliminary Experiments

PROCEDURE

1. Dilute 5.0 mL of 0.2 M KI solution with 10.0 mL of distilled water in a test tube, add three drops of starch solution and mix thoroughly, and then add 5.0 mL of 0.2 M $(NH_4)_2S_2O_8$ solution. Mix. Wait a while and observe color changes.
2. Repeat the procedure in (1), but when the solution changes color add four drops of 0.4 M $Na_2S_2O_3$, mix the solution, and note the effect that the addition of $Na_2S_2O_3$ has on the color.

B. Kinetics Experiment

Solution Preparation Prepare four reaction solutions as follows (one at a time):

Solution 1: 25.0 mL KI solution
    1.0 mL starch solution
    1.0 mL $Na_2S_2O_3$ solution
    48.0 mL KNO_3 solution
    1 drop EDTA solution
Total volume = 75.0 mL

Solution 3: 50.0 mL KI solution
    1.0 mL starch solution
    1.0 mL $Na_2S_2O_3$ solution
    23.0 mL KNO_3 solution
    1 drop EDTA solution
Total volume = 75.0 mL

Solution 2: 25.0 mL KI solution
        1.0 mL starch solution
        1.0 mL $Na_2S_2O_3$ solution
        23.0 mL KNO_3 solution
        1 drop EDTA solution
Total volume = 50.0 mL

Solution 4: 12.5 mL KI solution
        1.0 mL starch solution
        1.0 mL $Na_2S_2O_3$ solution
        35.5 mL KNO_3 solution
        1 drop EDTA solution
Total volume = 50.0 mL

Equipment Setup Set up two burets held by a clamp on a ring stand as shown in Figure 2. Use these burets to accurately measure the volumes of the KI and KNO_3 solutions. Use two separate 1-mL pipets for measuring the volumes of the $Na_2S_2O_3$ and starch solutions, and use 25-mL and 50-mL pipets to measure the volumes of the $(NH_4)_2S_2O_8$ solutions. Each solution must be freshly prepared to begin the rate study—that is, *prepare solutions 1, 2, 3, and 4 one at a time as you make your measurements.*

Rate Measurements Prepare solution 1 in a 250-mL Erlenmeyer flask that has been scrupulously cleaned and dried. Pipet 25.0 mL of $(NH_4)_2S_2O_8$ solution into a clean, dry 100-mL beaker. *Be ready* to begin timing the reaction when the solutions are mixed (READ AHEAD). The reaction starts the moment the solutions are mixed! BE PREPARED! ZERO TIME! Quickly pour the 25.0 mL of $(NH_4)_2S_2O_8$ solution into solution 1 and swirl vigorously; note the time you begin mixing to the nearest second. At the instant when the blue-black color appears, 2×10^{-4} mol of $S_2O_8^{2-}$ has reacted. IMMEDIATELY (be prepared!) add a 1-mL aliquot of $Na_2S_2O_3$ solution from the pipet and swirl the solution; the color will disappear. If you fill each of seven clean, dry test tubes with 1 mL of $Na_2S_2O_3$ solution, you then can add these aliquots to your reactions at the appearance of the blue color without loss of time.

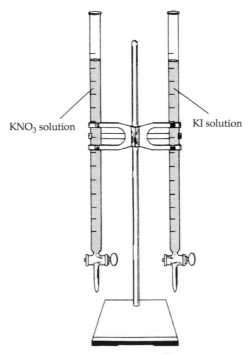

KNO₃ solution   KI solution

▲ FIGURE 2

Record the time for the reappearance of the blue-black color. Add another 1-mL aliquot of $Na_2S_2O_3$ solution and note the time for the reappearance of the color. The time interval being measured is that between appearances of the blue-black color. For good results, these aliquots of $Na_2S_2O_3$ must be measured as quickly, accurately, and reproducibly as possible. Continue this procedure until you have added seven (7) aliquots to solution 1.

You are finished with solution 1 when you have recorded all your times on the report sheet. *(The time intervals are cumulative.)*

Solutions 2, 3, and 4 should be treated in exactly the same manner except that 50.0-mL portions of $(NH_4)_2S_2O_8$ solutions should be added to solutions 2 and 4 and 25 mL of $(NH_4)_2S_2O_8$ solution should be added to solution 3. (CAUTION: *Be on guard—solution 2 will react much more rapidly than solution 1.*) In each of these reactions the final total solution volume is 100 mL.

Calculations

Tabulate on the data sheet for each aliquot of $Na_2S_2O_3$ added to each of the four solutions:

1. The time interval from the start of the reaction (addition of $S_2O_8^{2-}$) to the appearance of color for the first aliquot of $S_2O_3^{2-}$ and the time interval from the preceding color appearance for each succeeding aliquot (column 2).
2. The cumulative time from the start of the reaction to each appearance of color (column 3).
3. The corresponding numbers of moles $S_2O_8^{2-}$ consumed (column 4).

For each solution, plot on the graph paper provided the moles of $S_2O_8^{2-}$ consumed (as the ordinate, vertical axis) versus time in seconds (as the abscissa, horizontal axis), using the data in columns 3 and 4. Calculate the slope of each plot, and from these calculations answer the questions on your report sheet.

Waste-Disposal Instructions No wastes from this experiment should be flushed down the sink. Locate the special containers placed in the laboratory for the disposal of excess iodide and peroxydisulfate solutions as well as for the reaction mixtures from the test tubes or flasks. All wastes should be disposed of in these containers.

Before beginning this experiment in the laboratory, you should be able to answer the following questions:

PRE LAB QUESTIONS

1. What factors influence the rate of a chemical reaction?
2. What is the general form of a rate law?
3. What is the order of reaction with respect to A and B for a reaction that obeys the rate law rate $= k[A]^2[B]^3$?
4. Write the chemical equations involved in this experiment and show that the rate of disappearance of $[S_2O_8^{2-}]$ is proportional to the rate of appearance of the blue-black color of the starch-iodine complex.
5. It is found for the reaction A + B $\longrightarrow$ C that doubling the concentration of either A or B quadruples the rate of the reaction. Write the rate law for this reaction.

6. If 2×10^{-4} moles of $S_2O_8{}^{2-}$ in 50 mL of solution is consumed in 188 seconds, what is the rate of consumption of $S_2O_8{}^{2-}$?

7. Why are chemists concerned with the rates of chemical reactions? What possible practical value does this type of information have?

8. Suppose you were dissolving a metal such as zinc with hydrochloric acid. How would the particle size of the zinc affect the rate of its dissolution?

9. Assuming that a chemical reaction doubles in rate for each 10° temperature increase, by what factor would the rate increase if the temperature were increased 40°C?

10. A reaction between the substances A and B has been found to give the following data:

$$3A + 2B \longrightarrow 2C + D$$

[A] (mol/L)	[B] (mol/L)	Rate of appearance of C (mol/L-hr)
1.0×10^{-2}	1.0	0.3×10^{-6}
1.0×10^{-2}	3.0	8.1×10^{-6}
2.0×10^{-2}	3.0	3.24×10^{-5}
2.0×10^{-2}	1.0	1.20×10^{-6}
3.0×10^{-2}	3.0	7.30×10^{-5}

Using the above data, determine the order of the reaction with respect to A and B, the rate law and calculate the specific rate constant.

Name _____ Desk _____

Date _____ Laboratory Instructor _____

REPORT SHEET | EXPERIMENT

Rates of Chemical Reactions I: A Clock Reaction

A. Preliminary Experiments

1. What are the colors of the following ions:K^+ _____ ; I^- _____

2. The color of the starch $\cdot$ I_2 complex is _____

B. Kinetics Experiment

Solution 1.   Initial $[S_2O_8{}^{2-}]$ = 0.05 M; initial $[I^-]$ = 0.05 M. Time experiment started _____

Aliquot no.	Time (s) between appearances of color	Cumulative times(s)	Total moles of $S_2O_8{}^{2-}$ consumed
1	_____	_____	2.0×10^{-4}
2	_____	_____	4.0×10^{-4}
3	_____	_____	6.0×10^{-4}
4	_____	_____	8.0×10^{-4}
5	_____	_____	10.0×10^{-4}
6	_____	_____	12.0×10^{-4}
7	_____	_____	14.0×10^{-4}

Solution 2.   Initial $[S_2O_8{}^{2-}]$ = 0.10 M; initial $[I^-]$ = 0.05 M. Time experiment started _____

Aliquot no.	Time (s) between appearances of color	Cumulative time (s)	Total moles of $S_2O_8{}^{2-}$ consumed
1	_____	_____	2.0×10^{-4}
2	_____	_____	4.0×10^{-4}
3	_____	_____	6.0×10^{-4}
4	_____	_____	8.0×10^{-4}
5	_____	_____	10.0×10^{-4}
6	_____	_____	12.0×10^{-4}
7	_____	_____	14.0×10^{-4}

Solution 3. Initial $[S_2O_8^{2-}]$ = 0.05 M; initial $[I^-]$ = 0.10 M. Time experiment started _____

Aliquot no.	Time (s) between appearances of color	Cumulative time (s)	Total moles of $S_2O_8^{2-}$ consumed
1	_____	_____	2.0×10^{-4}
2	_____	_____	4.0×10^{-4}
3	_____	_____	6.0×10^{-4}
4	_____	_____	8.0×10^{-4}
5	_____	_____	10.0×10^{-4}
6	_____	_____	12.0×10^{-4}
7	_____	_____	14.0×10^{-4}

Solution 4. Initial $[S_2O_8^{2-}]$ = 0.10 M; initial $[I^-]$ = 0.025 M. Time experiment started _____

Aliquot no.	Time (s) between appearances of color	Cumulative time (s)	Total moles of $S_2O_8^{2-}$ consumed
1	_____	_____	2.0×10^{-4}
2	_____	_____	4.0×10^{-4}
3	_____	_____	6.0×10^{-4}
4	_____	_____	8.0×10^{-4}
5	_____	_____	10.0×10^{-4}
6	_____	_____	12.0×10^{-4}
7	_____	_____	14.0×10^{-4}

Calculations

1. Rate of reaction, $\Delta[S_2O_8^{2-}]/\Delta t$, as calculated from graphs (that is, from slopes of lines):

   Solution 1 _____   Solution 3 _____

   Solution 2 _____   Solution 4 _____

2. What effect does doubling the concentration of I^- have on the rate of this reaction?

3. What effect does changing the $[S_2O_8^{2-}]$ have on the reaction?

4. Write the rate law for this reaction that is consistent with your data.

5. From your knowledge of x and y in the equation (as well as the rate in a given experiment from your graph), calculate k from your data. Rate = $k[S_2O_8^{2-}]^x[I^-]^y$

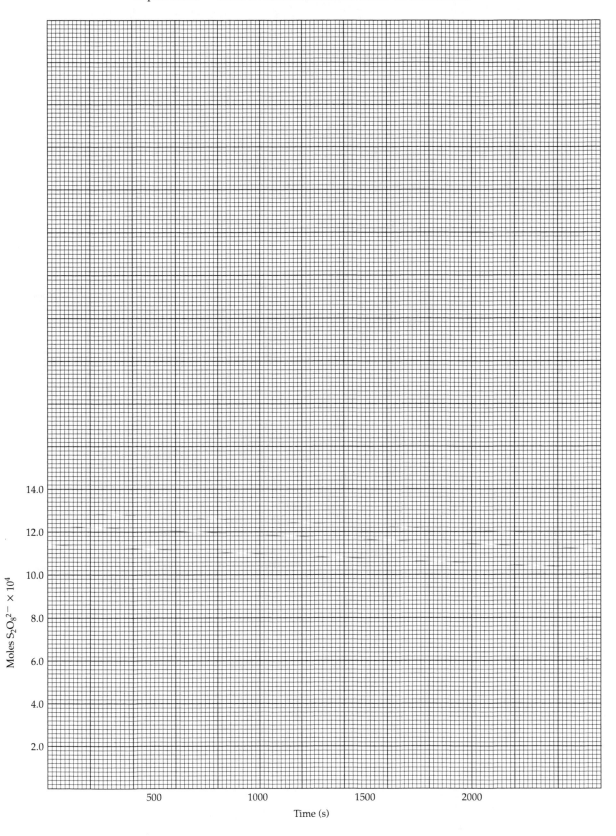

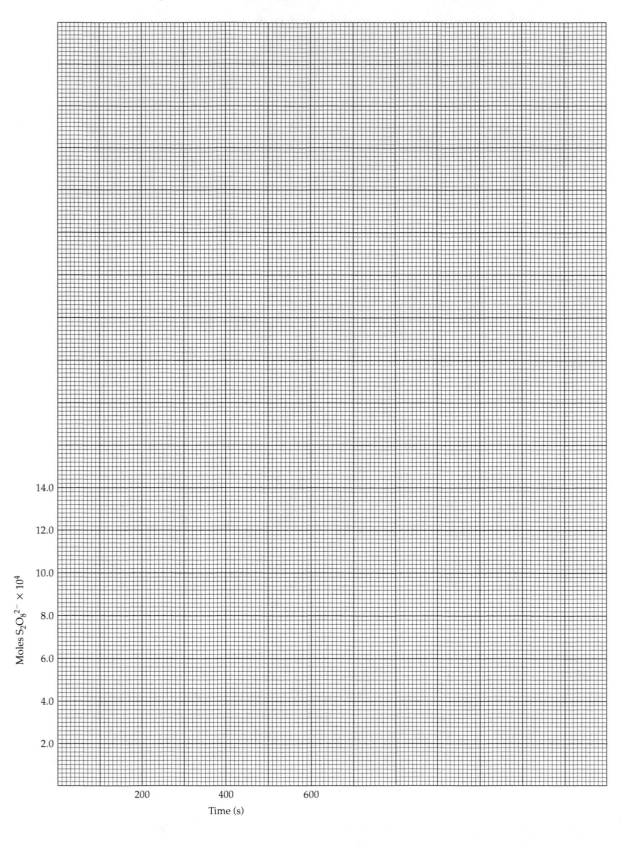

Moles $S_2O_8^{2-} \times 10^4$

Time (s)

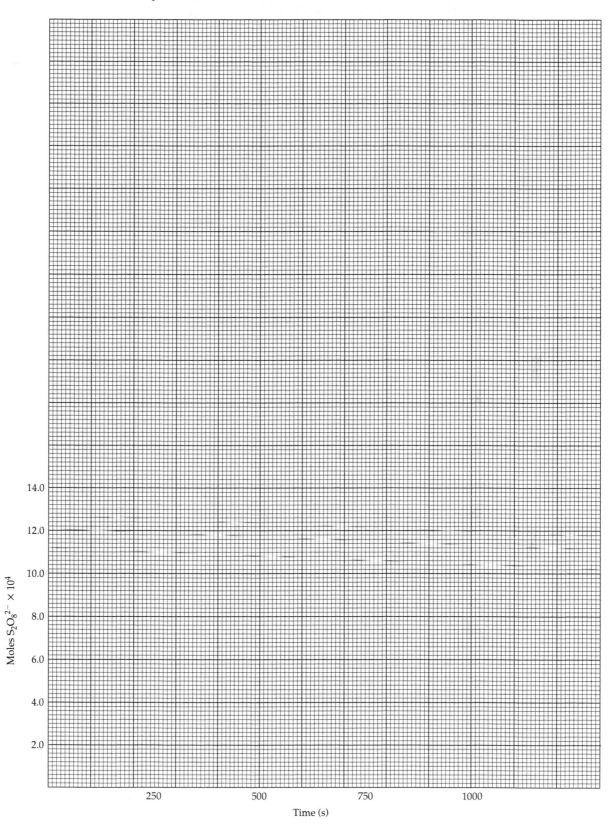

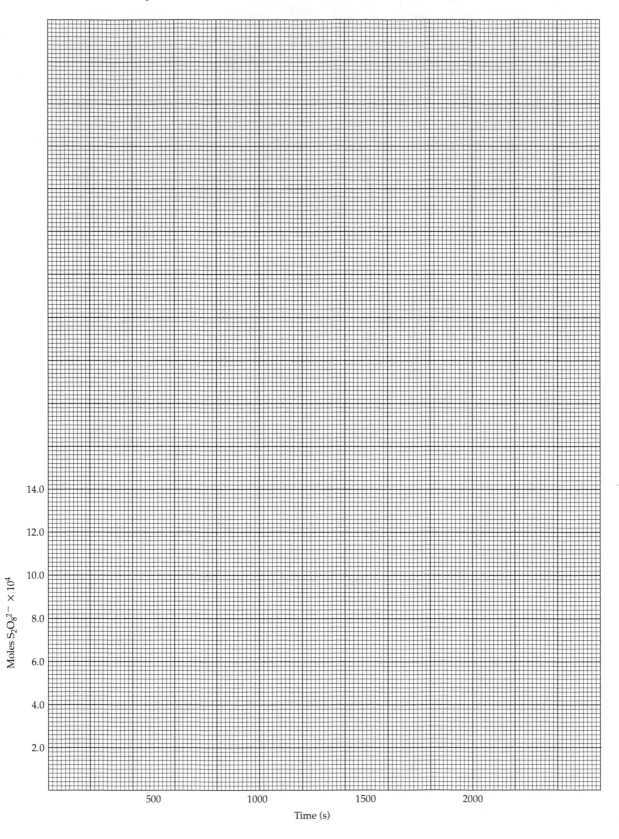

Time (s)

Moles $S_2O_8^{2-} \times 10^4$

Answers to Selected Pre Lab Questions

1. The factors that influence the rate of a chemical reaction are temperature, pressure, concentration, particle size, catalysts, and the nature of the species undergoing the reaction.

2. The general form of the rate law for the reaction $A + B \longrightarrow$ is. Rate $= k[A]^x[B]^y$.

3. A reaction that obeys the rate law of the form rate $= k[A]^2[B]^3$ is second order in A and third order in B. This reaction is fifth order overall.

4. The chemical reactions involved in this experiment are $S_2O_8^{2-} + 2I^- \longrightarrow I_2 + 2SO_4^{2-}$, $I_2 + 2S_2O_3^{2-} \longrightarrow 2I^- + S_4O_6^{2-}$, and $I_2 + $ starch $\longrightarrow$ starch $\cdot I_2$(blue), for which the rate of disappearance of $S_2O_3^{2-}$ is $k[S_2O_8^{2-}]^x[I^-]^y$ and the rate of appearance of blue color equals the rate of formation of the starch-iodine complex, which is proportional to the rate of appearance of iodine. Thus, the rate of appearance of iodine is $k[S_2O_8^{2-}]^x[I^-]^y$ and the rate of appearance of blue color is $k[I_2]^x$ $[$starch$]^y \alpha k[S_2O_8^{2-}]^x[I^-]^y$.

5. Rate $= k[A]^2[B]^2$.

6. Rate $= \left(\dfrac{2 \times 10^{-4}\,\text{mol}}{0.050\,\text{L}}\right)\left(\dfrac{1}{188\,\text{s}}\right)$

   $= 2.1 \times 10^{-5}\dfrac{\text{mol}}{\text{L-s}}$

7. From a knowledge of the rates of chemical reactions, chemists can determine how long to run a reaction in order to obtain the desired products. Clearly, this is of extreme practical value in the synthesis of new compounds.

Colorimetric Determination of an Equilibrium Constant in Aqueous Solution

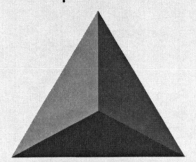

Experiment

To become familiar with the concept of equilibrium by determination of an equilibrium constant for a reaction in solution.

OBJECTIVE

Apparatus

6-50 mL volumetric flasks	10 mL graduated pipet
spectrophotometer	10 mL pipet
2 cuvettes	600 mL beaker
thermometer	6-18 × 150 mm test tubes

Chemicals

0.200 M $Fe(NO_3)_3$	0.10 M HNO_3
2.00×10^{-3} M NaSCN	

APPARATUS AND CHEMICALS

WORK IN GROUPS OF THREE OR FOUR, BUT ANALYZE THE DATA INDIVIDUALLY

If you have ever seen the beautiful stalactites and stalagmites that form in limestone caves, you must surely have wondered how they were formed. The key aspect of the formation of these primarily calcium carbonate natural wonders is the reversibility of chemical reactions. Calcium carbonate occurs in underground deposits as a remnant from ancient oceans. When water that contains dissolved CO_2 seeps through these deposits, they slowly dissolve as a result of the following reaction:

$$CaCO_3(s) + CO_2(g) + H_2O(l) \longrightarrow Ca^{2+}(aq) + 2HCO_3^-(aq) \qquad [1]$$

When the water saturated with $Ca(HCO_3)_2$ reaches a cave, the reverse reaction occurs, liberating gaseous CO_2 and very slowly depositing solid $CaCO_3$ as stalagtites and stalagmites. We write the expression for the *reversible* equilibrium reaction as Equation 2 with a double arrow to indicate that the reaction proceeds in both directions simultaneously.

$$CaCO_3(s) + CO_2(g) + H_2O(l) \rightleftharpoons Ca^{2+}(aq) + 2HCO_3^-(aq) \qquad [2]$$

All chemical equilibria are dynamic and are constantly proceeding in both directions. The system reaches a state of *equilibrium* when the rate of the reaction in the forward direction is equal to the rate of the reaction in the reverse direction. The *equilibrium expression* for this equilibrium with *equilibrium constant* K_c is:

$$K_c = \frac{[Ca^{2+}][HCO_3^-]^2}{[CaCO_3][CO_2][H_2O]} \qquad [3]$$

DISCUSSION

For the general equilibrium equation (4), where A, B, C, and D are the chemical species involved and a, b, c, and d are their coefficients in the balanced chemical equation, the equilibrium constant expression is

$$aA + bB \rightleftharpoons cC + dD \qquad [4]$$

$$K_{eq} = \frac{[C]^c[D]^d}{[A]^a[B]^b} \qquad [5]$$

The numerator in Equation 5 is the product of the molar concentrations of the products raised to the powers of their respective coefficients. The denominator is the product of the molar concentrations of reactants raised to the powers of their respective coefficients. In order to determine the value of an *equilib constant*, K_{eq}, we need to know the *equilibrium constant* of all the species involved in the equilibrium.

In this experiment you will determine the value of K_{eq} for the following equilibrium:

$$Fe^{3+}(aq,) + SCN^-(aq,) \rightleftharpoons FeNCS^{2+}(aq,)$$
$$\text{Pale yellow} \quad \text{colorless} \quad \text{blood red} \qquad [6]$$

Equilibrium 6 has been written in a simplified form. The pale yellow $Fe^{3+}(aq)$ is in reality $[Fe(H_2O)_6]^{3+}$. Actually, the $FeNCS^{2+}$, which contains the *ambidentate** thiocyanate ion bound to iron through nitrogen rather than sulfur, is in reality $[Fe(NCS)(H_2O)_5]^{2+}$. We have omitted the waters, both the coordinated and the free, from this equilibrium reaction.

If we determine the equilibrium $FeNCS^{2+}$ concentration in solutions of known initial concentrations of Fe^{3+} and SCN^- by simple stoichiometry, we may calculate the final equilibrium concentrations of all three species and hence the value of the equilibrium constant, K_{eq}. This is illustrated in Example 1.

EXAMPLE 1

If the equilibrium $FeNCS^{2+}$ concentration is 6.08×10^{-5} M in a solution that initially was 1.00×10^{-3} M in Fe^{3+} and 2.00×10^{-4} M in SCN^- calculate the equilibrium concentrations of Fe^{3+} and SCN^- and the value of K_{eq}.

SOLUTION: Equation 6 shows us that 1 mole of Fe^{3+} reacts with one mole of SCN^- to form 1 mole of $FeNCS^{2+}$. Because the volume does not change in this equilibrium reaction we may calculate the concentrations of all species by simple differences.

equilibrium $[Fe^{3+}]$ = initial $[Fe^{3+}]$ − equilibrium $[FeNCS^{2+}]$, therefore,

equilibrium $[Fe^{3+}]$ = 1.00×10^{-3} M − 6.08×10^{-5} M = 9.39×10^{-4} M

Similarly, equilibrium $[SCN^-] = 2.00 \times 10^{-4}$ M − 6.08×10^{-5} M $= 1.39 \times 10^{-4}$ M.

---

*An ambidentate ion is one that is capable of binding to a metal through two different sites.

Inserting these values into the equilibrium constant expression, we can calculate its value as follows:

$$K_{eq} = \frac{[FeNCS^{2+}]}{[Fe^{3+}][SCN^{-}]} = \frac{[6.08 \times 10^{-5}]}{[9.39 \times 10^{-4}][1.39 \times 10^{-4}]} = 466$$

We can determine the $FeNCS^{2+}$ concentration spectrophotometrically because it is highly colored. We will use a solution of iron(III) nitrate, $Fe(NO_3)_3$, as our source of Fe^{3+} ions and a solution of sodium thiocyanate, NaSCN, as our source of SCN^{-} ions. Equilibrium constants are somewhat dependent upon the total ionic concentration of the equilibrium mixture. Therefore, we will prepare all solutions using 0.10 M nitric acid, rather than water, to insure that all mixtures have comparable ionic concentrations. Because equilibrium constants are also temperature dependent, we will record the temperature at which our measurements are made.

Although the eye can discern differences in color intensity with reasonable accuracy, an instrument known as a *spectrophotometer*, which eliminates the "human" error, is commonly used for this purpose. Basically, it is an instrument that measures the fraction I/I_0 of an incident beam of light of a particular wavelength and of intensity I_0 that is transmitted by a sample. (Here, I is the intensity of the light transmitted by the sample.) A schematic representation of a spectrophotometer is shown in Figure 1. The instrument has these five fundamental components:

1. a light source that produces light with a wavelength range from about 375 to 650 nm

2. a monochromator, which *selects* a particular wavelength of light and sends it to the sample cell with an intensity of I_0

3. the sample cell, which contains the solution being analyzed

4. a detector that measures the intensity, I, of the light transmitted from the sample cell; if the intensity of the incident light is I_0 and the solution absorbs light, the intensity of the transmitted light, I, is less than I_0, and

5. a meter that indicates the intensity of the transmitted light

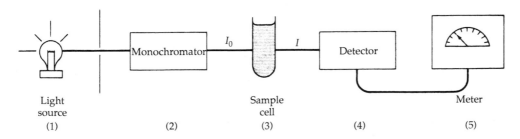

▲ FIGURE 1 Schematic representation of a spectrophotometer.

For a given substance, the amount of light absorbed depends on the

1. concentration
2. cell or path length
3. wavelength of light
4. solvent

Plots of the amount of light absorbed versus wavelength are called *absorption spectra*. There are two common ways of expressing the amount of light absorbed. One is in terms of *percent transmittance, %T*, which is defined as

$$\%T = \frac{I}{I_0} \times 100 \qquad [7]$$

As the term implies, percent transmittance corresponds to the percentage of light transmitted. When the sample in the cell is a solution, I is the intensity of light transmitted by the solution, and I_0 is intensity of light transmitted when the cell only contains solvent. Another method of expressing the amount of light absorbed is in terms of *absorbance, A*, which is defined by

$$A = \log\frac{I_0}{I} \qquad [8]$$

The term *optical density*, OD, is synonymous with absorbance. If there is no absorption of light by a sample at a given wavelength, the percent transmittance is 100, and the absorbance is 0. On the other hand, if the sample absorbs all of the light, $\%T = 0$ and $A = \infty$.

Absorbance is related to concentration by the Beer-Lambert law:

$$A = abc$$

where A is absorbance, b is solution path length, c is concentration in moles per liter, and a is molar absorptivity or molar extinction coefficient. There is a linear relationship between absorbance and concentration when the Beer-Lambert law is obeyed, as illustrated in Figure 2. However, since deviations from this law occasionally occur, it is wise to construct a calibration curve of absorbance versus concentration.

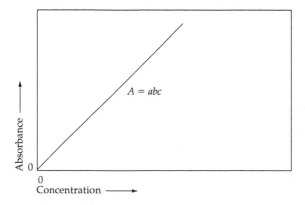

▲ FIGURE 2 Relationship between absorbance and concentration according to the Beer-Lambert law.

A. Preparation of the Calibration Curve

You will measure the absorbance of a series of solutions with known $FeNCS^{2+}$ ion concentrations to prepare a calibration curve. The experimental approach to this involves an interesting dilemma. The reaction that we will be using to prepare these solutions (Reaction 6) is reversible and does not proceed to completion. How then can solutions with known $FeNCS^{2+}$ concentrations be prepared? You will take advantage of LeChâtelier's principle to shift the equilibrium of Equation 6 to the right. By making an equilibrium mixture in which the Fe^{3+} ion concentration is relatively high, the equilibrium expression (see Example 1) indicates that the SCN^- concentration for this mixture will be relatively low. Consequently, by preparing a solution in which the initial Fe^{3+} ion concentration is much larger than that of the SCN^- ion, we can force the reaction to proceed nearly to completion. Under these conditions we will assume that all of the SCN^- is in the form of $FeNCS^{2+}$.

Label six 50.00-mL volumetric flasks 1 through 6. Pipet 10.00 mL of 2.00×10^{-1} M $Fe(NO_3)_3$ solution into each volumetric flask. Then, pipet 1.00, 2.00, 3.00, 4.00, and 5.00 mL of 2.00×10^{-3} M NaSCN solution into flasks 2 through 6, respectively.* *(Caution: Nitric acid and solutions containing it can cause burns and skin discoloration. If you come into contact with it, immediately wash the area with copious amounts of water.)* Add sufficient 0.10 M nitric acid to each flask to make the total volume 50.00 mL. Calculate the final $Fe(NO_3)_3$ concentrations and record them on your report sheet. Stopper the flasks. While holding the stopper firmly in the flask, invert the flask several times to thoroughly mix the solution. Use the information in Table 1 to calculate the $FeNCS^{2+}$ concentration in each flask assuming that all of the SCN^- is present as $FeNCS^{2+}$. Enter the results on your report sheet.

Obtain two cuvettes. Rinse one cuvette with solution 1, discarding the rinse into a 600-mL beaker labeled waste. Fill the rinsed cuvette with solution 1. Insert the cuvette into the spectrophotometer and adjust the light control knob until the meter reads zero absorbance (100 %T) at 447 nm. Save this reference cuvette for periodic calibration checks.

Rinse the second cuvette with solution 2, discarding the rinse into the waste beaker, then measure the absorbance and transmittance of solution 2

TABLE 1 Standard Solutions for $FeNCS^{2+}$ Ion Beer-Lambert Plot

Solution	mL of 2.00×10^{-3} M $Fe(NO_3)_3$ in 0.10 M HNO_3	mL of 2.00×10^{-3} M NaSCN in 0.10 M HNO_3	Total volume (mL)
1	10.00	0.00	50.00
2	10.00	1.00	50.00
3	10.00	2.00	50.00
4	10.00	3.00	50.00
5	10.00	4.00	50.00
6	10.00	5.00	50.00

Instructor: Time may be saved in this experiment by setting up several burets filled with $Fe(NO_3)_3$, NaSCN, and HNO_3 solutions on side tables in the laboratory. The students may obtain these solutions from these burets and refill the burets from bottles of stock solutions also located there.

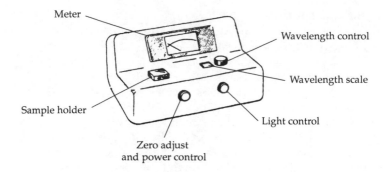

▲ **FIGURE 3** Spectrophotometer controls.

at 447 nm. Repeat this process with solutions 3 through 6. Prepare your calibration curve by plotting absorbance vs. concentration as in Figure 2. This curve should be turned in with your report sheet.

Operating Instructions for Spectronic 20

1. Turn the wavelength-control knob (Figure 3) to the desired wavelength (447 nm).
2. Turn on the instrument by rotating the power control clockwise and allow the instrument to warm up about 5 min. With no sample in the holder but with the cover closed, turn the zero adjust to bring the meter needle to zero on the "percent transmittance" scale.
3. Fill the cuvette about halfway with distilled water (or solvent blank) and insert it in the sample holder, aligning the line on the cuvette with that of the sample holder; close the cover and rotate the light-control knob until the meter reads 100% transmittance.
4. Remove the blank from the sample holder and replace it with the cuvette containing the sample whose absorbance is to be measured. Align the lines on the cuvette with the holder and close the cover. Read percent transmittance or absorbance from the meter.

B. Determination of the Equilibrium Constant

Label six clean, dry, 18×150-mm test tubes 1 through 6. Pipet 5.00 mL of 2.00×10^{-3} M $Fe(NO_3)_3$ solution into each of these test tubes. Add 1.00, 2.00, 3.00, 4.00, and 5.00 mL of 2×10^{-3} M NaSCN solution to test tubes 2 through 6, respectively. Add 5.00, 4.00, 3.00, 2.00, and 1.00 mL of 0.10 M HNO_3 to test tubes 1 through 6, respectively. The total volume in each test tube should now be 10 mL. Record the volumes of each of the component solutions in each of the test tubes on your report sheet. Measure and record the absorbances and transmittances of these solutions at 447 nm as described above for the determination of the calibration curve. From your calibration curve determine the equilibrium concentration of $FeNCS^{2+}$ in each of the test tubes.

Waste Disposal Instructions

The solutions used in this experiment are acidic and mildly oxidizing. Dispose of them in an appropriate waste container.

Before beginning this experiment in the laboratory you should be able to answer the following questions.

1. Write the reaction for the formation of $FeNCS^{2+}$.

2. Write the equilibrium constant expression for the formation of $FeNCS^{2+}$.

3. What are the $FeNCS^{2+}$ concentrations in solutions 1 through 6 used for the calibration curve?

4. Calculate the value of K_{eq} from the following equilibrium concentrations: $[FeNCS^{2+}] = 1.71 \times 10^{-4}$ M, $[Fe^{3+}] = 8.28 \times 10^{-4}$ M, and $[SCN^-] = 4.28 \times 10^{-4}$ M.

5. State the Beer-Lambert law and define all terms in it.

6. Why is a calibration curve constructed? How?

7. Briefly explain the meanings of the following terms as they relate to this experiment (a) reversible reactions, (b) state of dynamic equilibrium, (c) equilibrium constant expression, (d) equilibrium constant.

8. How are percent transmittance and absorbance related algebraically?

NOTES AND CALCULATIONS

REPORT SHEET | EXPERIMENT

Colorimetric Determination of an Equilibrium Constant in Aqueous Solution

A. Calibration Curve

Concentration of $Fe(NO_3)_3$ in 0.10 M HNO_3 solution _____

Concentration of NaSCN in 0.10 M HNO_3 solution _____

	Flask Number					
	1	2	3	4	5	6
Volume of NaSCN, mL Solution	_____	_____	_____	_____	_____	_____
Initial [SCN^-], M	_____	_____	_____	_____	_____	_____
Equil. [$FeNCS^{2+}$], M	_____	_____	_____	_____	_____	_____
Percent T	_____	_____	_____	_____	_____	_____
Absorbance	_____	_____	_____	_____	_____	_____

B. Equilibrium Constant Determination

Concentration of $Fe(NO_3)_3$ in 0.10 M HNO_3 solution _____

Concentration of NaSCN in 0.10 M HNO_3 solution _____

	Test Tube Number					
	1	2	3	4	5	6
Solution Temperature	_____					
Volume of $Fe(NO_3)_3$ Solution, mL	_____	_____	_____	_____	_____	_____
Volume of NaSCN Solution, mL	_____	_____	_____	_____	_____	_____
Initial [Fe^{3+}], M	_____	_____	_____	_____	_____	_____
Initial [SCN-], M	_____	_____	_____	_____	_____	_____
Absorbance	_____	_____	_____	_____	_____	_____

231

Equil. [FeNCS^{2+}], M _____ _____ _____ _____ _____ _____

Equil. [Fe^{3+}], M _____ _____ _____ _____ _____ _____

Equil. [SCN$^-$], M _____ _____ _____ _____ _____ _____

K$_{eq}$ (show calculations) _____ _____ _____ _____ _____ _____

Average K$_{eq}$ (show calculations) _____

QUESTIONS

1. How would the accuracy of your determined K$_{eq}$ change if all your volume measurements were made with graduated cylinders rather than pipets?

2. If all the SCN$^-$ were not converted completely to FeNCS^{2+} when the calibration curve was prepared, would this raise or lower the value of K$_{eq}$? Explain.

3. Use the mean value that you determined for K$_{eq}$ to calculate the SCN$^-$ concentration in a solution whose initial Fe^{3+} concentration was 4.00×10^{-2} M and initial SCN$^-$ concentration was 1.00×10^{-3} M. Is all of the SCN$^-$ in the form of FeNCS^{2+}?

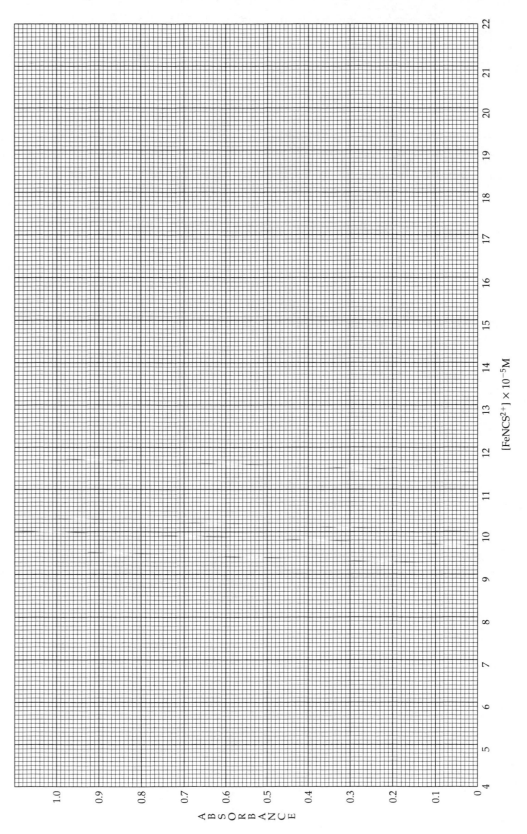

$[FeNCS^{2+}] \times 10^{-5}M$

ABSORBANCE

Answers to Selected Pre Lab Questions

1. $Fe^{3+}(aq) + SCN^-(aq) \rightleftharpoons FeNCS^{2+}(aq)$

3. Solution 2: Assume $[FeNCS^{2+}] = [SCN^-] = \dfrac{(1 \text{ mL})(2.00 \times 10^{-3} \text{ m})}{50 \text{ mL}}$
$$= 4.00 \times 10^{-5} \text{ M}$$

   Similarly, solutions 3, 4, 5, and 6 are 8.00×10^{-5} M, 1.20×10^{-4} M, 1.60×10^{-4} M and 2.00×10^{-4} M, respectively. Solution 1 has no $FeNCS^{2+}$.

5. The Beer-Lambert law is $A = abc$, where A is absorbance, b is solution path length, C is molar concentration of the absorbing species, and a is molar absorptivity.

7. (a) A reversible reaction is one that simultaneously proceeds in both directions.

   (b) A state of dynamic equilibrium is reached when the reaction rates in the forward and reverse directions are equal.

   (c) The equilibrium constant expression is the product of the molar concentrations of the reaction products raised to the power of their respective coefficients divided by the product of the reactants' molar concentrations raised to the powers of their respective coefficients. In this experiment

$$K_{eq} = \frac{[FeNCS^{2+}]}{[Fe^{3+}][SCN^-]}$$

   (d) The equilibrium constant, K_{eq}, is the numerical value of the equilibrium constant expression.

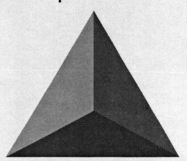

Chemical Equilibrium: LeChâtelier's Principle

To study the effects of concentration and temperature on equilibrium positions.

Apparatus

medicine droppers (4)	1 large test tube
250-mL beaker	ring stand, iron ring, and wire
100-mL graduated cylinder	gauze
3 small test tubes	Bunsen burner

Chemicals

0.1 M $CuSO_4$	0.01 M $AgNO_3$
0.1 M $NiCl_2$	6 M HNO_3
1.0 M $CoCl_2$	0.1 M HCl
0.1 M KI	1 M HCl
0.1 M Na_2CO_3	15 M NH_3

Many chemical reactions do not go to completion, that is, do not produce 100% yield of products. After a certain amount of time many of these reactions appear to "stop"—colors stop changing, gases stop evolving, and so forth. In several of these instances the process apparently stops before the reaction is complete, leading to a mixture of reactants and products.

For example, consider the interconversion of gaseous nitrogen oxides in a sealed tube:

$$N_2O_4(g) \rightleftharpoons 2NO_2(g) \qquad [1]$$
$$\text{colorless} \qquad \text{brown}$$

When frozen N_2O_4 is warmed above its boiling point (21.2 °C), the gas in a sealed tube progressively turns darker as colorless N_2O_4 dissociates into brown NO_2. The color change eventually stops even though there is still N_2O_4 present in the tube.

The condition in which the concentrations of all reactants and products in a closed system cease to change with time is called *chemical equilibrium*. Chemical equilibrium occurs when the rate at which products are formed from reactants equals the rate at which reactants are formed from products. For equilibrium to occur, neither reactants nor products can escape from the system.

If the concentration of any one of the reactants or products involved in a chemical equilibrium is changed, or if the temperature is changed, the position of the equilibrium shifts to *minimize the change*. For example, assuming the reaction represented by Equation [1] is at equilibrium, if more NO_2 is added, the probability of it reacting with other NO_2 molecules is increased, and the concentration of NO_2 decreases until a new state of equilibrium is attained. The equilibrium reaction is said to *shift to the left*. *LeChâtelier's principle* states that if a system at equilibrium is disturbed (by altering the concentration of reactants or products, the temperature, or pressure) the equilibrium will shift to minimize the disturbing influence. By this principle, if a reactant or product is added to a system at equilibrium, the equilibrium will shift to consume the added substance. Conversely, if reactant or product are removed, the equilibrium will shift to replenish the substance that was removed. The enthalpy change for a reaction indicates how a change in temperature affects the equilibrium. For an endothermic reaction an increase in temperature shifts the equilibrium to the right to absorb the added heat; for an exothermic reaction an increase in temperature shifts the equilibrium to the left. The equilibrium of equation [1] is endothermic, $\Delta H = +58$ kJ. Increasing the temperature will shift this equilibrium in the direction that absorbs the heat, and so the equilibrium shifts to the right.

It is important to remember that changes in concentrations, while causing shifts in the equilibrium positions, do not cause a change in the value of the equilibrium constant. Only changes in temperature affect the value of equilibrium constants.

In this experiment we will observe two ways that a chemical equilibrium can be disturbed: (1) by adding or removing a reactant or product, and (2) by changing the temperature. Your observations and conclusions will be interpreted using LeChâtelier's principle.

Part I: Changes in Reactant or Product Concentrations

A. Copper and Nickel Ions

Aqueous solutions of copper(II) and nickel(II) appear blue and green, respectively. However, when aqueous ammonia, NH_3, is added to these solutions, their colors change to dark blue and pale violet, respectively.

$$[Cu(H_2O)_4]^{2+}(aq) + 4NH_3(aq) \rightleftharpoons [Cu(NH_3)_4]^{2+}(aq) + 4H_2O(l)$$
$$\text{blue} \qquad\qquad\qquad\qquad\qquad\qquad \text{dark blue}$$

$$[Ni(H_2O)_6]^{2+}(aq) + 6NH_3(aq) \rightleftharpoons [Ni(NH_3)_6]^{2+}(aq) + 6H_2O(l)$$
$$\text{green} \qquad\qquad\qquad\qquad\qquad\qquad \text{pale violet}$$

Ammonia substitutes for water in these two reactions because the metal-ammonia bond is stronger than the metal-water bond, and the equilibria shift to the right, accounting for the color changes.

If a strong acid such as HCl is added to these ammoniacal solutions, their colors revert back to the original colors of blue and green. The equilibria shift left because the reactant ammonia, NH_3, is removed from the equilibria. It reacts with the acid to form ammonium ion according to reaction [2].

$$H^+(aq) + NH_3(aq) \rightleftharpoons NH_4^+(aq) \qquad\qquad [2]$$

Place about 1 mL of 0.1 M $CuSO_4$ in a small, clean test tube. Record the color of the solution on your report sheet (1). **(CAUTION: Concentrated NH_3 has a strong irritating odor; do not inhale. If you come in contact with it, immediately wash the area with copious amounts of water.)** Add 15 M NH_3 dropwise until a color change occurs and the solution is clear, not colorless.

Record your observation on your report sheet (2). Mix the solution in the test tube by "tickling" the test tube with your fingers as you add the NH_3. Add 1 M HCl dropwise while carefully mixing the solution in the test tube until the color changes. Note the color (3).

Repeat the same procedure using 0.1 M $NiCl_2$ in place of the $CuSO_4$ and record your corresponding observations on your report sheet.

Dispose of the solutions in the test tubes in the designated receptacles.

B. Cobalt Ions

Cobalt(II) ions in aqueous solution appear pale pink. In the presence of a large concentration of chloride ions, the solution changes color, and the following equilibrium is established:

$$[Co(H_2O)_6]^{2+}(aq) + 4Cl^-(aq) \rightleftharpoons [CoCl_4]^{2-}(aq) + 6H_2O(l) \qquad [3]$$

Place about 0.5 mL (10 drops) of 1 M $CoCl_2$ in a clean small test tube and note the color (7). **(CAUTION: Avoid inhalation and contact with concentrated HCl. If you come in contact with it, immediately wash the area with copious amounts of water.)** Add dropwise 12 M HCl to the test tube until a distinct color change occurs. Record the color on your report sheet (8). Slowly add water to the test tube while mixing. Record the color change on your report sheet (9).

Dispose of the solution in the test tube in the designated receptacle.

Part II. Equilibria Involving Sparingly Soluble Salts

Silver carbonate, silver chloride, and silver iodide salts are only very slightly soluble in water. They can be precipitated from silver nitrate solutions by the addition of sodium salts containing the corresponding anions. For example, silver carbonate will precipitate by mixing solutions of $AgNO_3$ and Na_2CO_3:

$$2AgNO_3(aq) + Na_2CO_3(aq) \rightleftharpoons Ag_2CO_3(s) + 2NaNO_3(aq)$$

for which the net ionic equation is:

$$2Ag^+(aq) + CO_3^{2-}(aq) \rightleftharpoons Ag_2CO_3(s) \qquad [4]$$

There is a dynamic equilibrium in the saturated solution of silver carbonate between the solid silver carbonate and its constituent silver and carbonate ions as shown in reaction [4]. In all saturated solutions a dynamic equilibrium exists between the solid and the ions in solution.

The silver carbonate precipitate can be dissolved by the addition of nitric acid. Protons, H^+, from the HNO_3 react with the carbonate ions, CO_3^{2-}, to form unstable carbonic acid

$$2H^+(aq) + CO_3^{2-}(aq) \rightleftharpoons H_2CO_3(aq); H_2CO_3(aq) \longrightarrow CO_2(g) + H_2O(l).$$

Removal of carbonate ions results in the dissolution of silver carbonate by a shift to the left of the equilibrium represented by reaction [4].

To 0.5 mL (10 drops) of 0.1 M Na_2CO_3 in a clean large test tube add 10 drops of 0.01 M $AgNO_3$. Record your observations on your report sheet (10). **(CAUTION: Avoid contact with nitric acid, HNO_3. If you come into contact with it, immediately wash the area with copious amounts of water.)** Cautiously add 6 M HNO_3 dropwise to the test tube until you observe a change in appearance of the contents of the test tube (11). Save the contents for the next steps.

The above solution contains silver ions and nitrate ions because the Ag_2CO_3 dissolved in the nitric acid. Addition of chloride ions to this solution, from HCl, results in the precipitation of AgCl. The precipitated AgCl is in dynamic equilibrium with Ag^+ and Cl^- ions:

$$Ag^+(aq) + Cl^-(aq) \rightleftharpoons AgCl(s) \qquad [5]$$

This dynamic equilibrium can be disturbed by removing the Ag^+ ions thereby forcing the equilibrium to shift to the left; and as a result, the AgCl dissolves. Silver ions can be removed by the addition of NH_3 because they react with NH_3 to form $[Ag(NH_3)_2]^+$:

$$Ag^+(aq) + 2NH_3(aq) \rightleftharpoons [Ag(NH_3)_2]^+(aq) \qquad [6]$$

Because the equilibrium of reaction [6] lies much farther to the right than that of reaction [5], the AgCl will dissolve.

Adding acid to this ammoniacal solution will remove the NH_3 by forming NH_4^+ (see Equation (2)). This causes equilibrium 6 to shift to the left. The released Ag^+ will combine again with Cl^- present to precipitate AgCl as shown in Equation [5]. The reprecipitated AgCl can be redissolved by the addition of excess NH_3 for the same reason given above (see Equation [6]).

To the solution saved from above add 0.1 M HCl dropwise until you observe a change in the appearance of the contents of the test tube. Record your observations on your report sheet (12). **(CAUTION: Concentrated NH_3 has a strong irritating odor; do not inhale. Do not get it on your skin. If you come into contact with it, immediately wash the area with copious amounts of water.)** While mixing the contents of the test tube, add 15 M NH_3 dropwise until evidence of a chemical change occurs (13). Acidify the solution by the dropwise addition of 6 M HNO_3 until there is evidence of a chemical change. Record your observations on your report sheet (14). Again while mixing, add 15 M NH_3 dropwise until there is no longer a change in the appearance of the contents of the test tube. Record your observations on your report sheet (15). Save the solution for the next step.

The equilibrium of Equation [6] can be disturbed by the addition of I^- from KI. Silver iodide will precipitate, removing Ag^+ causing the equilibrium to shift to the left. The reason that AgI will precipitate is because the equilibrium of Equation [7] lies much farther to the right than does the equilibrium of Equation [6].

$$I^-(aq) + Ag^+(aq) \rightleftharpoons AgI(s) \qquad [7]$$

To the solution from above continue to add 0.1 M KI dropwise until you see evidence of a chemical reaction. Record your observations on your report sheet (16).

Dispose of the silver salt solution in the designated receptacle.

Part III. Effect of Temperature on Equilibria

Heat about 75 mL of water to boiling in a 250 mL beaker on a ring stand. Place about 1 mL of 1.0 M $CoCl_2$ in a small test tube and place the test tube in the boiling water without spilling its contents. Compare the color of the cool cobalt solution to that of the hot solution (17).

Dispose of the solution in the designated receptacle.

Before beginning this experiment in the laboratory you should be able to answer the following questions.

PRE LAB QUESTIONS

1. Briefly state LeChâtelier's Principle.

2. Consider the following equilibrium:

$$BaSO_4(s) \rightleftharpoons Ba^{2+}(aq) + SO_4^{2-}(aq); \Delta H > 0$$

In which direction will the equilibrium shift if

a. H_2SO_4 is added? Why?
b. $BaCl_2$ is added? Why?
c. NaCl is added? Why?
d. Heat is added? Why?

3. Consider the following equilibrium for nitrous acid, HNO_2, a weak acid:

$$HNO_2(aq) + H_2O(l) \rightleftharpoons H_3O^+(aq) + NO_2^-(aq)$$

In which direction will the equilibrium shift if

a. NaOH is added?
b. $NaNO_2$ is added?
c. HCl is added?
d. The acid solution is made more dilute?

4. Complete and balance the following equations and then write balanced net ionic equations.

a. $AgNO_3(aq) + HCl(aq) \rightleftharpoons$
b. $NH_3(aq) + HCl(aq) \rightleftharpoons$
c. $Na_2CO_3(aq) + HNO_3(aq) \rightleftharpoons$

5. On the basis of LeChâtelier's Principle, explain why Ag_2CO_3 dissolves when HNO_3 is added.

NOTES AND CALCULATIONS

REPORT SHEET | EXPERIMENT

Chemical Equilibrium:
LeChâtelier's Principle

Part I. Changes in Reactant or *Product Concentrations*

A. Copper and Nickel Ions
Colors:

1. $CuSO_4(aq)$ _____
2. $[Cu(NH_3)_4]^{2+}(aq)$ _____
3. After HCl addition _____

4. $NiCl_2(aq)$ _____
5. $[Ni(NH_3)_6]^2(aq)$ _____
6. After HCl addition _____

Explain the effects of $NH_3(aq)$ and HCl (aq) on the $CuSO_4$ solution in terms of LeChâtelier's Principle. Consider the following equilibria:

B. Cobalt Ions

7. Color of $CoCl_2(aq)$ _____
8. Color after the addition of HCl(aq) _____
9. Color after the addition of H_2O _____

Account for the changes observed for the cobalt solutions in terms of LeChâtelier's Principle. Consider the following equilibrium:

Part II. Equilibria Involving Sparingly Soluble Salts

10. _____

11. _____

Account for your observations. Consider the following equilibria:

12. _____

Account for your observations. Consider the following equilibria:

13. Did the precipitated AgCl dissolve? Explain.

14. What effect did the addition of HNO_3 have on the contents of the test tube? Explain.

15. What effect did the addition of NH_3 have on the contents of the test tube? Explain.

16. Explain the effect of the addition of KI.

Part III. Effect of Temperature on Equilibria

17. Color of cool $CoCl_2$ _____

Color of hot $CoCl_2$ _____

Is the reaction exothermic? _____ Explain.

Answers to Selected Pre Lab Questions

2. (a) The reaction will shift to the left in order to decrease the $[SO_4^{2-}]$.
   (b) The reaction will shift to the left in order to decrease the $[Cl^-]$.
   (c) Same as b.
   (d) The reaction will shift to the right in order to absorb the added heat.

4. (a) $AgNO_3(aq) + HCl(aq) \rightleftharpoons AgCl(s) + HNO_3(aq)$;

   $$Ag^+(aq) + Cl^- \rightleftharpoons AgCl(s)$$

   (b) $NH_3(aq) + H^+(aq) \rightleftharpoons NH_4^+(aq) + H^+(aq) \rightleftharpoons N_4Cl^+(aq)$

   (c) $Na_2CO_3(aq) + 2HNO_3(aq) \rightleftharpoons 2NaNO_3(aq) + CO_2(g) + H_2O(l)$;

   $$CO_3^2(aq) + 2H^+(aq) \rightleftharpoons CO_2(g) + H_2O(l)$$

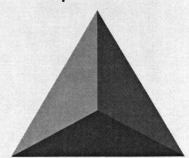

Determination of the Dissociation Constant of a Weak Acid

To become familiar with the operation of a pH meter and quantitative equilibrium constants.

Apparatus

pH meter with electrodes	600-mL Erlenmeyer flask
balance	250-mL Erlenmeyer flasks (3)
150-mL beakers (4)	25-mL pipet and pipet bulb
buret	buret clamp and ring stand
1-pint bottle and stopper	weighing bottle
Bunsen burner and hose	ring stand and ring
wire gauze	

Chemicals

potassium hydrogen phthalate (KHP)	0.1 M NaOH or 19 M NaOH
standard buffer solution	phenolphthalein indicator
unknown solution of a weak acid	solution
(~0.1 M)	

Acid-Base Equilibria

According to the Brønsted-Lowry acid-base theory, the strength of an acid is related to its ability to donate protons. All acid-base reactions are then competitions between bases of various strengths for these protons. For example, the strong acid HCl reacts with water according to Equation [1]:

$$HCl(aq) + H_2O(l) \longrightarrow H_3O^+(aq) + Cl^-(aq) \qquad [1]$$

This acid is a strong acid and is completely dissociated—in other words, 100% dissociated—in dilute aqueous solution. Consequently, the $[H_3O^+]$ concentration of 0.1 M HCl is 0.1 M.

By contrast, acetic acid, $HC_2H_3O_2$ (abbreviated HOAc), is a weak acid and is only slightly dissociated, as shown in Equation [2]:

$$H_2O(l) + HOAc(aq) \rightleftharpoons H_3O^+(aq) + OAc^-(aq) \qquad [2]$$

Its acid dissociation constant, as shown by Equation [3], is therefore small:

$$K_a = \frac{[H_3O^+][OAc^-]}{[HOAc]} = 1.8 \times 10^{-5} \qquad [3]$$

Acetic acid only partially dissociates in aqueous solution, and an appreciable quantity of undissociated acetic acid remains in solution.

For the general weak acid HA, the dissociation reaction and dissociation constant expression are

$$HA(aq) + H_2O(l) \rightleftharpoons H_3O^+(aq) + A^-(aq) \qquad [4]$$

$$K_a = \frac{[H_3O^+][A^-]}{[HA]} \qquad [5]$$

Recall that pH is defined as

$$-\log[H_3O^+] = pH \qquad [6]$$

Solving Equation [5] for $[H_3O^+]$ and substituting this quantity into Equation [6] yields

$$[H_3O^+] = K_a\frac{[HA]}{[A^-]} \qquad [7]$$

$$-\log[H_3O^+] = -\log K_a - \log\frac{[HA]}{[A^-]} \qquad [8]$$

$$pH = pK_a - \log\frac{[HA]}{[A^-]} \qquad [9]$$

where $pK_a = -\log K_a$

If we titrate the weak acid HA with a base, there will be a point in the titration at which the number of moles of base added is half the number of moles of acid initially present. This is the point at which 50% of the acid has been titrated to produce A^- and 50% remains as HA. At this point $[HA] = [A^-]$, the ratio $[HA]/[A^-] = 1$, and $\log[HA]/[A^-] = 0$. Hence, at this point in a titration, that is, at half the equivalence point, Equation [9] becomes

$$pH = pK_a \qquad [10]$$

By titrating a weak acid with a strong base and recording the pH versus the volume of base added, we can determine the ionization constant of the weak acid. From the resultant titration curve we obtain the ionization constant, as explained in the following paragraph.

From the titration curve (Figure 1), we see that at the point denoted as half the equivalence point, where $[HA] = [A^-]$, the pH is 4.3. Thus, from Equation [10], at this point $pH = pK_a$, or

$$pK_a = 4.3$$
$$-\log K_a = 4.3$$
$$\log K_a = -4.3$$
$$K_a = 5 \times 10^{-5}$$

(Your instructor will show you a graphical method for locating the equivalence point on your titration curves.)

Operation of the pH Meter

To measure the pH during the course of the titration, we shall use an electronic instrument called a pH meter. This device consists of a meter and two electrodes, as illustrated in Figure 2.

The main variations among different pH meters involve the positions of the control knobs and the types of electrodes and electrode-mounting devices. The

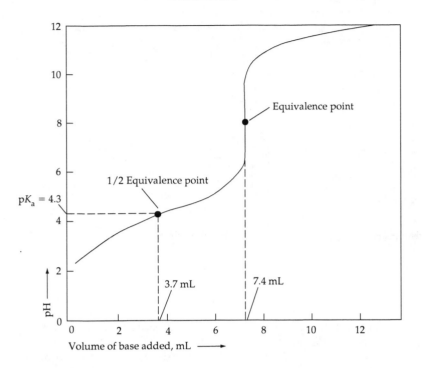

▲ FIGURE 1 Exemplary titration curve for the titration of a weak acid HA with a strong base.

measurement of pH requires two electrodes: a sensing electrode that is sensitive to H_3O^+ concentrations and a reference electrode. This is because the pH meter is really just a voltmeter that measures the electrical potential of a solution. Typical sensing and reference electrodes are illustrated in Figure 3.

The reference electrode is an electrode that develops a known potential that is essentially independent of the contents of the solution into which it is

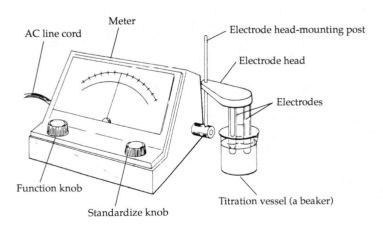

▲ FIGURE 2 An analog pH meter.

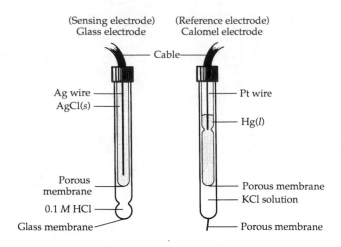

▲ **FIGURE 3** A typical sensing and reference electrode.

placed. The glass electrode is sensitive to the H_3O^+ concentration of the solution into which it is placed; its potential is a function of $[H_3O^+]$. It operates by transport of H_3O^+ ions through the glass membrane. This can be more precisely described, but for our purposes here it is sufficient for you to understand that two electrodes are required. These two electrodes are sometimes combined into an electrode called a combination electrode, which appears to be a single electrode. The combination electrode, however, does contain both a reference and a sensing electrode.

Preliminary Operations with the pH Meter

1. Obtain a buffer solution of known pH.
2. Plug in the pH meter to line current and allow at least 10 min for warm-up. It should be left plugged in until you are completely finished with it. *This does not apply to battery-operated meters.*
3. Turn the function knob on the pH meter to the standby position.
4. *Prepare the electrodes.* Make certain that the solution in the reference electrode extends well above the internal electrode. If it does not, ask your instructor to fill it with saturated KCl solution. Remove the rubber tip and slide down the rubber collar on the reference electrode. Rinse the outside of the electrodes well with distilled water.
5. *Standardize the pH meter.* Carefully immerse the electrodes in the buffer solution contained in a small beaker. *Remember that the glass electrode is very fragile; it breaks easily!* DO NOT touch the bottom of the beaker with the electrodes!! Turn the function knob to "read" or "pH." Turn the standardize knob until the pH meter indicates the exact pH of the buffer solution. Wait 5 s to be certain that the reading remains constant. *Once you have standardized the pH meter, don't readjust the standardize knob.* Turn the function knob to standby. Carefully lift the electrodes from the buffer and rinse them with distilled water. The pH meter is now ready to use to measure pH.

RECORD ALL DATA DIRECTLY ONTO THE REPORT SHEETS.

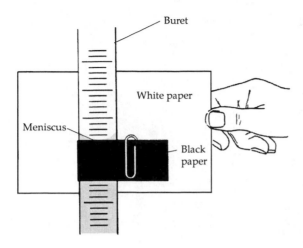

▲ FIGURE 4 Reading a buret.

A. Preparation of Approximately 0.100 *M* Sodium Hydroxide (NaOH)

PROCEDURE

Heat 500 mL of distilled water to boiling in a 600-mL flask* and, *after cooling under the water tap,* transfer to a 1-pint bottle fitted with a rubber stopper.† *(CAUTION: Concentrated NaOH can cause severe burns. If you come in contact with it, immediately wash the area with copious amounts of water).* Add 3 mL of stock solution of carbonate-free NaOH (approximately 19 *M*) and shake vigorously for at least 1 min.

Preparation of a Buret for Use   Clean a 50-mL buret with soap solution and a buret brush and thoroughly rinse with tap water. Then rinse with at least five 10-mL portions of distilled water. The water must run freely from the buret without leaving any drops adhering to the sides. Make sure that the buret does not leak and that the stopcock turns freely.

Reading a Buret   All liquids, when placed in a buret, form a curved meniscus at their upper surfaces. In the case of water or water solutions, this meniscus is concave (Figure 4), and the most accurate buret readings are obtained by observing the position of the lowest point on the meniscus on the graduated scales.

To avoid parallax errors when taking readings, the eye must be on a level with the meniscus. Wrap a strip of paper around the buret and hold the top edges of the strip evenly together. Adjust the strip so that the front and back edges are in line with the lowest part of the meniscus and take the reading by estimating to the nearest tenth of a marked division (0.01 mL). A simple way of doing this for repeated readings on a buret is illustrated in Figure 4.

---

*The water is boiled to remove carbon dioxide (CO_2), which would react with the NaOH and change its molarity.
†A rubber stopper should be used for a bottle containing NaOH solution. A strongly alkaline solution tends to cement a glass stopper so firmly that it is difficult to remove.

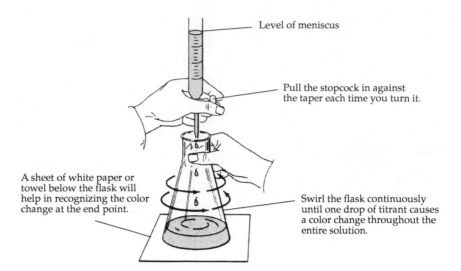

Level of meniscus

Pull the stopcock in against the taper each time you turn it.

A sheet of white paper or towel below the flask will help in recognizing the color change at the end point.

Swirl the flask continuously until one drop of titrant causes a color change throughout the entire solution.

▲ **FIGURE 5** Titration procedure.

B. Standardization of Sodium Hydroxide (NaOH) Solution

Prepare about 400 to 450 mL of CO_2-free water by boiling for about 5 min. Weigh from a weighing bottle (your lab instructor will show you how to use a weighing bottle if you don't already know) triplicate samples of between 0.4 and 0.6 g each of pure potassium hydrogen phthalate (KHP) into three separate 250-mL Erlenmeyer flasks; accurately weigh to four significant figures.* Do not weigh the flasks. Record the masses and label the three flasks in order to distinguish among them. Add to each sample about 100 mL of distilled water that has been freed from CO_2 by boiling, and warm gently with swirling until the salt is completely dissolved. Add to each flask two drops of phenolphthalein indicator solution.

Rinse the previously cleaned buret with at least four 5-mL portions of the approximately 0.100 M NaOH solution that you have prepared. Discard each portion into the designated receptacle. *Do not return any of the washings to the bottle.* Completely fill the buret with the solution and remove the air from the tip by running out some of the liquid into an empty beaker. Make sure that the lower part of the meniscus is at the zero mark or slightly lower. Allow the buret to stand for at least 30 s before reading the exact position of the meniscus. Remove any hanging drop from the buret tip by touching it to the side of the beaker used for the washings. Record the initial buret reading on your report sheet.

Slowly add the NaOH solution to one of your flasks of KHP solution while gently swirling the contents of the flask, as illustrated in Figure 5. As the NaOH solution is added, a pink color appears where the drops of the base come in contact with the solution. This coloration disappears with swirling. As the end point is approached, the color disappears more slowly,

---

*In cases where the mass of a sample is larger than 1 g, it is necessary to weigh only to the nearest milligram to obtain four significant figures. Buret readings can be read only to the nearest 0.02 mL, and for readings greater than 10 mL this represents four significant figures.

at which time the NaOH should be added drop by drop. It is most important that the flask be swirled constantly throughout the entire titration. The
end point is reached when one drop of the NaOH solution turns the entire
solution in the flask from colorless to pink. The solution should remain
pink when it is swirled. Allow the titrated solution to stand for at least 1
min so the buret will drain properly. Remove any hanging drop from the
buret tip by touching it to the side of the flask and wash down the sides of
the flask with a stream of water from the wash bottle. Record the buret
reading on your report sheet. Repeat this procedure with the other two
samples.

From the data you obtain in the three titrations, calculate the molarity of
the NaOH solution to four significant figures.

The three determinations should agree within 1.0%. If they do not, the
standardization should be repeated until agreement is reached. The average
of the three acceptable determinations is taken as the molarity of the NaOH.
Calculate the standard deviation of your results. SAVE your standardized
solution for the determination of the pK_a of the unknown acid.

C. Determination of pK_a of Unknown Acid

With the aid of a pipet bulb, pipet a 25-mL aliquot of your unknown acid solution into a 250-mL beaker and carefully immerse the previously rinsed
electrodes in this solution. Measure the pH of this solution by turning the
function knob to "read" or "pH." Record the pH on the report sheet. Begin
your titration by adding 1 mL of your standardized base from a buret and
record the volume of titrant and pH. Repeat with successive additions of
1 mL of base until you approach the end point; then add 0.1-mL increments
of base and record the pH and milliliters of NaOH added. When the pH no
longer changes upon addition of NaOH, your titration is completed. From
these data, plot a titration curve of pH versus mL titrant added. Repeat the
titration with two more 25-mL aliquots of your unknown acid and plot the
titration curves. From these curves calculate the ionization constant. Time
may be saved if the first titration is run with larger-volume increments of the
titrant to locate an approximate equivalence point; then the second and third
titrations may be run with the small increments indicated above. Turn the
function knob to standby, rinse the electrodes with distilled water, and wipe
them with a clean, dry tissue.

D. Concentration of Unknown Acid

Using the volume of base at the equivalence point, its molarity, and the fact
that you used 25.0 mL of acid, calculate the concentration of the unknown
acid and record this on the report sheet.

Before beginning this experiment in the laboratory, you should be able to
answer the following questions:

1. Define Brønsted-Lowry acids and bases.
2. Differentiate between the dissociation constant and equilibrium constant for the dissociation of a weak acid, HA, in aqueous solution.
3. Why isn't the pH at the equivalence point always equal to 7 in a neutralization titration? When is it 7?
4. What is the pK_a of an acid whose K_a is 6.5×10^{-6}?
5. Why must two electrodes be used to make an electrical measurement
   such as pH?

**PRE LAB
QUESTIONS**

6. What is a buffer solution?
7. The pH at one half the equivalence point in an acid-base titration was found to be 5.67. What is the value of K_a for this unknown acid?
8. If 30.15 mL of 0.0995 M NaOH is required to neutralize 0.302 g of an unknown acid, HA, what is the molecular weight of the unknown acid?
9. If K_a is 1.85×10^{-5} for acetic acid, calculate the pH at one half the equivalence point and at the equivalence point for a titration of 50 mL of 0.100 M acetic acid with 0.100 M NaOH.

REPORT SHEET | EXPERIMENT

Determination of the Dissociation Constant of a Weak Acid

B. Standardization of Sodium Hydroxide (NaOH) Solution

	Trial 1	Trial 2	Trial 3
Mass of bottle + KHP	_____	_____	_____
Mass of bottle	_____	_____	_____
Mass of KHP used	_____	_____	_____
Final buret reading	_____	_____	_____
Initial buret reading	_____	_____	_____
mL of NaOH used	_____	_____	_____
Molarity of NaOH	_____	_____	_____

Average molarity (show calculations and standard deviation) _____

Standard deviation _____

C. Determination of pK_a of Unknown Acid

First determination		*Second determination*		*Third determination*	
mL NaOH	pH	mL NaOH	pH	mL NaOH	pH
_____	_____	_____	_____	_____	_____
_____	_____	_____	_____	_____	_____
_____	_____	_____	_____	_____	_____
_____	_____	_____	_____	_____	_____
_____	_____	_____	_____	_____	_____
_____	_____	_____	_____	_____	_____
_____	_____	_____	_____	_____	_____
_____	_____	_____	_____	_____	_____
_____	_____	_____	_____	_____	_____
_____	_____	_____	_____	_____	_____
_____	_____	_____	_____	_____	_____
_____	_____	_____	_____	_____	_____
_____	_____	_____	_____	_____	_____
_____	_____	_____	_____	_____	_____
_____	_____	_____	_____	_____	_____
_____	_____	_____	_____	_____	_____
_____	_____	_____	_____	_____	_____
_____	_____	_____	_____	_____	_____
_____	_____	_____	_____	_____	_____
_____	_____	_____	_____	_____	_____
_____	_____	_____	_____	_____	_____
_____	_____	_____	_____	_____	_____
_____	_____	_____	_____	_____	_____
_____	_____	_____	_____	_____	_____
_____	_____	_____	_____	_____	_____
_____	_____	_____	_____	_____	_____

Volume at equivalence point _____ _____ _____

Volume at one half equivalence point _____ _____ _____

pK_a _____   pK_a _____   pK_a _____

K_a _____ K_a _____ K_a _____

Average K_a (show calculations) _____   Standard deviation of K_a _____

D. Concentration of Unknown Acid

	Trial 1	Trial 2	Trial 3
Volume of unknown acid	_____	_____	_____
Average molarity of NaOH from above	_____	_____	_____
mL of NaOH at equivalence point	_____	_____	_____
Molarity of unknown acid	_____	_____	_____

Average molarity (show calculations) _____ Standard deviation _____

QUESTIONS

1. What are the largest sources of error in this experiment?

2. What is the pH of the solution obtained by mixing 60.00 mL of 0.250 M HCl and 60.00 mL of 0.125 M NaOH?

3. What is the pH of a solution that is 0.50 M in sodium acetate and 0.75 M in acetic acid? (K_a for acetic acid is 1.85×10^{-5}.)

4. Calculate the pH of a solution prepared by mixing 15.0 mL of 0.10 M NaOH and 30.0 mL of 0.10 M benzoic acid solution. (Benzoic acid is monoprotic; its dissociation constant is 6.5×10^{-5}.)

5. K_a for hypochlorous acid, HClO, is 3.0×10^{-8}. Calculate the pH after 10.0, 20.0, 30.0, and 40.0 mL of 0.100 M NaOH have been added to 40.0 mL of 0.100 M HClO.

Titration curve

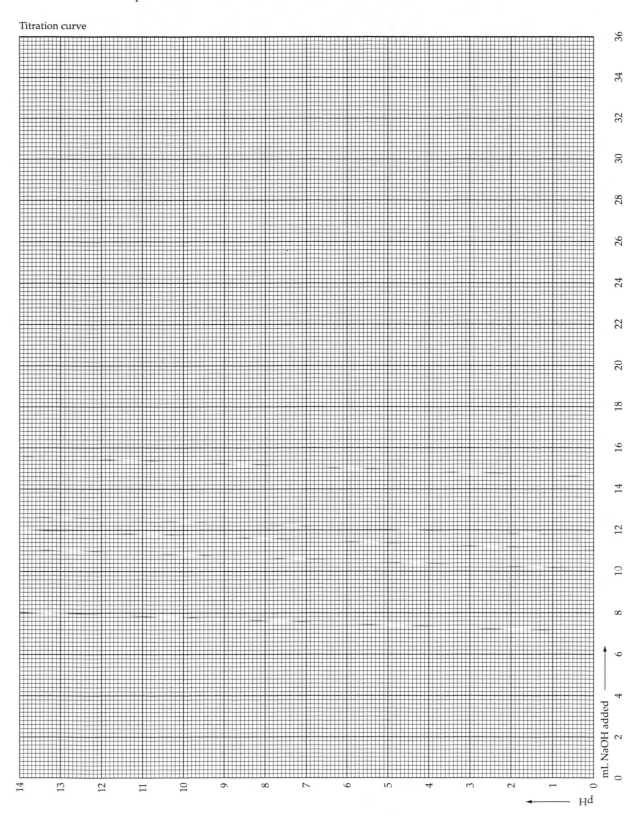

mL NaOH added

pH

Titration curve

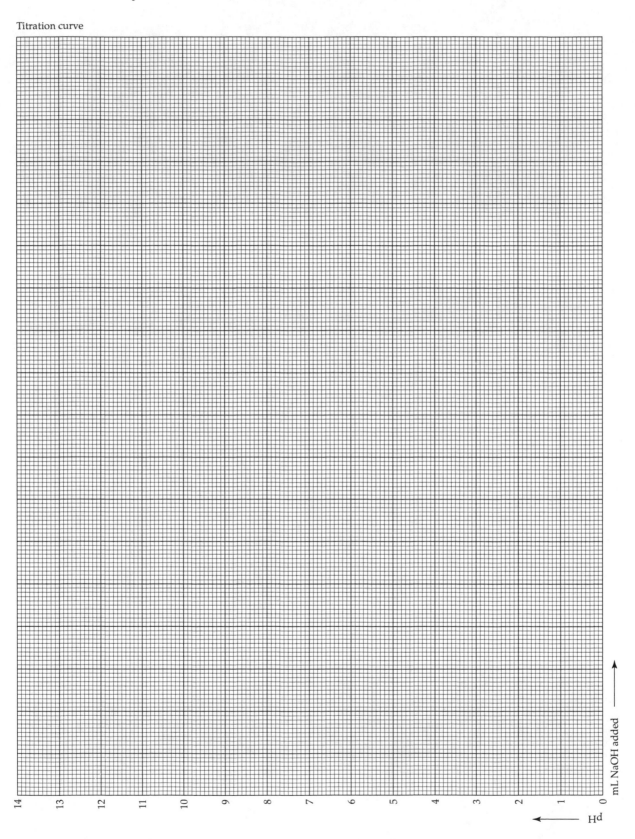

Titration curve

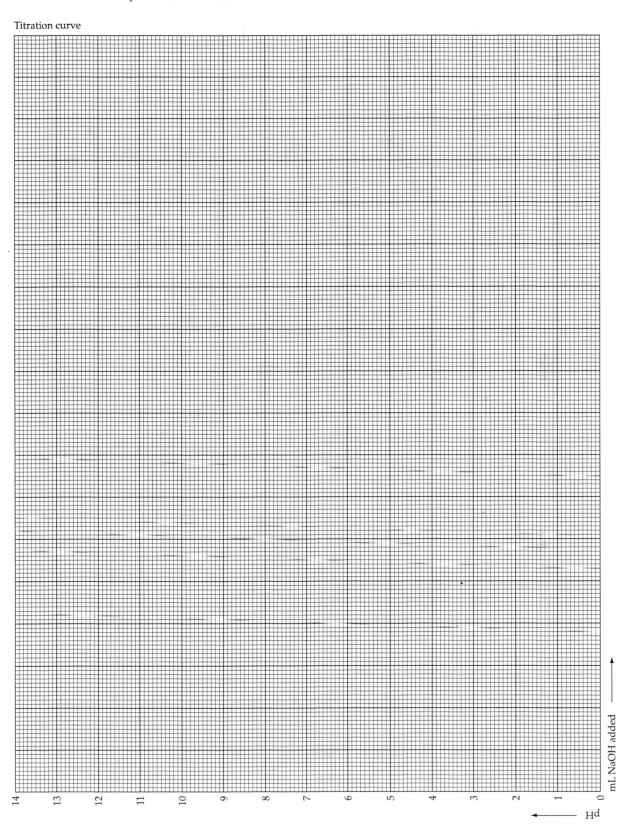

pH

mL NaOH added

NOTES AND CALCULATIONS

Answers to Selected Pre Lab Questions

1. According the Brønsted-Lowry definition, an acid is a proton donor and a base is a proton acceptor.

2. A weak acid dissociates in aqueous solution according to the equilibrium $HA + H_2O \rightleftharpoons H_3O^+ + A^-$, for which the equilibrium constant is $K_{eq} = [H_3O^+][A^-]/[HA][H_2O]$, and the dissociation constant is $K_a = [H_3O^+][A^-]/[HA]$ or $K_a = [H_2O]K_{eq}$.

3. The pH at the equivalence point in an acid-base titration depends upon the nature of the species present. For the titration of a strong acid and a strong base, the pH will be 7 because a salt that does not hydrolyze will be formed (for example, $NaOH + HCl$). For the titration of a strong acid with a weak base (for example, $HCl + NH_4OH$), the pH will be less than 7; and for the titration of a weak acid with a strong base (e.g., $HOAc + NaOH$), the pH will be greater than 7. This is so because the salt formed in each case (NH_4Cl and $NaOAc$) will undergo hydrolysis reactions with water.

4. $pK_a = -\log K_a = -\log(6.5 \times 10^{-6}) = 6 - \log 6.5 = 6 - 0.81 = 5.19$.

5. Two electrodes are necessary for an electrical measurement because some current flow must occur and this requires both a donor and an acceptor for the electrons.

6. A buffer solution is a solution that is resistant to a pH change. It always contains a weak electrolyte and normally is composed of two species, such as a weak acid and one of its salts or a weak base and one of its salts. Two specific examples are acetic acid plus sodium acetate and ammonium hydroxide plus ammonium chloride. An example of a single-component buffer solution is disodium hydrogen phosphate, Na_2HPO_4.

7. At one-half equivalence point $[HA] = [A^-]$. Because $HA \rightleftharpoons H^+ + A^-$ and $K_a = [H^+][A^-]/[HA]$, at one-half equivalence point, $K_a = [H^+]$. Therefore, $pK_a = pH$, so $pK_a = 5.67$, $K_a = $ antilog$(-5.67) = 2.1 \times 10^{-6}$.

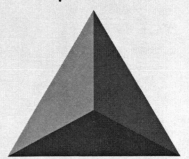

Hydrolysis of Salts and pH of Buffer Solutions

To learn about the concept of hydrolysis and to gain familiarity with acid-base indicators and the behavior of buffer solutions.

Apparatus

500-mL Erlenmeyer flask	pH meter
150-mL beakers (2)	balance
10- and 100-mL graduated cylinders	1-mL pipet
test tubes (6)	Bunsen burner and hose
test-tube rack	ring stand and iron ring
wire gauze	plastic wash bottle
stirring rods (2)	

Chemicals

$NaC_2H_3O_2 \cdot 3H_2O$	dropper bottles of:
0.1 M $ZnCl_2$	methyl orange
0.1 M NH_4Cl	methyl red
0.1 M $KAl(SO_4)_2$	bromothymol blue
0.1 M Na_2CO_3	phenolphthalein
0.1 M $NaCl$	alizarin yellow-R
0.1 M $NaC_2H_3O_2$	phenol red
6.0 M HCl	standard buffer solution (pH 4.5)
3.0 M $HC_2H_3O_2$	
6.0 M $NaOH$	

We expect solutions of substances such as HCl and HNO_2 to be acidic and solutions of $NaOH$ and NH_3 to be basic. However, we may be somewhat surprised at first to discover that aqueous solutions of some salts such as sodium nitrite, $NaNO_2$, and potassium acetate, $KC_2H_3O_2$, are basic, whereas others such as NH_4Cl and $FeCl_3$ are acidic. Recall that salts are the products formed in neutralization reactions of acids and bases. For example, when $NaOH$ and HNO_2 (nitrous acid) react, the salt $NaNO_2$ is formed:

$$NaOH(aq) + HNO_2(aq) \longrightarrow NaNO_2(aq) + H_2O(l)$$

Nearly all salts are strong electrolytes and exist as ions in aqueous solutions. Many ions react with water to produce acidic or basic solutions. The reactions of ions with water are frequently called *hydrolysis reactions*. We will see that anions such as CN^- and $C_2H_3O_2^-$ that are the conjugate bases of the weak acids HCN and $HC_2H_3O_2$, respectively, react with water to form OH^- ions. Cations such as NH_4^+ and Fe^{3+} come from weak bases and react with water to form H^+ ions.

Hydrolysis of Anions: Basic Salts

Let us consider the behavior of anions first. Anions of weak acids react with proton sources. When placed in water these anions react to some extent with water to accept protons and generate OH^- ions and thus cause the solution pH to be greater than 7. Recall that proton acceptors are Brønsted-Lowry bases. Thus, the anions of weak acids are basic in two senses: They are proton acceptors, and their aqueous solutions have pH's above 7. The nitrite ion, for example, reacts with water to increase the concentration of OH^- ions:

$$NO_2^-(aq) + H_2O(l) \rightleftharpoons HNO_2(aq) + OH^-(aq)$$

This reaction of the nitrite ion is similar to that of weak bases such as NH_3 with water:

$$NH_3(aq) + H_2O(l) \rightleftharpoons NH_4^+(aq) + OH^-(aq)$$

Thus, both NH_3 and NO_2^- are bases and as such have a basicity or base-dissociation constant, K_b, associated with their corresponding equilibria.

According to the Brønsted-Lowry theory, the nitrite ion is the conjugate base of nitrous acid. Let's consider the conjugate acid-base pair HNO_2 and NO_2^- and their behavior in water:

$$HNO_2 \rightleftharpoons H^+ + NO_2^- \qquad K_a = \frac{[H^+][NO_2^-]}{[HNO_2]}$$

$$NO_2^- + H_2O \rightleftharpoons HNO_2 + OH^- \qquad K_b = \frac{[HNO_2][OH^-]}{[NO_2^-]}$$

Multiplication of these dissociation constants yields:

$$K_a \times K_b = \left(\frac{[H^+][\cancel{NO_2^-}]}{[\cancel{HNO_2}]}\right)\left(\frac{[\cancel{HNO_2}][OH^-]}{[\cancel{NO_2^-}]}\right) = [H^+][OH^-] = K_w$$

where K_w is the ion-product constant of water.

Thus, the product of the acid-dissociation constant for an acid and the base-dissociation constant for its conjugate base is the ion-product constant for water:

$$K_a \times K_b = K_w = 1.0 \times 10^{-14} \qquad [1]$$

Knowing the K_a for a weak acid, we can easily find the K_b for the anion of the acid:

$$K_b = \frac{K_w}{K_a} \qquad [2]$$

By consulting a table of acid-dissociation constants, we can find that K_a for nitrous acid is 4.5×10^{-4}. Using this value, we can readily determine K_b for NO_2^-:

$$K_b = \frac{1.0 \times 10^{-14}}{4.5 \times 10^{-4}} = 2.2 \times 10^{-11}$$

We note that the stronger the acid is, the larger its K_a, and the weaker its conjugate base, the smaller its K_b. Likewise, the weaker the acid (the smaller the K_a), the stronger the conjugate base (the larger the K_b).

Anions derived from *strong acids*, such as Cl^- from HCl, do not react with water to affect the pH. Nor do Br^-, I^-, NO_3^-, SO_4^{2-}, and ClO_4^- affect the pH, for the same reason. They are spectator ions in the acid-base sense and can be described as neutral ions. Similarly, cations from strong bases, such as Na^+ from NaOH or K^+ from KOH, do not react with water to affect the pH. Hydrolysis of an ion occurs only when it can form a molecule or ion that is a weak electrolyte in the reaction with water. Strong acids and bases do not exist as molecules in dilute water solutions.

EXAMPLE 1

What is the pH of a 0.10 M NaClO solution if K_a for HClO is 3.0×10^{-8}?

SOLUTION: The salt NaClO exists as Na^+ and ClO^-. The Na^+ ions are spectator ions, but ClO^- ions undergo hydrolysis to form the weak acid HClO. Let x equal the equilibrium concentration of HClO (and OH^-):

$$ClO^-(aq) + H_2O(l) \rightleftharpoons HClO(aq) + OH^-(aq)$$
$$(0.10 - x)\,M \qquad\qquad xM \qquad\quad xM$$

The value of K_b for the reaction is $(1.0 \times 10^{-14})/(3.0 \times 10^{-8}) = 3.3 \times 10^{-7}$. Because K_b is so small, we can neglect x in comparison with 0.10 and thus $0.10 - x \approx 0.10$.

$$\frac{[HClO][OH^-]}{[ClO^-]} = K_b$$

$$\frac{x^2}{0.10} = 3.3 \times 10^{-7}$$

$$x^2 = 3.3 \times 10^{-8}$$

$$x = 1.8 \times 10^{-4}\,M$$

$$pOH = 3.74$$

$$\text{and } pH = 14 - 3.74 = 10.26$$

Anions with ionizable protons such as HCO_3^-, $H_2PO_4^-$, and HPO_4^{2-} may be either acidic or basic, depending on the relative values of K_a and K_b for the ion. We will not consider such ions in this experiment.

Hydrolysis of Cations: Acidic Salts

Cations that are derived from weak bases react with water to increase the hydrogen-ion concentration; they form acidic solutions. The ammonium ion is derived from the weak base NH_3 and reacts with water as follows:

$$NH_4^+(aq) + H_2O(l) \rightleftharpoons H_3O^+(aq) + NH_3(aq)$$

This reaction is completely analogous to the dissociation of any other weak acid, such as acetic acid or nitrous acid. We can represent this acid-dissociation of NH_4^+ more simply:

$$NH_4^+(aq) \rightleftharpoons NH_3(aq) + H^+(aq)$$

Here too the acid-dissociation constant is related to the K_b of NH_3, which is the conjugate base of NH_4^+:

$$NH_3(aq) + H_2O(l) \rightleftharpoons NH_4^+(aq) + OH^-(aq)$$

Knowing the value of K_b for NH_3, we can readily calculate the acid dissociation constant from Equation [3]:

$$K_a = \frac{K_w}{K_b} \qquad [3]$$

Cations of the alkali metals (Group 1A) and the larger alkaline earth ions, Ca^{2+}, Sr^{2+}, and Ba^{2+}, do not react with water, because they come from strong bases. Thus, these ions have no influence on the pH of aqueous solutions. They are merely spectator ions in acid-base reactions. Consequently, they are described as being neutral in the acid-base sense. The cations of most other metals do hydrolyze to produce acidic solutions. Metal cations are coordinated with water molecules, and it is the hydrated ion that serves as the proton donor. The following equations illustrate this behavior for the hexaaqua iron (III) ion:

$$Fe(H_2O)_6{}^{3+}(aq) + H_2O(l) \rightleftharpoons Fe(OH)(H_2O)_5{}^{2+}(aq) + H_3O^+(aq) \qquad [4]$$

We frequently omit the coordinated water molecules from such equations. For example, Equation [4] may be written as

$$Fe^{3+}(aq) + H_2O(l) \rightleftharpoons Fe(OH)^{2+}(aq) + H^+(aq) \qquad [5]$$

Additional hydrolysis reactions can occur to form $Fe(OH)_2{}^+$ and even lead to the precipitation of $Fe(OH)_3$. The equilibria for such cations are often complex, and not all species have been identified. However, equations such as [4] and [5] serve to illustrate the acidic character of dipositive and tripositive ions and account for most of the H^+ in these solutions.

Summary of Hydrolysis Behavior

Whether a solution of a salt will be acidic, neutral, or basic can be predicted on the basis of the strengths of the acid and base from which the salt was formed.

1. *Salt of a strong acid and a strong base*: Examples: $NaCl$, KBr, and $Ba(NO_3)_2$. Neither the cation nor anion hydrolyzes, and the solution has a pH of 7.
2. *Salt of a strong acid and a weak base*: Examples: NH_4Br, $ZnCl_2$, and $Al(NO_3)_3$. The cation hydrolyzes, forming H^+ ions, and the solution has a pH less than 7.
3. *Salt of a weak acid and a strong base*: Examples: $NaNO_2$, $KC_2H_3O_2$, and $Ca(OCl)_2$. The anion hydrolyzes, forming OH^- ions, and the solution has a pH greater than 7.
4. *Salt of a weak acid and a weak base*: Examples: NH_4F, $NH_4C_2H_3O_2$, and $Zn(NO_2)_2$. Both ions hydrolyze. The pH of the solution is determined by the relative extent to which each ion hydrolyzes.

In this experiment, we will test the pH of water and of several aqueous salt solutions to determine whether these solutions are acidic, basic, or neutral. In each case, the salt solution will be 0.1 M. Knowing the concentration of the salt solution and the measured pH of each solution allows us to calculate K_a or K_b for the ion that hydrolyzes. Example 2 illustrates such calculations.

EXAMPLE 2

Calculate K_b for OBr^- if a 0.10 M solution of NaOBr has a pH of 10.85.

SOLUTION: The spectator ion is Na^+. Alkali metal ions do not react with water and have no influence on pH. The ion OBr^- is the anion of a weak acid and thus reacts with water to produce OH^- ions:

$$OBr^- + H_2O \rightleftharpoons HOBr + OH^-$$

and the corresponding expression for the base dissociation constant is

$$K_b = \frac{[HOBr][OH^-]}{[OBr^-]} \qquad [6]$$

If the pH is 10.85, then

$$pOH = 14.00 - 10.85 = 3.15$$

and

$$[OH^-] = \text{antilog}\,(-3.15) = 7.1 \times 10^{-4}\ M$$

The concentration of HOBr that is formed along with OH^- must also be $7.1 \times 10^{-4}\ M$. The concentration of OBr^- that has not hydrolyzed is

$$[OBr^-] = 0.10\ M - 0.00071\ M \simeq 0.10\ M$$

Substituting these values into Equation [6] for K_b yields

$$K_b = \frac{[7.1 \times 10^{-4}][7.1 \times 10^{-4}]}{[0.10]}$$
$$= 5.0 \times 10^{-6}$$

We will use a set of indicators to determine the pH of various salt solutions. The dark areas in Figure 1 denote the transition ranges for the indicators you will use.

We will generally find that the solutions that we test will be more acidic than we would predict them to be. A major reason for this increased acidity is the occurrence of CO_2 dissolved in the solutions. CO_2 reacts with water to generate H^+:

$$CO_2(g) + H_2O(l) \rightleftharpoons H_2CO_3(aq) \rightleftharpoons H^+(aq) + HCO_3^-(aq)$$

The solubility of CO_2 is greatest in basic solutions, intermediate in neutral ones, and least in acidic ones. Even distilled water will therefore be somewhat acidic, unless it is boiled to remove the dissolved CO_2.

Buffer Solutions

Chemists, biologists, and environmental scientists frequently need to control the pH of aqueous solutions. The effects on pH caused by the addition of a small amount of a strong acid or base to water are dramatic. The addition of a mere 0.001 mole of HCl to 1 L of water causes the pH to drop instantly from 7.0 to 3.0 as the hydronium-ion concentration increases from 1×10^{-7} to 1×10^{-3} mol/L. And, on the other hand, the addition of 0.001 mole of NaOH

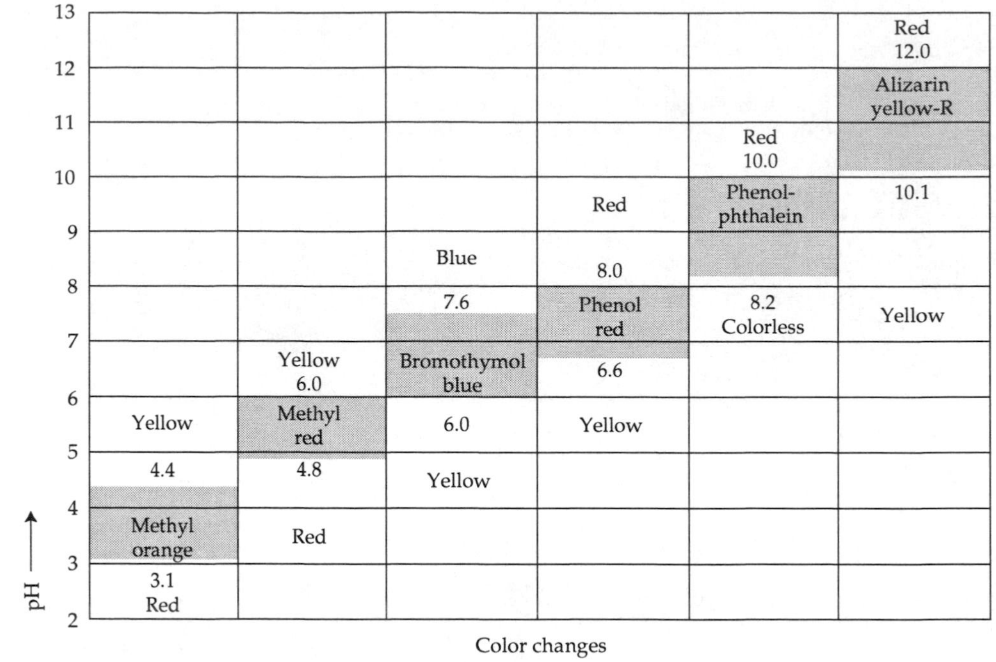

▲ **FIGURE 1** The color behavior of indicators.

to 1 L of water will cause the pH to increase from 7.0 to 11.0. That life could not exist without some mechanism for controlling or absorbing excess acid or base is indicated by the narrow normal range of blood pH, 7.35 to 7.45.

The control of pH is often accomplished by use of *buffer solutions* (often simply called *buffers*). A buffer solution has the important property of resisting large changes in pH upon the addition of small amounts of strong acids or bases. A buffer solution must have two components—one that will react with H^+, and the other that will react with OH^-. The two components of a buffer solution are usually a weak acid and its conjugate base, such as $HC_2H_3O_2$-$C_2H_3O_2^-$ or NH_4^+-NH_3. Thus, buffers are often prepared by mixing a weak acid or a weak base with a salt of that acid or base. For example, the $HC_2H_3O_2$-$C_2H_3O_2^-$ buffer can be prepared by adding $NaC_2H_3O_2$ to a solution of $HC_2H_3O_2$; the NH_4^+-NH_3 buffer can be prepared by adding NH_4Cl to a solution of NH_3. By the appropriate choice of components and their concentrations, buffer solutions of virtually any pH can be made.

Let's examine how a buffer works. Consider a buffer composed of a hypothetical weak acid HX and one of its salts MX, where M^+ could be Na^+, K^+, or other cations. The acid-dissociation equilibrium in this buffer involves both the acid, HX, and its conjugate base X^-:

$$HX(aq) \rightleftharpoons H^+(aq) + X^-(aq) \tag{1}$$

The corresponding acid-dissociation-constant expression is

$$K_a = \frac{[H^+][X^-]}{[HX]} \tag{2}$$

Solving this expression for $[H^+]$, we have

$$[H^+] = K_a \frac{[HX]}{[X^-]} \qquad [3]$$

We see from this expression that the hydrogen-ion concentration and therefore the pH is determined by two factors: the value of K_a for the weak acid component of the buffer, and the ratios of the concentrations of the weak acid and its conjugate base, $[HX]/[X^-]$.

If OH^- ions are added to the buffered solution, they react with the acid component of the buffer:

$$OH^-(aq) + HX(aq) \longrightarrow H_2O(l) + X^-(aq) \qquad [4]$$

This reaction results in a slight decrease in the $[HX]$ and a slight increase in the $[X^-]$, as long as the amounts of HX and X^- in the buffer are large compared to the amount of the added OH^-. In that case, the ratio $[HX]/[X^-]$ doesn't change much, and thus the change in the pH is small.

If H^+ ions are added to the buffered solution, they react with the base component of the buffer:

$$H^+(aq) + X^-(aq) \longrightarrow HX(aq) \qquad [5]$$

This reaction causes a slight decrease in the $[X^-]$ and a slight increase in the $[HX]$. Once again, as long as the change in the ratio $[HX]/[X^-]$ is small, the change in the pH will be small.

Buffers resist changes in pH most effectively when the concentrations of the conjugate acid-base pair, HX and X^-, are about the same. We see from examining Equation [3] that under these conditions their ratio is close to one, and thus the $[H^+]$ is approximately equal to K_a. For this reason we try to select a buffer whose acid form has a pK_a close to the desired pH.

Because we are interested in pH, let's take the negative logarithm of both sides of Equation [3] and obtain

$$-\log[H^+] = -\log K_a - \log\frac{[HX]}{[X^-]}$$

Because $-\log[H^+] = pH$ and $-\log[K_a] = pK_a$, we have

$$pH = pK_a - \log\frac{[HX]}{[X^-]}$$

and making use of the properties of logarithms (see Appendix A) we have

$$pH = pK_a + \log\frac{[X^-]}{[HX]} \qquad [6]$$

and in general

$$pH = pK_a + \log\frac{[\text{conjugate base}]}{[\text{weak acid}]} \qquad [7]$$

This relationship is known as the *Henderson-Hasselbalch equation*. Biochemists, biologists, and others who frequently work with buffers often use this equation to calculate the pH of buffers. What makes this equation particularly convenient is that we can normally neglect the amounts of the acid and base of the buffer that ionize. Therefore, we can use the *initial concentrations* of the acid and conjugate base components of the buffer directly in Equation [7].

271

EXAMPLE 3

What is the pH of a buffer that is 0.120 M in lactic acid, $HC_3H_5O_3$, and 0.100 M in sodium lactate, $NaC_3H_5O_3$? For lactic acid, $K_a = 1.4 \times 10^{-4}$.

SOLUTION: Because lactic acid is a weak acid, we will assume that its initial concentration is 0.120 M and that none of it has dissociated. We will also assume that the lactate ion concentration is that of the salt, sodium lactate, 0.100 M. Let x represent the concentration in mol/L of the lactic acid that dissociate. The initial and equilibrium concentrations involved in this equilibrium are

$$HC_3H_5O_3(aq) \rightleftharpoons H^+(aq) + C_3H_5O_3^-(aq)$$

Initial	0.120 M	0	0.100 M
Change	$-xM$	$+xM$	$+xM$
Equilibrium	$(0.120 - x)\,M$	$x\,M$	$(0.100 + x)\,M$

The equilibrium concentrations are governed by the equilibrium expression

$$K_a = 1.4 \times 10^{-4} = \frac{[H^+][C_3H_5O_3^-]}{[HC_3H_5O_3]} = \frac{x(0.100 + x)}{0.120 - x}$$

Because K_a is small and the presence of a common ion, we expect x to be small relative to 0.12 and 0.10 M. Thus, our equation can be simplified to give

$$1.4 \times 10^{-4} = \frac{x(0.100)}{0.120}$$

Solving for x gives a value that justifies our neglecting it:

$$x = [H^+] = \left(\frac{0.120}{0.100}\right)(1.4 \times 10^{-4}) = 1.7 \times 10^{-4}\,M$$

$$pH = -\log(1.7 \times 10^{-4}) = 3.77$$

Alternatively, we could have used the Henderson-Hasselbalch equation to calculate the pH directly:

$$pH = pK_a + \log\left(\frac{[\text{conjugate base}]}{[\text{weak acid}]}\right) = 3.85 + \log\left(\frac{0.100}{0.120}\right)$$

$$= 3.85 + (-0.08) = 3.77$$

Addition of Strong Acids or Bases to Buffers

Let's consider in a quantitative way the manner in which a buffer solution responds to the addition of a strong acid or base. Consider a buffer that consists of the weak acid HX and its conjugate base X^- (from the salt NaX). When a strong acid is added to this buffer, the H^+ is consumed by the X^- to produce HX; thus [HX] increases and $[X^-]$ decreases. Whereas, when a strong base is added to the buffer, the OH^- is consumed by HX to produce X^-; in this case, [HX] decreases and $[X^-]$ increases. There are basically two steps involved in calculating how the pH of the buffer responds to the addition of a strong acid or base. First consider the acid-base neutralization reaction and determine its effect on [HX] and $[X^-]$. And second, after performing this stoichiometric calculation, use K_a and the new concentrations of [HX] and $[X^-]$ to calculate the $[H^+]$. This second step in the calculation is a standard equilibrium calculation. This procedure is illustrated in Example 4.

EXAMPLE 4

A buffer is made by adding 0.120 mol $HC_3H_5O_3$ and 0.100 mol $NaC_3H_5O_3$ to enough water to make 1.00 liter of solution The pH of the buffer is 3.77 (see Example 3). Calculate the pH of the solution after 0.001 mol NaOH is added.

SOLUTION: Solving this problem involves two steps.

Stoichiometric calculation: The OH^- provided by the NaOH reacts with the $HC_3H_5O_3$, the weak-acid component of the buffer. The following table summarizes the concentrations before and after the neutralization reaction:

$$HC_3H_5O_3(aq) + OH^-(aq) \longrightarrow H_2O(l) + C_3H_5O_3^-(aq)$$

Before reaction	0.120 M	0.001 M	—	0.100 M
Change	-0.001 M	-0.001 M	—	$+0.001$ M
After reaction	0.119 M	0.0 M	—	0.101 M

Equilibrium calculation: After neutralization the solution contains different concentrations for the weak acid–conjugate base pair. We next consider the proton-transfer equilibrium in order to determine the pH of the solution:

$$HC_3H_5C_3(aq) + H_2O(aq) \rightleftharpoons H_3O^+(aq) + C_3H_5O_3^-(aq)$$

Before reaction	0.119 M	—	0	0.101 M
Change	$-xM$	—	$+xM$	$+xM$
After reaction	$(0.119 - x)$ M	—	x M	$(0.101 + x)$ M

$$K_a = \frac{[H_3O^+][C_3H_5O_3^-]}{[HC_3H_5O_3]} = \frac{(x)(0.101 + x)}{0.119 - x} \approx \frac{(x)(0.101)}{0.119} = 1.4 \times 10^{-4}$$

$$x = [H_3O^+] = \frac{(0.119)(1.4 \times 10^{-4})}{(0.101)} = 1.65 \times 10^{-4} \ M$$

$$pH = -\log(1.65 \times 10^{-4}) = 3.78$$

Note how the buffer resists a change in its pH. The addition of 0.001 mol of NaOH to a liter of this buffer results in a change in the pH of only 0.01 units, whereas the addition of the same amount of NaOH to a liter of water results in a change of pH from 7.0 to 11.0, a change of 4.0 pH units!

A. Hydrolysis of Salts

Boil approximately 450 mL of distilled water for about 10 min to expel dissolved carbon dioxide. Allow the water to cool to room temperature. While

PROCEDURE

the water is boiling and subsequently cooling, add about 5 mL of unboiled distilled water to each of six test tubes. Add three drops of a different indicator to each of these six test tubes (one indicator per tube) and record the colors on the report sheet. From these colors and the data given in Figure 1, determine the pH of the unboiled water to the nearest pH unit. (Remember that we would expect its pH to be below 7 because of dissolved CO_2.) Empty the contents of the test tubes and rinse the test tubes three times with about 3 mL of boiled distilled water. Then pour about 5 mL of the boiled distilled water into each of the six test tubes and add three drops of each of the indicators (one indicator per tube) to each tube. Record the colors and determine the pH. Empty the contents of the test tubes and rinse each tube three times with about 3 mL of boiled distilled water.

Repeat the same procedure to determine the pH of each of the following solutions that are 0.1 M: NaCl, $NaC_2H_3O_2$, NH_4Cl, $ZnCl_2$, $KAl(SO_4)_2$, and Na_2CO_3. Use 5 mL of each of these solutions per test tube. Do not forget to rinse the test tubes with boiled distilled water when you go from one solution to the next.

From the pH values that you determined, calculate the hydrogen- and hydroxide-ion concentrations for each solution. Complete the tables on the report sheets and calculate the K_a or K_b as appropriate.

Dispose of chemicals in designated receptacles.

B. pH of Buffer Solutions

1. Preparation of Acetic Acid–Sodium Acetate Buffer

Weigh about 3.5 g of $NaC_2H_3O_2 \cdot 3H_2O$ to the nearest 0.01 g, record its mass, and add it to a 150-mL beaker. Using a 10-mL graduated cylinder, measure 8.8 mL of 3.0 M acetic acid and add it to the beaker containing the sodium acetate. Using a graduated cylinder, measure 55.6 mL of distilled water and add it to the solution of acetic acid and sodium acetate. Stir the solution until all of the sodium acetate is dissolved. The pH of this solution will be measured using a pH meter. The operation and calibration of the pH meter are described in the next section. Calibrate the pH meter using a standard buffer with a pH of 4.5. After you have calibrated the pH meter, measure the pH of the buffer solution you have prepared and record the value. Save this buffer solution for part 2 below.

Operation and Calibration of the pH Meter

1. Obtain a buffer solution of known pH.
2. Plug in the pH meter to the line current and allow at least 10 min for warming up. It should be left plugged in until you are completely finished with it. *This does not apply to battery-operated meters.*
3. Turn the function knob on the pH meter to the standby position.
4. *Prepare the electrodes.* Make certain that the solution in the reference electrode extends well above the internal electrode. If it does not, ask your instructor to fill it with saturated KCl solution. Remove the rubber tip and slide down the rubber collar on the reference electrode. Rinse the outside of the electrodes well with distilled water.
5. *Standardize the pH meter.* Carefully immerse the electrodes in the buffer solution contained in a small beaker. *Remember that the glass electrode is very fragile; it breaks easily!* Do not touch the bottom of the beaker with the electrodes!! Turn the function knob to "read" or "pH." Turn the

standardize knob until the pH meter indicates the exact pH of the buffer solution. Wait 5 s to be certain that the reading remains constant. *Once you have standardized the* pH *meter, do not readjust the standardize knob.* Turn the function knob to standby. Carefully lift the electrodes from the buffer and rinse them with distilled water. The pH meter is now ready to use to measure pH.

2. Effect of Acid and Base on the Buffer pH

Pour half (32 mL) of the buffer solution you prepared above into another 150-mL beaker. Label the two beakers 1 and 2. (**CAUTION:** *Concentrated* **HCL** *can cause severe burns. Avoid contact with it. If you come in contact with it, immediately wash the area with copious amounts of water.*) Pipet 1.0 mL of 6.0 M HCl into beaker 1, mix, and then measure the pH of the resultant solution and record the pH. Remember to rinse the electrodes between pH measurements. (**CAUTION:** *Sodium hydroxide can cause severe burns. Avoid contact with it. If you come in contact with it, immediately wash the area with copious amounts of water.*) Similarly, pipet 1.0 mL of 6.0 M NaOH into beaker 2, mix, and then measure and record the pH of the resultant solution. Calculate the pH values of the original buffer solution, the values after the additions of the HCl and NaOH. How do the measured and calculated values compare? Dispose of the chemicals in the designated receptacles.

Before beginning this experiment in the laboratory, you should be able to answer the following questions:

PRE LAB QUESTIONS

1. Define Brønsted-Lowry acids and bases.

2. Which of the following ions will react with water in a hydrolysis reaction: Na^+, Ca^{2+}, Cu^{2+}, Zn^{2+}, F^-, SO_3^{2-}, Br^-?

3. For those ions in question 2 that undergo hydrolysis, write net ionic equations for the hydrolysis reaction.

4. The K_a for HCN is 4.9×10^{-10}. What is the value of K_b for CN^-?

5. What are the conjugate base and conjugate acid of $H_2PO_4^-$?

6. From what acid and what base were the following salts made: $CaSO_4$, NH_4Br, and $BaCl_2$?

7. Define the term *salt.*

8. Tell whether 0.1 M solutions of the following salts would be acidic, neutral, or basic: $BaCl_2$, $CuSO_4$, $(NH_4)_2SO_4$, $ZnCl_2$, NaCN.

9. If the pH of a solution is 8, what are the hydrogen- and hydroxide-ion concentrations?

10. The pH of a 0.1 M MCl (M^+ is an unknown cation) was found to be 4.7. Write a net ionic equation for the hydrolysis of M^+ and its corresponding equilibrium expression K_b. Calculate the value of K_b.

11. What is the pH of a solution that is 0.10 M $HC_2H_3O_2$ and 0.20 M $NaC_2H_3O_2$? K_a for acetic acid 1.8×10^{-5}.

NOTES AND CALCULATIONS

REPORT SHEET | EXPERIMENT

Hydrolysis of Salts and pH of Buffer Solutions

A. Hydrolysis of Salts

Solution	Ion expected to hydrolyze (if any)	Spectator ion(s) (if any)
0.1 M NaCl	_____	_____
0.1 M Na$_2$CO$_3$	_____	_____
0.1 M NaC$_2$H$_3$O$_2$	_____	_____
0.1 M NH$_4$Cl	_____	_____
0.1 M ZnCl$_2$	_____	_____
0.1 M KAl(SO$_4$)$_2$	_____	_____

Solution	Indicator Color*							pH	$[H^+]$	$[OH^-]$
	Methyl orange	Methyl red	Bromo-thymol blue	Phenol red	Phenol-phtha-lein	Alizarin yellow-R				
H$_2$O (unboiled)	___	___	___	___	___	___		___	___	___
H$_2$O (boiled)	___	___	___	___	___	___		___	___	___
NaCl	___	___	___	___	___	___		___	___	___
NaC$_2$H$_3$O$_2$	___	___	___	___	___	___		___	___	___
NH$_4$Cl	___	___	___	___	___	___		___	___	___
ZnCl$_2$	___	___	___	___	___	___		___	___	___
KAl(SO$_4$)$_2$	___	___	___	___	___	___		___	___	___
Na$_2$CO$_3$	___	___	___	___	___	___		___	___	___

* color key: org = orange; — = colorless; yell = yellow.

CALCULATIONS

Solution	Net-ionic equation for hydrolysis	Expression for equilibrium constant (K_a or K_b)	Value of K_a or K_b
$NaC_2H_3O_2$	_____	_____	_____
Na_2CO_3	_____	_____	_____
NH_4Cl	_____	_____	_____
$ZnCl_2$	_____	_____	_____
$KAl(SO_4)_2$	_____	_____	_____

QUESTIONS

1. Using the K_a's for $HC_2H_3O_2$ and HCO_3^- (from Appendix E), calculate the K_b's for the $C_2H_3O_2^-$ and CO_3^{2-} ions. Compare these values with those calculated from your measured pH's.

2. Using K_b for NH_3 (from Appendix F), calculate K_a for the NH_4^+ ion. Compare this value with that calculated from your measured pH's.

3. How should the pH of a 0.1 M solution of $NaC_2H_3O_2$ compare with that of a 0.1 M solution of $KC_2H_3O_2$? Explain briefly.

4. What is the greatest source of error in this experiment? How could you minimize this source of error?

B. pH of Buffer Solutions

Mass of $NaC_2H_3O_2 \cdot 3H_2O$ (FW = 136 g/mol) _____

pH of Original buffer solution _____

pH of Buffer + HCl _____

pH Buffer + NaOH _____

Calculate pH of original buffer. (Show calculations below.) _____

Calculate pH of buffer + HCl. (Show calculations below.)_____

Calculate pH of buffer + NaOH. (Show calculations below.) _____

NOTES AND CALCULATIONS

Answers to Selected Pre Lab Questions

1. According to the Brønsted-Lowry definitions, an acid is a proton donor and a base is a proton acceptor.

2. Cu^{2+}, Zn^{2+}, and SO_3^{2-} will undergo hydrolysis.

3. For example, $Cu^{2+}(aq) + 2H_2O(l) \rightleftharpoons Cu(OH)_2(s) + 2H^+(aq)$.

4. $K_b = 1.0 \times 10^{-14}/4.9 \times 10^{-10} = 2.0 \times 10^{-5}$

5. The conjugate base is HPO_4^{2-} and the conjugate acid is H_3PO_4.

6. For example, $CaSO_4$ may be made from $Ca(OH)_2$ and H_2SO_4.

11. $pK_a = -\log(1.8 \times 10^{-5}) = 4.74$ and $pH = 4.74 + \log(0.20/0.10) = 4.74 + (0.30) = 5.04$

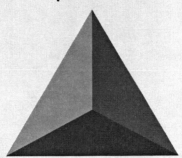

Introduction to Qualitative Analysis

CATIONS: Na^+, NH_4^+, Ag^+, Fe^{3+}, Al^{3+}, Cr^{3+}, Ca^{2+}, Mg^{2+}, Ni^{2+}, Zn^{2+}

ANIONS: SO_4^{2-}, NO_3^-, CO_3^{2-}, Cl^-, Br^-, I^-

To become acquainted with the chemistry of several elements and the principles of qualitative analysis.

OBJECTIVE

APPARATUS AND CHEMICALS

Apparatus

small test tubes (12)	droppers (6)
centrifuge	Bunsen burner and hose
evaporating dish or crucible	10-cm Nichrome wire with loop
red litmus	at end

Chemicals

6 M H_2SO_4	0.2 M NaCl
18 M H_2SO_4	Cl_2 water
3 M NaOH	mineral oil
6 M HCl	0.1 M $Ba(OH)_2$
12 M HCl	Solids: Na_2SO_4, $NaNO_3$, Na_2CO_3,
6 M NH_3	NaCl, NaBr, NaI
15 M NH_3	0.1 M NH_4NO_3
6 M HNO_3	0.1 M $AgNO_3$
15 M HNO_3	0.1 M $Fe(NO_3)_3$
5 M NH_4Cl	0.1 M $Cr(NO_3)_3$
3% H_2O_2	0.1 M $Al(NO_3)_3$
0.2 M $K_4Fe(CN)_6$	0.1 M $Ca(NO_3)_2$
0.1% Aluminon reagent*	0.1 M $NaNO_3$
1% dimethylglyoxime†	0.1 M $Zn(NO_3)_2$
0.2 M $BaCl_2$	0.1 M $Ni(NO_3)_2$
0.2 $M (NH_4)_2C_2O_4$	0.1 M $Mg(NO_3)_2$
Magnesium reagent‡	unknown cation solution
0.2 M $FeSO_4$ (stabilized with iron wire and 0.01 M H_2SO_4)	unknown anion salt, solid

ALL SOLUTIONS SHOULD BE PROVIDED IN DROPPER BOTTLES.

DISCUSSION

Qualitative analysis is concerned with the identification of the constituents contained in a sample of unknown composition. Inorganic qualitative analysis deals with the detection and identification of the elements that are present

---

*One gram of ammonium aurintricarboxylic acid in 1 L H_2O.

†In 95% ethyl alcohol solution.

††A solution of 0.1% (0.1 g/L) p-nitrobenzene-azoresorcinol in 0.025 M NaOH.

in a sample of material. Frequently this is accomplished by making an aqueous solution of the sample and then determining which cations and anions are present on the basis of chemical and physical properties. In this experiment you will become familiar with some of the chemistry of 10 cations (Ag^+, Fe^{3+}, Cr^{3+}, Al^{3+}, Ca^{2+}, Mg^{2+}, Ni^{2+}, Zn^{2+}, Na^+, NH_4^+) and six anions (SO_4^{2-}, NO_3^-, Cl^-, Br^-, I^-, CO_3^{2-}), and you will learn how to test for their presence or absence. Because there are many other elements and ions than those which we shall consider, we call this experiment an "abbreviated" qualitative-analysis scheme.

PART I: CATIONS

If a substance contains only a single cation (or anion), its identification is a fairly simple and straightforward process, as you may have witnessed in Experiments 7 and 10. However, even in this instance additional confirmatory tests are sometimes required to distinguish between two cations (or anions) that have similar chemical properties. The detection of a particular ion in a sample that contains several ions is somewhat more difficult because the presence of the other ions may interfere with the test. For example, if you are testing for Ba^{2+} with K_2CrO_4 and obtain a yellow precipitate, you may draw an erroneous conclusion because if Pb^{2+} is present, it also will form a yellow precipitate. Thus, the presence of lead ions interferes with this test for barium ions. This problem can be circumvented by first precipitating the lead as PbS with H_2S, thereby removing the lead ions from solution prior to testing for Ba^{2+}.

The successful analysis of a mixture containing 10 or more cations centers about the systematic separation of the ions into groups containing only a few ions. It is a much simpler task to work with two or three ions than with 10 or more. Ultimately, the separation of cations depends upon the differences in their tendencies to form precipitates, to form complex ions, or to exhibit amphoterism.

The chart in Figure 1 illustrates how the 10 cations you will study are separated into groups. Three of the 10 cations are colored: Fe^{3+} (rust to yellow), Cr^{3+} (blue-green), and Ni^{2+} (green). Therefore, a preliminary examination of an unknown that can contain any of the 10 cations under consideration yields valuable information. If the solution is colorless, you know immediately that iron, chromium, and nickel are absent. You are to take advantage of all clues that will aid you in identifying ions. However, in your role as a detective in identifying ions, be aware that clues can sometimes be misleading. For example, if Fe^{3+} and Cr^{3+} are present together, what color would you expect this mixture to display? Would the color depend upon the proportions of Fe^{3+} and Cr^{3+} present? Could you assign a *definite* color to such a mixture?

The group-separation chart (Figure 1) shows that silver can be separated from all the other cations (what are they?) as an insoluble chloride by the addition of hydrochloric acid. Iron, chromium, and aluminum are separated from the decantate as their corresponding hydroxides by precipitating them from a buffered ammonium hydroxide solution. Next, calcium can be isolated by precipitating it as insoluble calcium oxalate. Finally, magnesium and nickel can be separated from the remaining ions (Zn^{2+} and Na^+) as their insoluble hydroxides. Examination of the chart shows that in achieving these separations, reagents containing sodium and ammonium ions are used; therefore, tests for these ions must be made prior to their introduction into the solution.

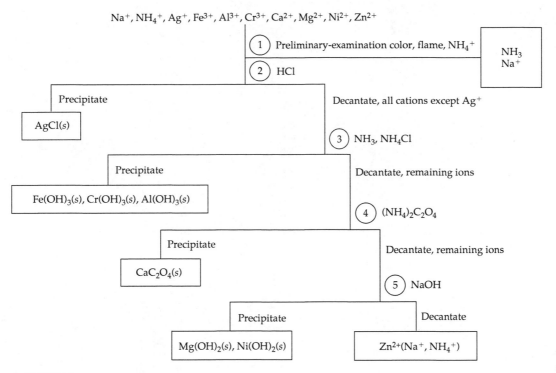

Na^+, NH_4^+, Ag^+, Fe^{3+}, Al^{3+}, Cr^{3+}, Ca^{2+}, Mg^{2+}, Ni^{2+}, Zn^{2+}

(1) Preliminary-examination color, flame, NH_4^+

NH_3
Na^+

(2) HCl

Precipitate

AgCl(s)

Decantate, all cations except Ag^+

(3) NH_3, NH_4Cl

Precipitate

$Fe(OH)_3(s)$, $Cr(OH)_3(s)$, $Al(OH)_3(s)$

Decantate, remaining ions

(4) $(NH_4)_2C_2O_4$

Precipitate

$CaC_2O_4(s)$

Decantate, remaining ions

(5) NaOH

Precipitate

$Mg(OH)_2(s)$, $Ni(OH)_2(s)$

Decantate

$Zn^{2+}(Na^+, NH_4^+)$

▲ **FIGURE 1** Flow chart for group separation.

To derive the maximum benefit from this exercise, you should be thoroughly familiar with the group-separation chart in Figure 1. You should know not only which 10 cations (by formula and charge) you are studying but also how they are separated into groups. More details regarding the identification of these cations are provided in the flow chart for cations (Figure 2) and in the following discussion about the chemistry of the analytical scheme. Make frequent referrals to the flow charts while learning about the chemistry of the qualitative analysis scheme.

1 Detection of Sodium and Ammonium

Sodium salts and ammonium salts are added as reagents in the analysis of your general unknown. Hence, tests for Na^+ and NH_4^+ must be made on the original sample before performing tests for the other cations. Remember, your unknown may contain up to 10 cations, and you do not want inadvertently to introduce any of them into your unknown.

CHEMISTRY OF THE QUALITATIVE ANALYSIS SCHEME

Sodium Most sodium salts are water-soluble. The simplest test for the sodium ion is a flame test. Sodium salts impart a characteristic yellow color to a flame. The test is *very* sensitive, and because of the prevalence of sodium ions, much care must be exercised to keep equipment clean and free from contamination by these ions.

Ammonium The ammonium ion, NH_4^+, is the conjugate acid of the base ammonia, NH_3. The test for NH_4^+ takes advantage of the following equilibrium:

$$NH_4^+(aq) + OH^-(aq) \rightleftharpoons NH_3(g) + H_2O(l)$$

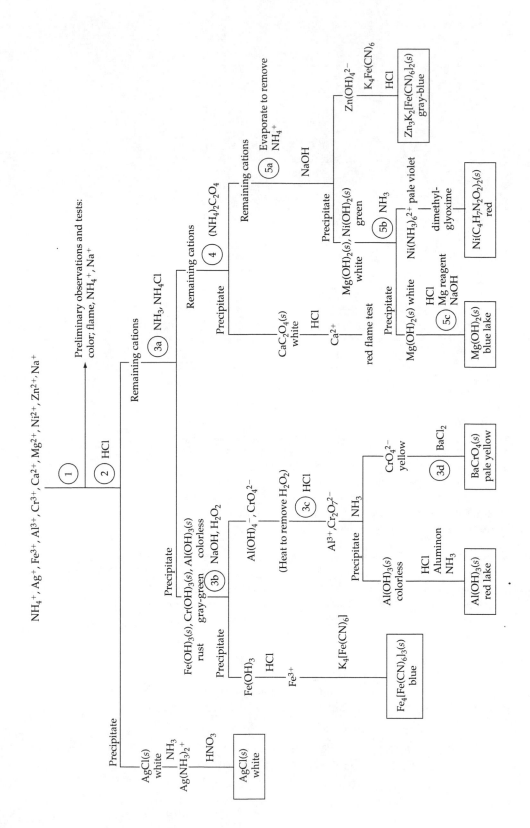

▲ **FIGURE 2** Cation flow chart.

Thus, when a strong base such as sodium hydroxide is added to a solution of an ammonium salt, and this solution is heated, NH_3 gas is evolved. The NH_3 gas can easily be detected by its effect upon moist red litmus paper.

2 Separation and Detection of Silver

All chloride salts are soluble in water except those of Pb^{2+}, Hg_2^{2+}, and Ag^+. Silver can be precipitated and separated from the other nine cations that we are considering by the addition of HCl to the original unknown:

$$Ag^+(aq) + Cl^-(aq) \longrightarrow \mathbf{AgCl}(s)$$
$$\text{white}$$

A slight excess of HCl is used to ensure the complete precipitation of silver ions and to reduce their solubility by the common-ion effect; an excess of chloride ions drives the above equilibrium to the right. However, a large excess of chloride ions must be avoided because AgCl tends to dissolve by forming a *soluble-complex ion:*

$$\mathbf{AgCl}(s) + Cl^-(aq) \longrightarrow AgCl_2^-(aq)$$

To be absolutely certain that the white precipitate is AgCl ($PbCl_2$ and Hg_2Cl_2 are also insoluble, and they are also white), NH_3 is added to the precipitate. If the precipitate is indeed AgCl, it will dissolve and then re-precipitate when the ammoniacal solution is made acidic:

$$\mathbf{AgCl}(s) + 2NH_3(aq) \longrightarrow Ag(NH_3)_2^+(aq) + Cl^-(aq)$$

$$Ag(NH_3)_2^+(aq) + 2H^+(aq) + Cl^-(aq) \longrightarrow \mathbf{AgCl}(s) + 2NH_4^+(aq)$$

The other two insoluble chlorides do not behave this way. Thus we can be assured that the white chloride precipitate is silver chloride.

3a Separation and Detection of Iron, Aluminum, and Chromium

Iron, aluminum, and chromium can be separated from the other ions (Ca^{2+}, Mg^{2+}, Ni^{2+}, and Zn^{2+}) by making the solution alkaline and precipitating these cations as their corresponding hydroxides:

$$Fe^{3+}(aq) + 3NH_3(aq) + 3H_2O(l) \longrightarrow \mathbf{Fe(OH)_3}(s) + 3NH_4^+(aq)$$
$$\text{rust}$$

$$Cr^{3+}(aq) + 3NH_3(aq) + 3H_2O(l) \longrightarrow \mathbf{Cr(OH)_3}(s) + 3NH_4^+(aq)$$
$$\text{gray-green}$$

$$Al^{3+}(aq) + 3NH_3(aq) + 3H_2O(l) \longrightarrow \mathbf{Al(OH)_3}(s) + 3NH_4^+(aq)$$
$$\text{colorless}$$

The hydroxide-ion concentration required to precipitate these three ions must be carefully controlled, because if it is too high, $Mg(OH)_2$ will also precipitate. An alkaline buffer of NH_3 and NH_4Cl provides a hydroxide-ion concentration that is high enough to precipitate Fe^{3+}, Cr^{3+}, and Al^{3+} and yet is low enough to prevent precipitation of $Mg(OH)_2$. Aqueous ammonia is a weak base:

$$NH_3(aq) + H_2O(l) \rightleftharpoons NH_4^+(aq) + OH^-(aq)$$

289

By itself, it would provide too high of a hydroxide-ion concentration, and $Mg(OH)_2$ would precipitate along with the other cations. However, the NH_4^+ ions derived from the NH_4Cl causes this equilibrium to shift to the left; this reduces the hydroxide-ion concentration sufficiently to prevent Mg^{2+} from precipitating.

3b   Separation and Detection of Iron

Iron hydroxide can be separated from the other hydroxides by treating the precipitate with the strong base NaOH and hydrogen peroxide, H_2O_2. These reagents do not react with the insoluble $Fe(OH)_3$; however, $Al(OH)_3$ is amphoteric and dissolves, forming the soluble complex ion $Al(OH)_4^-$. The $Cr(OH)_3$ also dissolves, being oxidized by H_2O_2 to form CrO_4^{2-}:

$$\textbf{Al(OH)}_3(s) + OH^-(aq) \longrightarrow Al(OH)_4^-(aq)$$

$$\textbf{2Cr(OH)}_3(s) + 3H_2O_2(aq) + 4OH^-(aq) \longrightarrow 2CrO_4^{2-}(aq) + 8H_2O(l)$$
$$\text{yellow}$$

The rust-colored $Fe(OH)_3$ remains undissolved. That the rust-colored precipitate is in fact iron hydroxide can be confirmed by dissolving it in acid and then adding potassium hexacyanoferrate(II), $K_4[Fe(CN)_6]$, and noting the formation of a dark blue precipitate (Prussian blue):

$$\textbf{Fe(OH)}_3(s) + 3H^+(aq) \longrightarrow Fe^{3+}(aq) + 3H_2O(l)$$

$$4Fe^{3+}(aq) + 3Fe(CN)_6^-(aq) \longrightarrow \textbf{Fe}_4[\textbf{Fe(CN)}_6]_3(s)$$
$$\text{blue}$$

3c and 3d   Separation and Detection of Chromium and Aluminum

While iron was being precipitated as the hydroxide, chromium was oxidized to the yellow chromate ion, CrO_4^{2-}, and aluminum was converted to the soluble complex aluminate ion, $Al(OH)_4^-$, which is colorless. These two ions are in the supernatant liquid, which upon acidification converts the chromate ion to the orange dichromate ion and the aluminate to the colorless solvated aluminum ion:

$$2CrO_4^{2-}(aq) + 2H^+(aq) \rightleftharpoons H_2O(l) + Cr_2O_7^{2-}(aq)$$
$$4H^+(aq) + Al(OH)_4^-(aq) \longrightarrow 4H_2O(l) + Al^{3+}(aq)$$

When this solution is treated with aqueous ammonia, aluminum precipitates as $Al(OH)_3$, which can be separated from the chromate ion in the supernatant liquid. (Note: the CrO_4^{2-} ion is stable in neutral or alkaline solution but is reversibly converted to the dichromate ion, $Cr_2O_7^{2-}$, in acidic solution.) The formation of a yellow precipitate, $BaCrO_4$, upon the addition of barium chloride, confirms the presence of chromium:

$$Ba^{2+}(aq) + CrO_4^{2-}(aq) \longrightarrow \textbf{BaCrO}_4(s)$$
$$\text{yellow}$$

Aluminum hydroxide is a clear, colorless substance and is difficult to see in this analysis. A confirmatory test for aluminum involves dissolving the aluminum hydroxide in acid and then re-precipitating it with ammonia in the presence of Aluminon reagent. As the aluminum hydroxide precipitates, it absorbs the Aluminon reagent and assumes a red coloration known as a "lake."

$$Al^{3+}(aq) + 3NH_3(aq) + 3H_2O(l) + \underset{\text{reagent}}{\text{Aluminon}} \longrightarrow \underset{\text{red lake}}{Al(OH)_3(s)} + 3NH_4^+(aq)$$

4   Separation and Detection of Calcium

Calcium   Calcium can be separated from the remaining cations (Mg^{2+}, Ni^{2+}, and Zn^{2+}) by precipitating it as an insoluble oxalate salt:

$$Ca^{2+}(aq) + C_2O_4^{2-}(aq) \longrightarrow CaC_2O_4(s)$$

If magnesium is present, it is possible that it will precipitate and be mistaken for calcium. To confirm that the precipitate is that of calcium and not magnesium, it is dissolved in acid and a flame test is performed on the solution.

$$CaC_2O_4(s) + 2H^+(aq) \longrightarrow Ca^{2+}(aq) + H_2C_2O_4(aq)$$

A transient brick-red flame verifies the presence of calcium ions. Magnesium ions do not impart any color to a flame.

5a Separation and Detection of Zinc

Separation of zinc from magnesium and nickel can be accomplished by precipitating $Mg(OH)_2$ and $Ni(OH)_2$ from a strongly alkaline solution. Excess ammonium ions must be removed before the precipitation of these hydroxides because ammonium ions interfere with the confirmatory test for magnesium. Ammonium ions are easily removed by evaporating the solution, which has been acidified with nitric acid to dryness:

$$NH_4Cl(s) \overset{\Delta}{\longrightarrow} NH_3(g) + HCl(g)$$

$$NH_4NO_3(s) \overset{\Delta}{\longrightarrow} N_2O(g) + 2H_2O(g)$$

Although magnesium and nickel form insoluble hydroxides in the presence of a strong base, zinc is amphoteric and forms the soluble complex ion $Zn(OH)_4^{2-}$:

$$Ni^{2+}(aq) + 2OH^-(aq) \longrightarrow Ni(OH)_2(s)$$
$$Mg^{2+}(aq) + 2OH^-(aq) \longrightarrow Mg(OH)_2(s)$$
$$Zn^{2+}(aq) + 4OH^-(aq) \longrightarrow Zn(OH)_4^{2-}(aq)$$

The presence of zinc is confirmed by precipitating it from an acidic solution as a gray-blue salt, $Zn_3K_2[Fe(CN)_6]_2$:

$$3Zn(OH)_4^{2-}(aq) + 12H^+(aq) + 2K^+(aq) + 2Fe(CN)_6^{4-}(aq) \longrightarrow$$
$$\underset{\text{gray-blue}}{Zn_3K_2[Fe(CN)_6]_2(s)} + 12H_2O(l)$$

5b   Separation and Detection of Nickel

Because nickel forms the soluble complex ion hexaamminenickel(II), $Ni(NH_3)_6^{2+}$, in the presence of aqueous ammonia, it can be separated from $Mg(OH)_2$:

$$Ni(OH)_2(s) + 6NH_3(aq) \longrightarrow Ni(NH_3)_6^{2+}(aq) + 2OH^-(aq)$$

It is confirmed by forming a strawberry red precipitate, $Ni(C_4H_7N_2O_2)_2$, with an organic reagent, dimethylglyoxime.

$$Ni(NH_3)_6^{2+}(aq) + 2HC_4H_7N_2O_2(aq) \longrightarrow \underset{\text{strawberry red}}{\textbf{Ni(C}_4\textbf{H}_7\textbf{N}_2\textbf{O}_2\textbf{)}_2(s)} + 4NH_3(aq) + 2NH_4^+(aq)$$

5c Detection of Magnesium

Magnesium is confirmed by dissolving the hydroxide with acid and then re-precipitating it in the presence of an organic compound called "Magnesium reagent." The presence of Mg^{2+} is indicated by formation of a blue lake.

$$\textbf{Mg(OH)}_2(s) + 2H^+(aq) \longrightarrow Mg^{2+}(aq) + 2H_2O(l)$$
$$Mg^{2+}(aq) + 2OH^-(aq) + Mg\text{ reagent} \longrightarrow \underset{\text{blue lake}}{\textbf{Mg(OH)}_2(s)}$$

PROCEDURE

First you will analyze a known that contains all ten cations. Record on your report sheet the reagents used in each step, your observations, and the equations for each precipitation reaction. After completing this practice analysis, obtain an unknown. Follow the same procedures as with the known, again recording reagents and observations. Also record conclusions regarding the presence or absence of all cations. *Before beginning this experiment, review the techniques used in qualitative analysis found in Appendix I: heating solutions, precipitation, centrifugation, washing precipitates, and testing acidity.*

Waste Disposal Instructions All waste from this experiment should be placed in appropriate containers in the laboratory.

1 Initial Observations and Tests for Sodium and Ammonium

Note the color of your sample and record any conclusions about what cations are present or absent on your report sheet.

The flame test for sodium is very sensitive, and traces of sodium ion will impart a characteristic yellow color to the flame. Just about every solution has a trace of sodium and thus will give a positive result. On the basis of the intensity and duration of the yellow color, you can decide whether Na^+ is merely a contaminant or present in substantial quantity. To perform the flame test, obtain a piece of platinum or Nichrome wire that has been sealed in a piece of glass tubing. Clean the wire by dipping it in 12 M HCl that is contained in a small test tube and heat the wire in the hottest part of your Bunsen burner flame. Repeat this operation until no color is seen when the wire is placed in the flame. Several cleanings will be required before this is achieved. Then place 10 drops of the solution to be analyzed in a clean test tube and perform a flame test on it. If the sample being tested is your unknown, run a flame test on distilled water and then another on a 0.2 M NaCl solution. Compare the tests; this should help you make a decision as to the presence of sodium in your unknown.

Place 10 drops of the original sample to be analyzed in an evaporating dish or a crucible. Moisten a strip of red or neutral litmus paper with distilled water and place the paper on the bottom of a small watch glass. Add 10 drops of 3 M NaOH to the unknown, swirl the evaporating dish or crucible, and immediately place the watch glass on it with the litmus paper down. Let stand for a few minutes. The presence of NH_4^+ ions is confirmed if the paper turns blue.

2 Separation and Detection of Silver

Place 10 drops of the original solution to be analyzed in a small test tube, add five drops of distilled water, and two drops of 6 M HCl. Stir well, centrifuge, and reserve the decantate for Procedure 3. Wash the precipitate with 10 drops of distilled water, centrifuge, and add the washings to the decantate. Dissolve the precipitate in four drops of 6 M NH$_3$;* then add 6 M HNO$_3$ to the ammoniacal solution until it is acidic to litmus. (*CAUTION: nitric acid can cause severe burns: Avoid contact with it. If you come in contact with it, immediately wash the area with copious amounts of water*) A curdy white precipitate of AgCl confirms the presence of Ag$^+$ ions.

3a Separation and Detection of Iron, Aluminum, and Chromium

To the decantate from Procedure 2 add two drops of NH$_4$Cl solution and 6 M NH$_3$ until the solution is basic to litmus. Centrifuge and reserve the decantate for Procedure 4. Wash the precipitate with 10 drops of distilled water, centrifuge, and add the washings to the decantate.

3b Separation and Detection of Iron

To the precipitate from Procedure 3a, add five drops of distilled water, 10 drops of 3 M NaOH, and five drops of 3% H$_2$O$_2$. Stir well, centrifuge, and reserve the decantate for Procedure 3c. Wash the precipitate with 10 drops of distilled water and add the washings to the decantate. Dissolve the reddish-brown precipitate in two drops of 6 M HCl and add 10 drops of K$_4$[Fe(CN)$_6$] solution. A blue precipitate of Fe$_4$[Fe(CN)$_6$]$_3$ confirms the presence of Fe^{3+} ions.

3c Separation and Detection of Aluminum

If the decantate from Procedure 3b is yellow in color, place it in an evaporating dish or a crucible and evaporate almost to dryness to remove excess H$_2$O$_2$ (see Note 1 below). Add 10 drops of distilled water and 6 M HCl until acid to litmus. Then add 6 M NH$_3$ until the solution is basic to litmus. Centrifuge and reserve the decantate for Procedure 3d. Wash the precipitate with 10 drops of distilled water, centrifuge, and add the washings to the decantate. Dissolve the precipitate in two drops of 6 M HCl, add two drops of Aluminon reagent, and 6 M NH$_3$ until basic to litmus. Centrifuge the solution. A red "lake" confirms the presence of Al^{3+} ions.

Note 1   Hydrogen peroxide is a reducing agent in acid solutions, so CrO$_4^{2-}$ ions could be reduced to Cr^{3+} when the solution is acidified. When NH$_3$ is added, Cr(OH)$_3$ will be precipitated and could be incorrectly reported as Al(OH)$_3$. Also, Cr^{3+} would not be confirmed in the proper procedure.

3d Separation and Detection of Chromium

Add two drops of BaCl$_2$ solution to the decantate from Procedure 3c. A yellow precipitate of BaCrO$_4$ confirms the presence of Cr^{3+} ions.

4 Separation and Detection of Calcium

Add three drops of (NH$_4$)$_2$C$_2$O$_4$ solution to the decantate from Procedure 3a and centrifuge. Reserve the decantate for Procedure 5a. Wash the precipitate with 10 drops of distilled water, centrifuge, and add the washings to the

---

*Bottles may be labeled 6 M NH$_4$OH.

decantate. Dissolve the precipitate of CaC_2O_4 in two drops of 6 M HCl and carry out a flame test with the solution. A brick-red flame confirms Ca^{2+} ions (see Note 2 below).

Note 2 If magnesium ions are present, they may be precipitated as MgC_2O_4.

To determine if MgC_2O_4 is precipitated, test the acid solution for Mg^{2+} as described in Procedure 5c.

5a Separation and Detection of Zinc

Place the decantate from Procedure 4 in an evaporating dish and carefully evaporate to dryness using a burner flame. *(CAUTION: Concentrated HNO₃ can causes severe burns: Avoid contact with it. If you come in contact with it, immediately wash the area with copious amounts of water.)* Add five to six drops of 16 M HNO_3 and heat again until no more fumes are observed (you are removing excess NH_4^+ ions that would interfere with the tests for Mg^{2+} ions). Dissolve the residue in five drops of 6 M HCl. Add 10 drops of distilled water to the HCl solution and transfer it to a small test tube. Wash out the evaporating dish with 10 drops of distilled water, and add the wash to the acid solution. Add 3 M NaOH until the solution is basic to litmus; centrifuge, and reserve the precipitate for Procedure 5b. Wash the precipitate with 10 drops of distilled water and add the washings to the decantate. Add three drops of $K_4[Fe(CN)_6]$ to the decantate and acidify with 6 M HCl; a gray-blue coloration or precipitate of $Zn_3K_2[Fe(CN)_6]_2$ confirms the presence of Zn^{2+} ions.

5b Separation and Detection of Nickel

(Caution: Concentrated NH₃ has a strong irritating odor and causes severe burns: Avoid inhaling it. If you come in contact with it, immediately wash the area with copious amounts of water.)

Add five drops of distilled water and five drops of 15 M NH_3 to the precipitate from Procedure 5a; centrifuge, and reserve the precipitate for Procedure 5c. Wash the precipitate with 10 drops of distilled water, and add the wash to the decantate. Add one drop of dimethylglyoxime solution to the decantate; a strawberry-red precipitate of $Ni(C_4H_7N_2O_2)_2$ confirms the presence of Ni^{2+} ions.

5c Detection of Magnesium

If Ni^{2+} ions were confirmed in Procedure 5b, add 15 M NH_3 to the precipitate saved from Procedure 5b until a negative result for Ni^{2+} is obtained. Dissolve the hydroxide precipitate in two drops of 6 M HCl; add two drops of "Magnesium reagent" and 3 M NaOH until the solution is basic. A blue lake confirms the presence of Mg^{2+} ions.

PRE LAB QUESTIONS

Before beginning Part I of this experiment in the laboratory, you should be able to answer the following questions:

1. What are the names and formulas of the 10 cations you will identify?
2. Why are confirmatory tests necessary in identifying ions?
3. Which of the 10 cations are colored, and what are their colors?
4. Which salt is insoluble: $FeCl_3$, $ZnCl_2$, NaCl, or AgCl?
5. How could you separate Fe^{3+} from Ag^+?
6. How could you separate Cr^{3+} from Mg^{2+}?

7. How could you separate Al^{3+} from Ag^+?

8. Complete and balance the following:

$$NH_4^+(aq) + OH^-(aq) \longrightarrow$$

$$AgCl(s) + NH_3(aq) \longrightarrow$$

PART II: ANIONS

DISCUSSION

A systematic scheme based on the kinds of principles involved in cation analysis can be designed for the analysis of anions. Because we shall limit our consideration to only six anions (SO_4^{2-}, NO_3^-, Cl^-, Br^-, I^-, and CO_3^{2-}) and will not consider mixtures of the ions, our method of analysis is quite simple and straightforward. It is based on specific tests for the individual ions and does not require special precaution to eliminate interferences that may arise in mixtures.

Initially you will make a general test on a solid salt with concentrated sulfuric acid (H_2SO_4). The results of this test should strongly suggest what the anion is. You will then confirm your suspicions by performing a specific test for the ion you believe to be present.

Table 1 summarizes the behavior of anions (as dry salts) with concentrated sulfuric acid.

PROCEDURE

Perform the general sulfuric acid test described below on the individual anions. Then perform the specific tests on each of the ions. Record your

TABLE 1 Behavior of Anions with Concentrated Sulfuric Acid, H_2SO_4

A. Cold H_2SO_4

SO_4^{2-}	No reaction.
NO_3^-	No reaction.

CO_3^{2-} A colorless, odorless gas forms.

$$CO_3^{2-}(s) + 2H^+(aq) \longrightarrow H_2O(l) + CO_2(g)$$

Cl^- A colorless gas forms. It has a sharp-pungent odor, gives an acidic test result with litmus, and fumes in moist air.

$$Cl^-(s) + H^+(aq) \longrightarrow HCl(g)$$

Br^- A brownish-red gas forms. It has a sharp odor, gives an acidic test result with litmus, and fumes in moist air. The odor of SO_2 may be detected.

$$2Br^-(s) + 4H^+(aq) + SO_4^{2-}(aq) \longrightarrow Br_2(g) + SO_2(g) + 2H_2O(l)$$

$$(HBr \text{ is also liberated})$$

I^- Solid turns dark brown immediately with the slight formation of violet fumes. The gas has the odor of rotten eggs, gives an acidic test result with litmus, and fumes in moist air.

$$2I^-(s) + 4H^+(aq) + SO_4^{2-}(aq) \longrightarrow I_2(g) + SO_2(g) + 2H_2O(l)$$

$$(HI \text{ and } H_2S \text{ are also liberated})$$

B. Hot Concentrated H_2SO_4

There are no additional reactions with any of the anions except NO_3^-, which forms brown fumes of NO_2 gas.

$$4NO_3^-(s) + 4H^+(aq) \longrightarrow 4NO_2(g) + O_2(g) + 2H_2O(l)$$

observations and equations for the reactions that occur. After completing these tests on the six anions, obtain a solid salt unknown and identify its anion. Record your observations and conclusion. Only one anion is present in the salt.

Sulfuric Acid Test

Place a small amount of the solid (about the size of a pea) in a small test tube. Add one or two drops of 18 M H_2SO_4 and observe everything that occurs, especially the color and odor of gas formed. (**CAUTION:** *Concentrated* **H_2SO_4** *causes severe burns. Do not get it on your skin or clothing. If you come in contact with it, immediately wash the area with copious amounts of water.*) DO NOT place your nose directly over the mouth of the test tube, but carefully fan gases toward your nose. Then *carefully* heat the test tube, but not so strongly as to boil the H_2SO_4. (**CAUTION:** *If you heat the acid too strongly, it could come shooting out!*) Note whether or not brown fumes of NO_2 are produced. (**CAUTION:** *Do not look down into the test tube. Do not point the test tube at yourself or at your neighbors.* **SAFETY GLASSES MUST BE WORN.**)

Specific Tests for Anions

When an anion is indicated by the preliminary test result with concentrated H_2SO_4, it is confirmed using the appropriate specific test. Make an aqueous solution of the solid unknown and perform the following tests on portions of this solution.

Sulfate   Place 10 drops of a solution of the anion salt in a test tube, acidify with 6 M HCl, and add a drop of $BaCl_2$ solution. The formation of a white precipitate of $BaSO_4$ confirms SO_4^{2-} ions.

$$Ba^{2+}(aq) + SO_4^{2-}(aq) \longrightarrow \textbf{BaSO}_4(s)$$

Nitrate   Place 10 drops of a solution of the anion salt in a small test tube and add five drops of $FeSO_4$ solution; mix the solution. Carefully, without agitation, pour concentrated H_2SO_4 down the inside of the test tube so as to form two layers. The formation of a brown ring between the two layers confirms NO_3^- ions.

(1) $3Fe^{2+}(aq) + NO_3^-(aq) + 4H^+(aq) \longrightarrow 3Fe^{3+}(aq) + NO(g) + 2H_2O(l)$

(2) $NO(g) + Fe^{2+}(aq)(excess) \longrightarrow Fe(NO)^{2+}(aq)(brown)$

Chloride   Place 10 drops of a solution of the anion salt in a test tube and add a drop of $AgNO_3$ solution. A white, curdy precipitate confirms Cl^- ions.

$$Ag^+(aq) + Cl^-(aq) \longrightarrow \textbf{AgCl}(s)$$

Bromide   Place 10 drops of a solution of the anion salt in a test tube, add three drops of 6 M HCl, then add five drops of Cl_2 water and five drops of mineral oil. Shake well. Br^- ions are confirmed if the mineral-oil (top) layer is colored orange to brown. Wait 30 s for the layers to separate.

$$2Br^-(aq) + Cl_2(aq) \rightleftharpoons Br_2(aq) + 2Cl^-(aq)$$

Iodide   Repeat the test as described for Br$^-$ ions. If the mineral-oil layer is colored violet, I$^-$ ions are confirmed.

$$2I^-(aq) + Cl_2(aq) \rightleftharpoons I_2(aq) + 2Cl^-(aq)$$

Carbonate   Place a small amount of the solid anion salt in a small test tube and add a few drops of 6 M H$_2$SO$_4$. If a colorless, odorless gas evolves, hold a drop of Ba(OH)$_2$ solution over the mouth of the test tube using either an eyedropper or Nichrome wire loop; CO$_3$$^{2-}$ ions are confirmed if the drop turns milky.

$$(1)\ 2H^+(aq) + CO_3^{2-}(s) \longrightarrow CO_2(g) + H_2O(l)$$
$$(2)\ CO_2(g) + Ba(OH)_2(aq) \longrightarrow BaCO_3(s) + H_2O(l)$$

Before beginning Part II of this experiment in the laboratory, you should be able to answer the following questions:

PRE LAB QUESTIONS

1. Give the names and formulas of the anions to be identified.
2. Describe the behavior of each solid containing the anions toward concentrated H$_2$SO$_4$.
3. If you had a mixture of NaCl and Na$_2$CO$_3$, would the action of concentrated H$_2$SO$_4$ allow you to decide that both Cl$^-$ and CO$_3$$^{2-}$ were present?

NOTES AND CALCULATIONS

REPORT SHEET | EXPERIMENT

Introduction to
Qualitative Analysis

Part I: Cations

A. Known

Record the reagent used in each step, your observations, and the equations for each precipitation reaction.

	Reagent	Observations	Equations
1			
2			
3a			
3b			
3c			

	Reagent	Observations	Equations
3d			
4			
5a			
5b			
5c			

B. Unknown (Cation unknown no._____)

Record reagent used, your observations, and the equations for each precipitate formed.

Reagent   *Observations*   *Equations*

Cations in unknown _____

PART II: ANIONS
A. Known

Concentrated H_2SO_4 test.

Ion	Observations and equations
SO_4^{2-}	
NO_3^-	
CO_3^{2-}	
Cl^-	
Br^-	
I^-	
NO_3^- (heated)	

B. Known

Specific tests.

Ion	Observations and equations
SO_4^{2-}	
NO_3^-	
CO_3^{2-}	
Cl^-	
Br^-	
I^-	

C. Unknown (Anion unknown no. _____)

Observations and equations

1 H$_2$SO$_4$ test:

2 Specific test(s):

Anion in unknown _____

Answers to Selected Pre Lab Questions

I Cations

1. Ammonium, NH_4^+; silver, Ag^+; ferric or iron(III), Fe^{3+}; aluminum, Al^{3+}; chromic or chromium(III), Cr^{3+}; calcium, Ca^{2+}; magnesium, Mg^{2+}; nickel or nickel(II), Ni^{2+}; zinc, Zn^{2+}; and sodium, Na^+.

2. Sometimes ions behave very similarly. For example, Ba^{2+} and Pb^{2+} both form yellow precipitates with K_2CrO_4. Hence, other additional confirmatory tests would be required to distinguish between these ions. For example, Pb^{2+} forms a white precipitate with HCl, whereas Ba^{2+} does not.

3. Only three of the ions are colored as follows: Fe^{3+}, rust to yellow; Cr^{3+}, blue-green; Ni^{2+}, green.

4. Because only AgCl precipitates on the addition of HCl to a solution of the ten cations, all chlorides of these ions except AgCl must be soluble.

5. Based on the group separation chart (Figure 1) Ag^+ can be separated from all of the other ions by the addition of HCl. Silver forms insoluble AgCl.

6. Examination of the group separation chart shows that in the presence of the buffer NH_3—NH_4Cl, Cr^{3+} precipitates as $Cr(OH)_3$ while Mg^{2+} remains in solution.

7. Addition of chloride ions to a solution containing Al^{+3} and Ag^+ would precipitate AgCl, while Al^{3+} would remain in solution. HCl would be a good source of chloride ions, and the H^+ would help retard hydrolysis of Al^{3+}.

8. $NH_4^+(aq) + OH^-(aq) \rightleftharpoons NH_3(aq) + H_2O(l)$; $AgCl(s) + 2\,NH_3$
   $(aq) \rightleftharpoons [Ag(NH_3)_2]^+(aq) + Cl^-(aq)$.

II Anions

1. Sulfate, SO_4^{2-}; nitrate, NO_3^-; carbonate, CO_3^{2-}; chloride, Cl^-; bromide, Br^-; and iodide, I^-.

2. See Table 1: behavior of anions with concentrated sulfuric acid.

3. No. Because HCl is pungent and forms on the addition of H_2SO_4 to chloride salts, it would be impossible to tell that a second gas that is odorless is also present. Hence you would not be aware of the presence of CO_3^{2-} in the mixture.

REMOVE GRAPH PAPER BEFORE USING, OR INSERT CARDBOARD BEHIND THE DUPLICATE PAGE.

REMOVE GRAPH PAPER BEFORE USING, OR INSERT CARDBOARD BEHIND THE DUPLICATE PAGE.

REMOVE GRAPH PAPER BEFORE USING, OR INSERT CARDBOARD BEHIND THE DUPLICATE PAGE.

Laboratory/Experiment:_____ Date:_____

Student:_____ Instructor:_____ Course & Lab Section:_____

REMOVE GRAPH PAPER BEFORE USING, OR INSERT CARDBOARD BEHIND THE DUPLICATE PAGE.

REMOVE GRAPH PAPER BEFORE USING, OR INSERT CARDBOARD BEHIND THE DUPLICATE PAGE.

REMOVE GRAPH PAPER BEFORE USING, OR INSERT CARDBOARD BEHIND THE DUPLICATE PAGE.

REMOVE GRAPH PAPER BEFORE USING, OR INSERT CARDBOARD BEHIND THE DUPLICATE PAGE.

Laboratory/Experiment: _____ Date: _____

Student: _____ Instructor: _____ Course & Lab Section: _____

REMOVE GRAPH PAPER BEFORE USING, OR INSERT CARDBOARD BEHIND THE DUPLICATE PAGE.

Laboratory/Experiment:_____ Date:_____

Student:_____ Instructor:_____ Course & Lab Section:_____

REMOVE GRAPH PAPER BEFORE USING, OR INSERT CARDBOARD BEHIND THE DUPLICATE PAGE.

REMOVE GRAPH PAPER BEFORE USING, OR INSERT CARDBOARD BEHIND THE DUPLICATE PAGE.

REMOVE GRAPH PAPER BEFORE USING, OR INSERT CARDBOARD BEHIND THE DUPLICATE PAGE.

REMOVE GRAPH PAPER BEFORE USING, OR INSERT CARDBOARD BEHIND THE DUPLICATE PAGE.

REMOVE GRAPH PAPER BEFORE USING, OR INSERT CARDBOARD BEHIND THE DUPLICATE PAGE.